AUSTRALIAN TELEVISION

Previous titles in the series

AUSTRALIAN TELEVISION

Programs, Pleasures and Politics

Edited by
John Tulloch and Graeme Turner

Australian Cultural Studies
Editor: John Tulloch

Routledge
Taylor & Francis Group

LONDON AND NEW YORK

First published 1989 by Allen & Unwin

Published 2020 by Routledge
2 Park Square, Milton Park, Abingdon, Oxon OX14 4RN
605 Third Avenue, New York, NY 10017

Routledge is an imprint of the Taylor & Francis Group, an informa business

National Library of Australia
Cataloguing-in-Publication:

Australian television: programs, pleasures & politics.
  Includes index.
  ISBN 0 04 380030 0.

  1. Television broadcasting — Social aspects — Australia.
  2. Television programs — Australia.   I. Tulloch, John,
  1942–   II. Turner, Graeme. (Series: Australian
  cultural studies).

302.2'345'0994

Library of Congress Catalog Card Number: 89-83597

Set in 10½/11½ Plantin by Best-set Typesetter Co. Ltd

ISBN–13: 9780043800300 (pbk)

Contents

v

General Editor's Preface

Nowadays the social and anthropological definition of 'culture' is probably gaining as much public currency as the aesthetic one. Particularly in Australia, politicians are liable to speak of the vital need for a domestic film industry in 'promoting our cultural identity'—and they mean by 'cultural identity' some sense of Australianness, of our nationalism as a distinct form of social organisation. Notably, though, the emphasis tends to be on Australian *film* (not popular television); and not just *any* film, but those of 'quality'. So the aesthetic definition tends to be smuggled back in—on top of the kind of cultural nationalism which assumes that 'Australia' is a unified entity with certain essential features that distinguish it from 'Britain', the 'USA' or any other national entities which threaten us with 'cultural dependency'.

This series is titled 'Australian Cultural Studies', and I should say at the outset that my understanding of 'Australian' is not as an essentially unified category; and further, that my understanding of 'cultural' is anthropological rather than aesthetic. By 'culture' I mean the social production of meaning and understanding, whether in the inter-personal and practical organisation of daily routines or in broader institutional and ideological structures. I am *not* thinking of 'culture' as some form of universal 'excellence', based on aesthetic 'discrimination' and embodied in a pantheon of 'great works'. Rather, I take this aesthetic definition of culture itself to be part of the *social mobilisation of discourse* to differentiate a cultural 'élite' from the 'mass' of society—as evidenced for instance in the Australian Senate Inquiry into 'Children and Television' discussed by Bob Hodge in this book.

Unlike the cultural nationalism of our opinion leaders, 'Cultural Studies' focusses not on the essential unity of national cultures, but on the meanings attached to social difference (as in the distinction between 'élite' and 'mass' taste). It analyses the construction and

ix

mobilisation of these distinctions to maintain or challenge existing power differentials, such as those of gender, class, age, race and ethnicity. In this analysis, terms designed to socially differentiate people (like 'élite' and 'mass') become categories of discourse, communication and power. Hence our concern in this series is for an analytical understanding of the meanings attached to social difference within the *history* and *politics* of discourse.

It follows that the analysis of 'texts' needs to be untied from a single-minded association with 'high' culture (marked by 'authorship'), but must include the 'popular' too—since these distinctions of 'high' and 'popular' culture themselves need to be analysed, not assumed. Both of the books published in the series so far—*National Fictions* and *Myths of Oz* reject the assumed distinction between 'high' and 'popular' culture, Graeme Turner drawing on both popular film and recognised 'Literature' for his analysis of 'produced texts', and John Fiske, Bob Hodge and Graeme Turner examining, on the one hand, opera house and art gallery, and on the other, pubs, beaches and shopping centres in their study of 'lived texts'. *Australian Television* follows in the same tradition, examining 'Art' and 'serious' science documentaries on the one hand, popular quiz shows and soap opera on the other. Curthoys and Docker, for instance, speak in their chapter against high culture critics who dismiss **Prisoner** as 'an insult to the intelligence—nothing but nasty people behaving nastily in a nasty situation'. 'How different', the authors note of this high/popular culture double-standard, 'must *Macbeth* and *King Lear* and *Hamlet* be—nothing but nice people behaving nicely in nice situations'.

Culture, as Fiske, Hodge and Turner say in *Myths of Oz*, grows out of the *divisions* of society, not its unity. 'It has to work to *construct* any unity that it has, rather than simply celebrate an achieved or natural harmony.' *Australian* culture is then no more than the temporary, embattled construction of 'unity' at any particular historical moment. The 'readings' in this series of 'Australian Cultural Studies' inevitably (and polemically) form part of the struggle to make and break the boundaries of meaning which, in conflict and collusion, dynamically define our culture.

John Tulloch

Preface

It is well over 30 years since television began transmission in Australia. In that time it has been the subject of a wide range of diverse and contradictory claims: it is both trivial and powerful; it is an important element in socialisation and a dangerous influence on children; it is passively consumed but it can teach four-year-olds to read. While there have been a number of chatty histories of Australian television, this book, despite the growth of media studies and despite the growing reputation of Australian media researchers, is the first collection of articles to deal with a wide range of Australian television through the perspectives and methodologies of television studies.

Both the editors have attempted to teach courses on television by using the only texts available: British or American readers which employ unfamiliar examples of television programs and inappropriate models of cultural relations. There has long been a need for a collection centred around the texts produced for and transmitted through Australian television. *Australian Television: Programs, Pleasures and Politics*, it is hoped, is the first of many such collections.

While we have tried to cover as many topics as possible this volume cannot hope to be comprehensive. The state of Australian television programming as well as of television theory is constantly changing. When this collection was first planned in 1986, it seemed unlikely that **Neighbours** would become an international success or that Kylie Minogue would become something of an institution. Further, the pressures of time and other commitments have reduced even our original list of topics and contributors; a particularly regrettable effect of the withdrawal of some of the original contributors has been the exacerbation of the gender imbalance.

What follows is nevertheless a substantial collection of some of the best work being done in television studies in Australia at the moment. Many of the contributors have developed their work within Australia, around such journals as *The Australian Journal of Screen Theory*, and the *Australian Journal of Cultural Studies*. Many have worked in collaboration with one or more of the other contributors, exploring the benefits of a range of theoretical traditions. Common to all the chapters is a firm awareness of the interrelation between industry and text, production and reception. The collection is further informed by the contemporary recovery of the importance of pleasure, as well as meanings, as a product of television.

While the enterprise of television studies may be singular, the approaches are extremely various. Tom O'Regan and Albert Moran offer institutional histories of the television industry in their chapters, while Graeme Turner's discussion of 'transgressive' television suggests a different, discursive history of a mode of Australian production. The codes and conventions of particular genres are the focus of the chapters by Stuart Cunningham, Ann Curthoys and John Docker, John Fiske, Dugald Williamson, and Philip Bell and Kathe Boehringer. John Hartley and John Tulloch both examine the space *between* programs, in discussions of continuity and sequencing. The way in which audiences make over the television message has become central to television studies today; the influence of ethnographic and psychoanalytic studies of audiences can be seen in the chapters by Ann Curthoys and John Docker, John Fiske, Bob Hodge, and the Afterword by John Tulloch. Finally, Theo van Leeuwin introduces musicology as a means of understanding the function of television signature tunes. The chapters offer readings of documentaries, game shows, variety and Tonight shows, mini-series, soap opera, station identification links, advertising sequencing, science shows, and signature tunes, while advancing theoretical discussions of the pleasures of television, their relation to notions of popularity, the role of the audience, and the ways in which the television message is implicated in the ideological systems of the culture.

Australian cultural studies have produced a great deal of interesting work on television; much of it has appeared in small journals, unseen by many of those who could benefit from it. This book is the first step towards making this work more accessible and more usable; it is our hope that it will open up a space for others like (and unlike) it, and for the expansion of television studies in secondary schools and tertiary institutions.

Graeme Turner and John Tulloch
August 1988.

Contributors

Albert Moran is the author of a number of books on Australian television, including *Images and Industry*, (with John Tulloch) *Quality Soap: A Country Practice*, and the editor (with Tom O'Regan) of *An Australian Film Reader*, and *Australian Screen*. He is a senior lecturer in the School of Humanities at Griffith University.

Tom O'Regan is editor of *Continuum*, and co-editor (with Albert Moran) of *An Australian Film Reader*, and *Australian Screen*. He teaches in the School of Humanities at Murdoch University.

Graeme Turner is the author of *National Fictions: Literature, Film, and the Construction of Australian Narrative*, *Film as Social Practice*, and co-author (with Bob Hodge and John Fiske) of *Myths of Oz: Reading Australian Popular Culture*. He is an editor of the journal *Cultural Studies*, and an Associate Professor in English at the University of Queensland.

Stuart Cunningham has published numerous important articles on Australian film and, more recently, television in such journals as *Filmnews*, *The Australian Journal of Screen Theory*, the *Australian Journal of Cultural Studies*, and *Media Information Australia*. He is currently working on an account of Kennedy-Miller's productions for film and television, while researching for the Communication Law Centre.

Ann Curthoys is a social historian who is perhaps best known for her work in labour history, and her current work on post-war working women. She co-edited two collections of left history with John Merritt: *Australia's First Cold War*, and *Better Dead Than Red*. She is an Associate Dean in Humanities and Social Sciences at the University of Technology, Sydney.

John Docker has been trying to convince intellectuals to take Australian popular culture seriously since the early 1970s. His publications include *Australian Cultural Elites*, and his study of the institutionalisation of Australian literary studies, *In a Critical Condition*. John Docker is a freelance writer.

John Fiske has established an international reputation for his work on television. His publications include (with John Hartley) *Reading Television, Introduction to Communication Studies*, (with Bob Hodge and Graeme Turner) *Myths of Oz: Reading Australian Popular Culture*, and most recently, *Television Culture*. John Fiske is now professor in Television Studies at the University of Wisconsin-Madison, USA.

Dugald Williamson has primarily published on film theory, and his work includes articles in *Screen* and a monograph for Local Consumptions, *Authorship*. He is currently completing a study of obscenity and literature with Ian Hunter and David Saunders, to be published by Macmillan. Dugald is a senior lecturer in the School of Humanities at Griffith University.

Philip Bell teaches Mass Communication at Macquarie University.

Kathe Boehringer is a sociologist and lawyer, teaching in the School of Law at the same institution. They have collaborated on a number of studies of politics, social and scientific issues in the Australian media. They are the authors (with Stephen Crofts) of *Programmed Politics: A Study of Australian Television* (1982).

John Hartley has published widely on television and popular culture; his publications include *Understanding News* and (with John Fiske) *Reading Television*. He has recently co-edited a collection of essays on television in Western Australia with Tom O'Regan, *The Moving Image*. He is a senior lecturer in the School of Humanities at Murdoch University.

John Tulloch is Associate Professor of Mass Communications at Macquarie University. His publications include *Legends on the Screen, Australian Cinema: Industry, Narrative, Meaning*, (with Albert Moran) *Quality Soap: A Country Practice*. He is currently working on a book on TV drama.

Robert Hodge has published on literature, linguistics, the media, Aboriginal writing, and popular culture. His publications include (with Gunther Kress) *Language As Ideology*, (with David Tripp) *Children and Television*, (with Graeme Turner and John Fiske) *Myths of Oz: Reading Australian Popular Culture*, and most recently (with Gunther Kress) *Social Semiotics*. He is an Associate Professor in Humanities at Murdoch University.

Theo van Leeuwen is a senior lecturer in Mass Communication at Macquarie University. He has published articles on language, visual communication and music in the mass media, and regularly performs as a jazz pianist in Sydney.

1

Three Stages of Australian Television

Albert Moran

Australia is a 'region of recent (white) settlement' whose staple-based economy has been linked to that of Argentina and Canada. Australian television is locked into international television in terms of the flow of technology, programs and programming practices. The 30-odd years since the introduction of television in 1956 seems like one continuous period. Certainly the period is unified as one of television broadcasting; the television narrowcasting, now developing in the United States has not yet begun in Autralian television.[1] But when we survey these years of Australian television in more detail it is apparent that there are many breaks and discontinuities. Australian television from this perspective falls into three stages: the first to 1965 can be called 'radio with pictures', the second from 1965 to 1975/6 sees the emergence of a local TV drama production industry. Since 1975, Australian television has been marked by the introduction of new technologies, the rise of new media conglomerates, growing internationalisation and an increasing overlap with the Australian feature film production industry. This third stage is still with us.

Radio with pictures

The first stage of Australian television seems both familiar and remote from a present day point of view. All programs were broadcast

1

in black and white. Under an agreement with the major Hollywood film companies, films made before 1948 were available to television and the great majority of these, too, were in black and white. Many other programs, especially variety shows, were broadcast live. The only form of recording available, a system known as kinneying, filmed images off a TV monitor but these images were poor in quality and the system was not widely used.

The hours of television transmission were restricted. Initially stations in Sydney and Melbourne opened in the later afternoon and broadcast until shortly before midnight. The hours of broadcasting on the weekend were more extended, because of live sport broadcasts. Such practices as breakfast shows and midnight-to-dawn news, sport and movies lay many years into the future.

Australian television developed according to a pre-arranged pattern. Two commercial television licences were awarded to operators in Sydney, Melbourne, Brisbane and Adelaide and one each in Canberra, Perth and Hobart. One commercial licence was awarded in smaller cities and towns throughout the rest of the country. This development occurred in several stages. Following the implementation of Stage 4 of the Development of Television Services in 1964/65 nearly 80 per cent of the country came within the net of television. The service extended to smaller cities and towns such as Kempsey in New South Wales and Bunbury in Western Australia.[2]

The granting of two licences in Sydney, Melbourne, Brisbane and Adelaide both facilitated the development of networking arrangements in the four most populous cities and restricted these arrangements to those cities. Networking here was understood as combining, for the purposes of cost sharing, on program buying and program production. Frank Packer's Consolidated Press had, before the coming of television, some informal arrangements with the Herald and Weekly Times Group for the purpose of buying newspaper comics, overseas news and other press material. The link continued into television—Packer's TCN Channel 9 had links with HSV Channel 7 from 1956 to 1960. However, Packer had ambitions to establish a television network chain, initially applying unsuccessfully for commercial licences in Brisbane and in country areas of New South Wales. In 1960 he bought GTV Channel 9 in Melbourne and the Nine Network came into being. Later in the decade the Seven Network emerged.

The ABC was unaffected by these developments. Single ABC television stations began in Sydney and Melbourne in late 1956–early 1957 and other ABC stations rippled out across the country. Under its long-serving general manager, Sir Charles Moses, the ABC gave little thought to its new television service. By and large, it saw television as an extension of radio so that nowhere was it truer to say that television was simply radio with pictures. Television owners and station executives in this first stage of television did not give a great deal of thought to programs. Instead their main concern was with the capital cost of establishing and operating a station. Although several would-be licensees made expressions of commitment to the idea of locally produced programs at both the hearings of the Royal Commission on Television (1953) and at the Licence Inquiries (1955–59), their early practice did not encourage local production. Instead the economics of this first stage of television were that in order to buy the necessary kind of equipment to set up television stations the commercial operators offset capital costs against the relatively cheap costs of imported American material. They commissioned one of the cheapest forms of local content, namely variety shows, as a way of further underwriting establishment costs. This made most commercial television stations highly profitable, leading operators to echo the famous dictum of Lord Thompson that having a television station was like having a licence to print money.

The television stations were both distributors and producers of programs, like supermarkets which also manufactured the goods they sold. The programs were made at the station by the station. The most notable of the stations for in-house production were ATN Channel 7 Sydney and GTV Channel 9 in Melbourne. GTV Channel 9 would continue with its successful *In Melbourne Tonight* for several years after the Packer takeover but gradually its drama production fell away. ATN Channel 7 persisted with in-house production until 1970.

The early television schedule was constructed on units of a quarter hour. News programs, soap opera and some early teenage music programs were fifteen minutes in length, although most programs were a half hour in length. A few imported drama series, such as *Perry Mason* and *Wagon Train*, plays and variety programs were longer, running 60 or 90 minutes. The programming schedule was dominated by half-hour programs such as *The Mickey Mouse Club*, *The Cisco Kid*, *The Lone Ranger*, *Sergeant Bilko*, *Hancock's Half Hour* and others. Many of these would be stripped (programmed in the same time slot over the five days of the week) in the early evening for children viewers. Thus when we find them in prime time they project a childish image in the schedule.

The dominant drama genres were westerns, crime and situation comedies. Popular westerns included *Rawhide, Wagon Train, Cheyanne, Sugarfoot, Wanted Dead or Alive* and *Bonanza*; popular crime series included *77 Sunset Strip, The Untouchables* and **Dragnet**; *Leave it to Beaver*, **Father Knows Best**, **Life of Riley** and *I Love Lucy* were favourite situation comedies. Of these genres the latter two have remained a staple of the television schedule over the remaining periods while the western had faded from mass popularity.

The period was also marked by the popularity of the one-off television play. There were two kinds of play: the first, emanating from the BBC, was dominated by a West End conception of drama and theatre. It favoured theatrical works of famous British playwrights such as Shakespeare, Shaw and, in the modern period, Noel Coward and Terence Rattigan. This model was the one adopted by ABC television. From the late 1950s it combined imports from the BBC with television versions of some famous Australian plays. But essentially it was working on the basis of adapting pre-existing theatrical materials to television. The frame of mind of the drama department of the ABC at that time is well conveyed by Colin Dean, a producer with the ABC, responsible for its first television drama series, *The Hungry Ones*, in 1960:

> The ABC has a very honourable place in the life of the Australian theatre. During the war, in the 1950s and early 1960s, the ABC in its live dramas kept alive the traditions of the theatre giving work to actors, writers and others, giving them the opportunity to practice their craft.[3]

The other kind of play came from American television. In the early 1950s, in programs such as *The US Steel Hour* and *Playhouse 90*, playwrights such as Sterling Stilliphant, Paddy Chayefsky and Tod Mostel had written a series of original social realist plays for television including *Marty*, *The Miracle Worker* and *Requiem for a Heavyweight*. The model was adopted in Australian television by ATN Channel 7 and its partner station, first GTV Channel 9 and then HSV Channel 7, under the sponsorship of both Shell and General Motors. Notable plays written for television under the aegis of these sponsors include *Other People's Houses*, *Tragedy in a Temporary Town* and *Thunder of Silence*.

An absence from the television schedule in this early period was current affairs. *Four Corners*, modelled on the BBC's *Panorama*, did not begin on the ABC until 1961. In its earliest form it was more of a newsreel or news digest program with several items in each episode rather than the hard-hitting investigative program we have become more familiar with. Its first producer, Bob Raymond, left the ABC in 1963 and began *Project 63* on TCN Channel 9. These programs can be seen as forerunners to the kind of current affairs television that blossomed in the later 1960s and 1970s.

Instead of investigative current affairs, this period had a more sedate form of public affairs television, well exemplified in TCN Channel 9's *Meet the Press*. *Meet the Press* was scheduled at a late hour on Sunday evening and featured a discussion *cum* interview between an eminent visitor to Australia or distinguished guests and senior newspaper executives of Consolidated Press. The discussion was usually polite and dignified, the questions were never probing or uncomfortable and the general atmosphere was usually one of exclusivity and smugness. The fact that the journalists were press journalists rather than television journalists is a sign of how far the concept of current affairs television has shifted since this first stage of television.

There was little in the way of locally oriented documentary films on Australian television at this particular time. Such material was mostly brought in from elsewhere. The ABC did not establish a filmmaking pool, consisting of teams of cameramen available to both news and documentary program, until 1959. There was an enormous reliance on overseas material.

If there was any kind of presence of what we might call 'Australian Content' on Australian television in this period, it occurred in cheaper production genres such as variety and quiz shows. Indeed there was a boom in local variety shows. Programs such as *In Melbourne Tonight*, *The Graham Kennedy Show*, *In Sydney Tonight*, *Delo and Daly*, *Startime*, *Revue 60* and *Revue 61*, *Bandstand*, *Six O'Clock Rock*, *Sing Sing Sing*, *Curtain Call*, *The Bobby Limb Late Show*, *The Mobil-Limb Show* and *The Johnny O'Keefe Show* were important landmarks. In Brisbane and Adelaide local *Tonight* Shows were hosted by figures such as George Wallace Junior, Gerry Gibson and Ernie Sigley. Among early successful local quiz shows were *Wheel of Fortune*, *Concentration* and *Tic-Tac-Dough*, all packaged for TCN Channel 9 by Reg Grundy. The success of these variety and quiz shows meant that, despite the overwhelming presence of American and British programs, Australian programs had a distinct place in the television schedule. It was through the presence of this variety cycle that Australian television was given a local look or flavour and developed a deliberate programming mix between overseas drama and local variety. But variety shows often had international guests, so that even if they qualified under Broadcasting Control Board regulations as Australian content, nevertheless they had a distinctly international flavour.

This period, both in Australia and elsewhere, was marked by the attempt to switch various formats, programs and personalities that had worked well in radio across to television. Some of the familiar kinds of genres, shows and personalities once heard on radio took on visible material form. Overseas programs such as *Gunsmoke*, *The Nelsons* and *Hancock's Half Hour*, and Australian programs such as *Consider Your Verdict*, *Pick-A-Box* and *Wheel of Fortune*, made a successful transition from radio to television. There was also an attempt to move soap opera from radio to television in the late 1950s when ATN Channel 7 produced *Autumn Affair* and *The Story of Peter Grey*. But these found neither sponsors nor audience. Although several personalities, including Bob Dyer and Graham Kennedy, moved successfully across, a notable casualty of the new medium was Jack Davey.

Enter Hector's inspectors

The second period of Australian television between 1964 and 1975 was marked by a good deal of stability. The novelty phase of television was at an end, the Box had become part of the lounge-room, and young children who had never known a world without television were now teenagers.

Between 1963 and 1965 a new commercial station appeared in Sydney, Melbourne, Brisbane, Adelaide and Perth. The new stations formed themselves into the 0–10 network so that east coast Australia now had three commercial networks. Of these, the new-comer was the weakest in terms of audience and ratings—so much so that in 1973 a new federal Labor government briefly contemplated taking away the licences. Apart from the licensing of the 0–10 stations there was no other change to the structure of Australian television.

The advent of the new network meant that there was barely enough imported program material for the commercial networks and the ABC. This was an important factor in the sudden rise of local television drama. The new cycle began with the rather unexpected success of the police series *Homicide*, made in Melbourne by Crawford Productions, and which began production in late 1964. By the end of the 1960s there were three police series (*Homicide*, *Division 4*, *Matlock Police*) on the different commercial networks. The ABC also had a police drama series, *Contrabandits*, dealing with activities of the customs department on Sydney Harbour.

Homicide was the most successful drama series produced for Australian television. The series, dealing with different homicide investigators, ran for eleven years. In all 509 one-hour episodes were made, initially in black and white, later in colour. The early episodes were produced on an integrated system of filmed locations and electronically recorded interiors, while later episodes were shot on an all-film basis. Sixteen different actors played members of the Homicide squads at different times.

Homicide ushered in a new look to Australian television. It presented audiences with a different, more factual, view of Australia than anything available hitherto. The increased use of Australian film footage in news programs undoubtedly assisted the factual tone and the authenticity of location and detail. As a local critic put it:

> In *Homicide* and *Division 4*, the dramatic character, action and ethic are embedded in a world we know—the sub-industrial landscape of narrow-guttered South Melbourne timber cottages, Carlton back streets and lanes, the Victoria docks, the Dynon Road railway yard. . . More than anything else, the location shooting makes the series good to look at. . . and again it all sustains that constancy of tone I've been talking about. If a smalltime drunk-roller is being pursued by the boys in blue, then he'll be hunted down through smalltime back streets, alleys and courtyards. . . the squalidness of the settings echoes the squalidness of the crime.[4]

This authenticity of detail and locale was not restricted to the police series. It could be found across a wide range of locally produced drama including *Bellbird*, *You Can't See Around Corners*, *My Name's McGooley*, *The Battlers* and *Dynasty*. In labelling these series as local programs, we mean several things. The familiarity of the locations and characters for local audiences has already been mentioned. But these programs were made with Australian audiences in mind. Because they were in black and white and shot on the integrated basis, they did not export particularly well and so the producers worked very much to Australian audiences in terms of language, accents, references and visual icons. These programs were distinctively Australian.

With the rise in popularity of Australian programs there was a shift in the economies of local commercial television. In the first stage of television, cheap imports subsidised the capitalisation, equipping and maintenance of new television stations. In this second stage, cheap imports allowed commercial stations and networks to underwrite the costs of local productions. It was on the basis of their Australian programs that the commercial stations rose or fell in the ratings. However the popularity of local drama series resulted in an equally dramatic downturn in variety. From 1965 variety production effectively ceased in Brisbane, Adelaide and Perth. Fewer shows came out of Sydney and Melbourne, and Graham Kennedy and Bobby Limb, the biggest stars in the variety cycle, were seen infrequently.

This period, too, saw a marked increase in the importance of current affairs television and documentary. After a shaky start, the weekly *Four Corners* settled down to a new kind of investigative television journalism. In 1967 the ABC started the daily current affairs series *This Day Tonight*—modelled on the BBC series *Today Tonight*. *This Day Tonight* (TDT) was hard-hitting investigative journalism that dared to examine political and social issues in ways never imagined by a programme such as *Meet the Press*. It was a very big success for the ABC and helped to markedly improve its ratings performance. *This Day Tonight* was enormously influential in extending the range of current affairs television, not just on the ABC, but also on commercial stations. In the 1970s many ABC journalists and reporters, of whom Mike Willesee is the most famous, would move to current affairs work on commercial stations. The ABC's *Chequerboard* introduced *cinéma vérité* into Australian television documentary and, like TDT, it expanded significantly the range of social concerns and issues that could be examined on television. *A Big Country* also expanded the audience's sense of what constituted the nation.

The state, through the Australian Broadcasting Control Board, played a part in securing the place of Australian content on television in this period. The first content regulations which operated between 1956 and the early 1960s had required that television stations should whenever possible employ Australians for the production and transmission of programs. But this regulation was too general. It also assumed that programs would be live and thus was irrelevant to the actual situation where many programs were recorded. In 1965 the Control Board changed the system to one based on a quota. Stations were required to screen three hours per week[5] of Australian content in prime time. A precedent for the quota lay in the requirement introduced by the Board in 1960 that all commercials screened on Australian television be produced in Australia. This amounted to a quota of 100 per cent. Clearly the three hours was a fairly limited quota compared with the blanket protection offered through the advertising regulation.

The quota rose slowly throughout the rest of the 1960s. In 1972 it stood at 50 per cent during the hours 6–10 p.m., and in 1973 the Board introduced a points system. This system still operated on a quota basis but it attempted to discriminate in favour of local program forms such as drama which had the highest production values. These measures did not bring about the big upsurge in Australian television production already noticed. But they did set a minimum threshold for the scheduling of local productions, below which commercial television stations could not fall. In other words, the quota and then the points system were to help guarantee at least part of the market for Australian program producers.

With the rise in local production, commercial television stations redefined their activities and packages emerged. In the first stage of Australian television, stations had mostly produced programs in-house. They had done this to guarantee ownership of programs. In Australian radio of the 1930s, 1940s and 1950s, where advertisers had owned the programs, stations and networks had come close to ruin when advertisers or their agencies had switched programs to rival stations. By 1964, television stations felt less threatened by this possibility and were content to farm out production to packagers. Packagers were program producers who guaranteed to deliver programs at a set cost and time. The most successful packager in this period was Crawford Productions, established in Melbourne by Hector Crawford in 1945 to package radio programs. By 1973 Crawfords had six programs in production—*Homicide*, *Division 4*, *Matlock*, *The Box*, *Ryan* and *Showcase*. The company had over 500 employees and was a scaled-down Hollywood on the Yarra. Its biggest rival, Reg Grundy Productions, had begun in 1958 in quiz program packaging, moving successfully, in 1973, into television drama with the serial *Class of 73*. Other important local packagers to emerge at this time included Fauna and Cash-Harmon.

The ABC continued to produce its own programs in-house. However, with the retirement of Sir Charles Moses in 1965, a major restructuring of ABC television and radio took place. Television drama severed many of its links with the theatre. Following a BBC example, drama was organised into three strands—series, serials and plays. The series strand gave rise to several successful series including *Contrabandits* and *Delta* (a series of investigations involving a scientific team from the CSIRO). By 1967, the serial strand initiated *Bellbird*, an on-going serial set in a rural Australian town and the most successful serial ever to play on Australian television. It ran for nearly eleven years. In the early 1970s it was joined by another on-going serial, produced by the ABC in Sydney, *Certain Women*. The play strand was of lesser importance. It was most active in the late 1960s when it produced several successful seasons of *Australian Playhouse*, an anthology series of one-off hour and half-hour plays written for television.

Television in a new age

The environment of Australian television since 1975 has been markedly different to that in earlier periods. Briefly, there has been the entry of new players; new technologies; several of the ground rules and strategies for survival in the industry have changed; Australian television has become more integrated into international television; and firm links have developed between the television and film industries.

In 1980 the Special Broadcasting Service (SBS) television service was inaugurated in Sydney and Melbourne, and later spread to other capital cities. Multicultural or ethnic television, as it was called, was conceived on lines very different to that of ethnic radio. The first managing director of the service, Bruce Gyngell, did much to establish the programming policies and scheduling practices of the service. Much of Gyngell's background was in Australian commercial television and he saw the task of the new service as that of providing ethnically-diverse entertainment for its multicultural audience. To this end, he secured television programs from the major non-English television production and distribution centres such as France, Italy, Germany, Russia and China. The result has been a schedule that mixes together such ingredients as art films, soccer broadcasts, Greek variety shows, Chinese cooking programs and Latin American soap operas in varying amounts. However, SBS has significantly failed to attract any large migrant audience; instead it has drained off some of the middle class audience of ABC television.

The most recent stage of Australian television has seen a significant downturn in the fortunes of the ABC. The recession which began in 1974/75 and which shows no signs of abating has led the federal government, both conservative and Labor, to cut the budget of the ABC. The ABC has lost staff steadily, with some of the most creative people moving to commercial television. The reconstitution of the ABC as a Corporation in 1983 has not halted this process. The output of the drama department has suffered badly, falling as low as 40 hours in 1984/85. Compared to the second stage of television, ABC drama has little in the way of distinctive achievements to point to in this period.

Other new players in Australian television have emerged around the buying and selling of commercial stations. Rupert Murdoch bought the two Channel 10 stations in Sydney and Melbourne in the late 1970s. Within five years, his company has succeeded in turning the Ten Network into the ratings leader of east coast television. However an enormous carve up of Australian media empires occurred in 1986/7 leading to the disappearance of the large long-established media groups and the emergence of new ones. Kerry Packer sold his television and broadcasting interests to the Bond Corporation. Christopher Skase took control of much of the Seven Network from Fairfax, while Murdoch's News Corporation turned over its television holdings to a regional, hitherto small group, Northern Star.

The scramble for television stations in the mid 1980s was linked to the networking possibilities that the Aussat satellite made available to Australian television. But the satellite was only one of several new communications technologies introduced into the domain of television in the most recent stage. Australian television switched to colour in 1976. This change was in its own way as profound a change as the coming of sound to the movies in the late 1920s. One effect of colour has been to inhibit the circulation of earlier, black and white material on Australian television. Colour has also had the effect of codifying black and white footage as old, belonging to the past, the domain of history rather than contemporary experience. This coding was used in the introductory credits to Crawford's series, *The Sullivans*, which began on television in late 1975.

A second technology appeared in the early 1980s with the marketing of low priced, domestic video recorders. Sales of VCRs were very high: by the mid 1980s, it was estimated that half of all Australian households with television sets also had VCRs. The VCR did not affect program content or the television programming schedule, but it did alter the audience's relationship with television. The VCR made it possible to time-shift, to 'zap' commercials and to store programs. It also enabled audiences to use their television set as a display monitor for the playing of pre-recorded material. Overall its effect has been to lessen the power of television programmers over the domestic routines and schedules of the viewer.

The first Aussat satellite was launched in 1986, the second in 1987. Using satellite facilities, television operators in Sydney and Melbourne now had the ability to network programs over the length and breadth of Australia. Country television stations were most affected by the satellite—they faced competition from the commercial networks where previously they had enjoyed a monopoly. But under the Equalisation Scheme developed by the federal government in 1986/7, these operators were to be issued with two auxiliary licences so that they would become local agents for the three commercial networks. The concept of networking had changed considerably; it now closely resembled the broadcast networking that obtained in the United States. It was in the wake of the new marketing possibilities made available by the satellite that the upheavals in commercial television ownership took place.

The third stage of television has seen a new body and a new philosophy in the area of regulation. In 1976/7, the Australian Broadcasting Control Board was abolished and the Australian Broadcasting Tribunal established. The change was part of a new approach to broadcasting by the state which has generally moved in the direction of deregulation. Under the Tribunal, commercial television licences were given control of such areas as program standards and advertising although the stations were now meant to be publicly accountable for their actions and practices. Australian content levels have remained regulated under the Points System although stations have lobbied vigorously to be allowed to set their own content levels.

Scheduling practices have changed significantly in the most recent stage of Australian television. Where the first two decades were marked by the series as a staple of the programming schedule, the present era has seen a different pattern. The programming of series offered the regular repetition of a particular experience (recalling characters, situations, locations, themes and kinds of stories). It set in train a loyal viewer who tuned in again and again, week after week. Following developments in American network television during 1976, there is now an emphasis on the special. The special can take a variety of forms—a sports program, a variety special, a mini-series, the screening of a blockbuster movie over several nights. The special has been usefully defined as the long run over a short term: it will usually be screened in large amounts of prime time (two or three hours) over several succeeding nights of the week. The practice developed around the televising on American network television of the 1976 Olympics. In drama, the practice gave rise to the mini-series.

These scheduling practices were taken up by Australian commercial television in the late 1970s and 1980s. The prime time schedule of Australian television in 1987/8 is dominated by programs of two hours or more—movies, specials, mini-series, sports programs, compilations of video clips and so on. Various other half-hour and one-hour forms complete the schedule: news, current affairs, quiz shows (all local), comedy series (almost all imported) and soap operas (some local and imported). The mini-series, both imported and locally produced, has been a major programming form in the most recent stage of Australian television. Beginning in 1978 with *Against the Wind*, Australian television packagers have mostly concentrated on the historical mini-series (*A Town Like Alice, For the Term of His Natural Life, Waterfront, Shout!—The Johnny O'Keefe Story* and others) although there have been occasional variants such as the adventure/thriller (*Silent Running*) and the romantic melodrama (*Return to Eden*). As I have suggested elsewhere,[6] the historical mini-series typically links the personal history of one or two individuals to a set of more public, historical events and situations (the Castle Hill convict rebellion, World War Two, the convict era in Australian history, the Vietnam War and so on).

The mini-series has had high production values and budgets. It has been aided by the provisions of the 10BA tax legislation introduced by the federal government in the early 1980s to subsidise the Australian film industry. Indeed (as Tom O'Regan explains in Chapter 2) there has been a good deal of recent crossover between this kind of television, the quality end of the spectrum, and the film industry. History has been an important subject area for both. There has been a crossover of film production personnel—most especially directors (Phil Noyce, Stephen Wallace, John Duigan and others). There has also emerged new, smaller packagers of which Kennedy-Miller are the most important (in television the company has produced *The Dismissal, Bodyline, Cowra Breakout* and *Vietnam*, while in film it has made the *Mad Max* trilogy and *The Witches of Eastwick*).

The bread and butter end of local television drama has been the soap opera. Notably long-running Australian soaps have included *The Sullivans, The Young Doctors, The Restless Years, Sons and Daughters, Neighbours, Prisoner* and *A Country Practice*. The Australian soapie has mostly been concerned with the home and the family rather than with more public or historical events. And unlike the mini-series, the family in these soap operas has generally been one without hierarchy, in a state of chaos and confusion; characters in the mini-series seek and find a stable and permanent domestic identity, but characters in the soap operas never do.

The last feature of the most recent stage concerns the export fate of these two drama forms. Both have sold well overseas, especially the mini-series. Sales of the mini-series have undoubtedly been helped by the recent international reputation of Australian feature films. But other factors have also been important: the stories have sometimes concerned other places and nations; much of the story material has been deliberately universalised; the mini-series in particular, have high production values; and there has been a world-wide expansion of the market for television product.

What has been more surprising has been the good export sales of Australian television soaps. *Prisoner* for example sold to several cable stations in the United States. By the mid 1980s, British commercial television ran such Australian serials as *The Sullivans* and *A Country Practice* in its weekday afternoon schedule. *Neighbours* is currently the top-rating program in the United Kingdom, and is screened twice daily. Unlike the mini-series which were Australian in terms of well-known events, situations and figures but more universal in story terms, these serials were more specifically Australian and were not originally intended for other markets. Their success in those other places is more an indication of the expansion of international demand for programs (more stations and longer hours of broadcasting) rather than any reflection, one way or the other, on their quality.

This discussion has suggested that far from being monolithic, the 30-odd-year history of Australian television is marked by a series of distinct shifts and changes. Television as an institution is composed of many elements—stations, networks, technologies, programs, scheduling practices, government regulation, audience viewing habits and so on. In turn these are embedded in that larger totality that is society. The theme of this chapter has been that these elements are in flux but changing at different speeds, sometimes rapidly, sometimes appearing to stand still. Overall I have been concerned to link these changes into significant bundles to suggest that we can think of Australian television history as consisting of three stages.

Notes

1 Various communication scholars have commented on the shift in television from broadcasting to narrowcasting. See for example Paul Atallah, *Music Television* (Working Papers in Communication, McGill University, Montreal, 1986).

2 See *Sixteenth Annual Report of the Australian Broadcasting Control Board for the year ending 30 June 1964* (Commonwealth Government Printer, Canberra, 1964).

3 Andrew Willoughby, 'Interview with Colin Dean', Sydney, September 1982.

4 John C. Murray, 'Defending the defenders', *Lumiere*, April 1973, p.18.

5 See my *Images and Industry: Television Drama Production in Australia* (Currency Press, Sydney, 1985), especially Chapter 1.

6 Ibid., chapter 11.

2

The Converging of Film and Television

Tom O'Regan*

The year 1981 saw the beginning of a rapprochement between the TV and film industries. The convergence of TV and film in the 1980s led to greater opportunities within TV for an independent production industry. A number of factors were responsible for this convergence. It was the product of a change in federal film policy; within both TV and cinema markets; and among the film and TV producers themselves.

The federal film policy in question was the tax concessions for feature film, documentary and TV mini-series production. This policy was first mooted in the 1980 election campaign (and enacted in June 1981). It was designed to assist the financing of feature films—with mini-series and documentaries being added as an afterthought. Although never intended to alter the shape of the industry, to change government attitudes to it, or to reincorporate TV drama (and the documentary) within the arena of 'subsidised production', the concessions did all three. It led to a sustained production boom from October 1980 to the middle of 1987. The average number of feature films made per year doubled from 15 in the 1970s to 27 in the 1980s. Some 65 mini-series were made in the same period. There was also a steady increase in the numbers of documentaries,

---

* This is an edited excerpt from a much longer article on the film and television interface in Australia.—Eds.

15

peaking at 110 in 1986/7.[1] Additionally, the budgets for all these rose sharply. Most importantly, this boom privatised the subsidised film industry sector thus permitting private investors (including TV networks) to invest in projects on their own terms. Depending on one's viewpoint, 'cautious investors' wishing to 'minimise' their tax—or 'speculative capital'—became the backbone of the film industry in the 1980s, effectively displacing government subvention.

The tax concessions enabled people to pay less tax by investing in an Australian film. It did so by allowing investors to write-off their films outlays against the income they earned in their usual occupations. This created in the Australian Film Corporation's (AFC) words 'a safety net, protecting investors from the possibility of total loss'.[2] The concessions permitted investors to claim as part of their taxable income more than the full amount they invested. During the life of the scheme this varied from 150 per cent (at the start), to 130 per cent (from August 1983) to 120 per cent (September 1985). Investors could also claim a certain percentage of the film's returns as being exempt from tax: this varied from 50 per cent to 30 per cent to 20 per cent in line with the above changes. In addition, investors looked to further minimise their risk by selling the production—whether TV mini-series or feature film—before it was completed. This pre-selling brought the film industry closer to the TV networks on the one hand and to international film distribution on the other. In the process the 'film industry' lost some of its independence.

At the same time the Australian TV market was changing. The late 1970s and the 1980s saw the slow but inexorable move towards (higher-budgeted) national programming and away from (lower-budgeted) local programming in all but news and current affairs. Scheduling was becoming more fragmented as stations sought to get the edge over their commercial rivals in ratings periods. This opened the way for 'event programming': mini-series and simultaneously screened national programming like Packer cricket. Also the networks were now functioning as semi-autonomous bodies rather than groupings of stations—they were commanding both more money and more centralised decision-making power. This coincided with the successful appearance of the TV mini-series with *Roots* (USA, 1977) and *Against the Wind* (Australian, 1978). As a consequence the networks were not only prepared to underwrite mini-series projects but, given their high production cost, were also looking for partners to share those costs. If the mini-series is related to the fragmentation of the TV schedule and rating sweeps, it is also related to the rapid rise in the standard of TV presentation during the 1980s. These standards, and their cost to the stations, can be measured not only by the size of mini-series' budgets but also by the high production values sought in other areas. For example, sports coverage by the early 1980s required multi-camera set-ups, action replays and special effects to be credible.

In the 1980s the commercial networks were open to screening and underwriting limited episode serials and one-off productions for national distribution. Of course, the commercial networks would not have been prepared to open their schedules in this way if national and multi-national advertisers had not been prepared to pay a premium price to associate themselves with this 'event' programming. The logic of this 'out of the ordinary' TV—both in terms of its high cost and its scheduling (typically stripped across the week)—was that it provided an intensity of viewing and bigger, 'quality', audiences—made up of occasional viewers, ABC and SBS viewers, and (hopefully) rival networks' viewers. Take the mini-series as an example: MacNair Anderson has reckoned that Australian mini-series rate 10 points higher than imported series with an average capital city rating of 31 points—some 8 points above the average. Indeed, in Melbourne, both *All The Rivers Run* and *Bodyline* rated 50 when screened.[3]

Another important set of possibilities was generated by the addition of a second non-commercial TV network in late 1980. Multicultural TV—SBS—was first introduced in Sydney and Melbourne and was gradually introduced to Canberra and the other major capital cities over the next five years. Although never attracting significant ratings it helped expand the definitions of TV. Not only did it screen foreign language films and TV series, cover minority sports and expand the definition of the newsworthy, but it also screened what had previously been seen as non-commercial features and documentaries. These films had had only marginal theatrical and non-theatrical release up to that time. And unlike the ABC which had its own production house, the SBS was open to purchasing new programs from independent producers. In the process, SBS permitted broadcast TV to appear in the forefront of social, cultural and aesthetic transformations.

The cinema market was also changing. In the 1980s the cinema trade was increasingly reliant upon blockbuster films to make up its revenues—and Australian producers increasingly looked to the production of such blockbusters. The prevalence of blockbusters, however, meant there was not the same demand for product that there had been. In the process the ground was progressively eroded from under the feet of the middle-budgeted 'quality' Australian film with a modest promotional budget. Thus viability was increasingly found in either the high-budgeted, extensively promoted, more internationally oriented 'kidult' ends of production—for example *The Man from Snowy River* (1984) and *Crocodile Dundee* (1986/7) —or in the lower budgeted, modestly promoted, Australian and international art-house film—for example Paul Cox's *Man of Flowers* (1983) and *My First Wife* (1986). Given these circumstances it's not surprising that filmmakers looked to TV—particularly the mini-series—as a means of maintaining the 1970s industry norm of the 'quality' Australian film. From a critical perspective the Australian blockbusters were not as amenable to the enthusiastic, culturalist readings and aesthetic claims as the quality film had been. As a consequence some of the importance of the feature film to cultural definitions lapsed with the slack being taken up by the mini-series.

Just as it was important for TV, SBS was an equally important event for Australian filmmaking. Not only did it accustom audiences and filmmakers alike to art-cinema protocols but it expanded the ways in which Australia could be represented in film. Both *Moving Out* (1982) and *Street Hero* (1984) are good examples of mainstream films which could, because of SBS presence, employ Italian and English actors and focus on ethnic Australia.

Put all these changes within cinema and TV industries together with economic recession and the film industry's privatisation through the tax concessions and we get a scenario which demanded a change of direction on the part of federal and state film bodies. In the 1970s they had provided some 50 per cent of production finance: in the 1980s this figure looked closer to 10–15 per cent. The state government film institutions—be they Film Victoria or the South Australian Film Corporation (SAFC)—increasingly looked to TV as a stable revenue source. It was visible enough (unlike the art film) and did not entail too significant a risk on funds committed. TV also had gained in importance for these bodies because many feature films produced for the cinema were gaining international release through TV anyway. TV could also, it was felt, provide steadier work opportunities in each state's local production industry. This reorientation was justified in terms reminiscent of the Vincent Report by John Morris of the SAFC: TV was where the mass audience was, it need not be so bad, government production help could make it better.[4] The Victorians, citing Crawford Productions' Melbourne base and worrying about a 'brain drain' to Sydney, saw their TV involvement as a means of maintaining existing employment opportunities in that state. It was in this context that the Victorian body provided some $200 000 towards the production of *A Town Like Alice*. The AFC, for its part, saw its role as one of 'seed bedding' projects be they film or TV. In one sense, the 1980s actually saw the coming to fruition of the 1960s policy dream of an independent film industry producing limited episode serials (mini-series) for TV and thus maintaining a feature film industry.

The interpenetration of film and TV

With the upper ends of TV being brought together with the feature industry in the 1980s to form a single 'film industry', the cultural agenda began to incorporate TV; personnel from one medium began to work in the other and vice versa. The process began dramatically in 1981 with the production of the mini-series, *A Town Like Alice*. This mini-series achieved the kind of international TV exposure and acclaim previously enjoyed only by *Skippy* (1967–69). It marked a watershed: no longer did the feature film have a mortgage on any cultural ambassadorial role on 'quality' audio-visual production. Hereafter feature film and the mini-series—and in 1978/9 the documentary—seemed bound up in the task of defining or reconstructing (depending on your perspective) Australian cultural and national identity. As Sue Dermody and Liz Jacka put it: 'In a remarkable way the mini-series inherited the nationalist mantle of the feature industry; even more remarkably, they formed a link back to its earlier phases, with remakes of classics like *A Town Like Alice* and *Robbery Under Arms*.[5] Some, like Beth Quinlivan, went so far as to say that Australians' film-making capacities were better suited to the TV mini-series and the tele-movie than to feature production.[6]

An interesting confirmation of this reconstruction of TV's cultural role came from Professor Leonie Kramer whilst Chairperson of the ABC. She articulated a role for the ABC as a producer of TV which would show the best of Australia to the world:

> I would hope that we'd be able to recover sufficiently to a point where we could produce several high quality dramas that we could sell overseas. I think the ABC has a real opportunity to make our creative talents known overseas. The foreign image of us does not do us justice. When I am abroad I am still meeting people who think of us as not very informed, not very bright, ill-mannered and boorish. I feel I have to tell them that we are: a modern, sophisticated and inventive community, even though I still have anxieties about Australia's culture.[7]

Reading between the lines we can see the 'high quality dramas'—i.e. mini-series—offered an Australian replication of the 'quality' BBC serial productions that significant sections of Australia's literate public held in high esteem. Also we can see that 'quality TV drama' allowed for the kinds of character development associated with the film of culture and quality, thus sidestepping the problems feature producers were having in contending with kidult films.

The most important cross-over from film to TV in the 1980s was provided by the Kennedy-Miller organisation. Named after its founders—the producer and the director of the *Mad Max* cycle of feature films, Kennedy-Miller produced a set of extraordinary mini-series: *The Dismissal* (1983) on the downfall of the Whitlam government: *Bodyline* (1984) on the controversial cricket series between Australia and England in the 1930s; *Cowra Breakout* (1985) which dealt with a massacre of Japanese prisoners-of-war at Cowra during the Second World War; and finally *Vietnam* (1987) which dealt with the circumstances and aftermath of Australia's involvement in that war. All represented major historical events in new ways and confirmed the vanguard role of the mini-series. All four series employed a distinguished group of directors drawn from feature film, TV and, in the case of George Ogilvie, the theatre. The first three series were particularly innovative in terms of their collaborative writing and acting workshops. All four used a cinematic style of production. Not only was TV being directed by the makers of *Mad Max*, but also by the makers of such acclaimed features as *Newsfront* (Phil Noyce) and *Winter of Our Dreams* (John Duigan, 1981) on adequate budgets.

The traffic though was not only one way. The involvement of mainstream TV personnel in feature films was also a feature of the 1980s. Indeed TV personnel were responsible for the two biggest Australian films of the 1980s: *The Man from Snowy River* (1982) and *Crocodile Dundee* (1986). Both became in their times the biggest money-earning films at the Australian box office. Both brought to feature filmmaking a populist and avowedly commercial taste. *Snowy River's* director, George Miller, and producers Geoff Burrowes and Simon Wincer all came from Crawfords. It also mixed actors better known from Australian TV soaps with its 'international actors', Jack Thompson and Kirk Douglas. *Crocodile Dundee* starred the TV comic and ad personality Paul Hogan, was produced by his manager and former TV partner, John Cornell and directed by TV 'event' specialist, Peter Faiman. Faiman was, even before *Crocodile Dundee*, the logical candidate for the four hour bicentennial show *Australia Live* (1988).

Film versus TV

It is true to say that the 1980s witnessed something of a rediscovery of the advantages of TV over features by investors and government authorities. Its principal advantage lay in that it was a safer, if less profitable, bet. TV offered the chance to be seen—regardless of whether the production was on the commercial networks or on the ABC and SBS. A mini-series or documentary was visible in a way that only the occasional feature film was. Further, it would not sink without trace in the way that many features had. A TV rating failure was still seen by a lot of people; the TV stations still had to purchase it and therefore less money was lost on it than with an unsuccessful film. In addition, the cost of feature film as opposed to a limited episode series was considerably higher per unit of screen time. In a TV series, the cost could be amortised over a number of units. No such economic advantages were available with features. Additionally a series was easily and cheaply advertised on the exhibiting network through filler spots between programs or at ad breaks. It could also, up until the November 1986 ownership changes, be promoted in the magazines and newspapers owned by the networks. The mini-series and documentary did not put all the investors' eggs in the one basket whereas the cinema film tended to do just that. A film could be trialled in one market and if it did not succeed then it had the kiss of death; it could have a blanket release with a big advertising budget and a large number of prints but if it did not succeed then the loss would be considerable. TV mini-series by contrast could build audiences more slowly—and be screened again. Cinema promotion, by contrast, was expensive. Ads had to be paid for and audiences are not already built-in in the way they were for TV: but the returns were significantly higher.

Generally, then, TV production was less risky than feature film production. As John Morris, Director of the SAFC, put it:

> This thing about TV is that there is a clearly defined upper limit. If you are highly successful in TV you know how much money you'll get; and if you're just good you know how much money you'll get; if you're bad, of course, you get nothing! In cinema there is no upper limit because a film, if it takes off, can make millions and millions and millions. So theoretically there is much more money to be got out of cinema than out of TV but the risks are much greater. That's the true answer. So there's more money in cinema if you make *Mad Max* but if you make *Weekend of Shadows* or *Dawn* you make nothing. Whereas if they had been made especially for TV that would probably have at least got their money back, if not made a slight profit. But if *Mad Max* had been made for TV, and been successful on TV it wouldn't have made anything like the money it's made out of cinema. Which was millions.[8]

It had been clear as early as *Breaker Morant* (1980) and *Gallipoli* (1982) that even a major Australian (and to a lesser extent, international) film success could have trouble recovering its costs in the short term. To be successful, extraordinary national and international box-office figures were required. The *Mad Max* cycle and *Crocodile Dundee I* and *II* proved the rule: producers could not expect to be extraordinarily successful, although extraordinary film successes do happen from time to time. And we find the international TV success of *A Town Like Alice* leaving its producers not much better off than before; its film equivalent at the other end of the 1980s, *Crocodile Dundee*, made its investors and producers very rich indeed.

After 1983, investors had increasingly required the 'pre-sale' of the production to guarantee the recoupment of a portion of the budget. But pre-sales are not just the province of TV. Increasingly, feature films were being pre-sold. Indeed by 1988, mini-series and feature films were increasingly in the same boat. In part this is because profits on mini-series production, already low, were further squeezed by the changes to the tax concessions (which accounts for the 1985/6 downturn in mini-series production from 24 to 5); and also because pre-sales had become a more important film financing instrument with the development of international video markets, pay TV, and pre-sales to the cinema trade.

By 1987, cinema and TV production faced problems getting the 65 per cent of budget in pre-sales required to break even. Both looked to international involvement through co-productions to obtain the level of pre-sales required; just as they had in the early 1960s in TV with *Whiplash* (1961) and in the cinema with *They're a Weird Mob* (1966). After the long film industry boom of the 1980s, feature film, like TV, was facing a financial crisis. 'Internationalism' was set to make its return—and, once again, the government announced the establishment of a 'film bank—or film finance corporation'. Through the 1980s, the mini-series had provided a way of remaining Australian; ironically, by the end of the 1980s, it too was feeling the pressure to internationalise. The tax concessions which had protected the Australian face of the industry now look set to encourage the industry's internationalisation.

Conclusion

Most of the developments within Australian TV from 1960 on were predicated in part upon government measures: be they content provisions or (after 1969) direct (and later indirect) subsidies to production. Although it has been argued that the Australian content provisions were mostly symbolic gestures, they were important in ensuring an Australia-wide market for Australian productions. These provisions were especially important in getting the 30 per cent of the

Australian TV market (that could get all the overseas drama material they needed for their schedules) to obtain local drama programming. The content provisions in the major capital city markets created a bottom line below which stations could not go. They thus encouraged levels of Australian content in excess of the requirements. Recently these government regulations and government-subsidised support for film production have come under attack. In 1987 advertisers were freed to show as many ads as they liked. The tax concessions have been targeted as an iniquitous tax haven which needs to be pared back. Government instrumentalities, like the AFC, are seen to be areas of unnecessary wastage of scarce government funds. Taken together these deregulatory, minimal government impulses pose significant challenges. If they were to successfully challenge the authority of the Broadcasting Tribunal and its Australian content provisions, and if we also were to see the demise of direct and indirect production subsidies, then two of the crucial planks sustaining a film and TV production industry would be removed. And this at a time when TV broadcasting is losing some of its dominance to competing uses for the TV monitor. Such actions, if not counterbalanced by other instruments, could devastate local production and turn the clock back 30 years. What needs to be remembered is that the initial decisions taken in TV policy that were so prejudicial to Australian produced TV were not taken out of a desire to denigrate the local product. They were taken for a host of other reasons—to ensure economic viability and to meet concerns for the quality of TV. This is a salutary reminder that legitimate demands for deregulation, an equitable tax system and reduced government expenditure, could have further, unintended, effects on the complexion of cultural production in Australia.

Notes

1 *Film Assistance: Future Options* (Sydney: George Allen and Unwin, 1987), p.2. This AFC report goes on to note that 'production grew from a base of between 50 and 1000 hours per annum to a new benchmark of around 250 hours, divided in broadly equal measure between cinema and TV'.
2 *Film Assistance*, p.1.
3 *Film Assistance*, p.2.
4 John Morris quoted in Michele Fryar, 'Australian Film: An Interview with John Morris', in Michele Fryar and Joost Daalder, *Aspects of Australian Culture* (Adelaide: Abel Tasman Press, 1982), p.118.
5 Sue Dermody and Liz Jacka, *The Screening of Australia* (Sydney: Currency Press, 1987), pp.189–90.
6 Beth Quinlivan, 'Up from Nowhere to Stardom and Back in Ten Years',

Far Eastern Economic Review, 3 May 1984, p.71.
7 Professor Leonie Kramer quoted in Deirdre Macken, 'Leonie Kramer: A Fighter not a Killer', *The Age*, 12 May 1982.
8 Michele Fryar, 'Australian Film', p.119.

3

Transgressive TV: From *In Melbourne Tonight* to *Perfect Match*

Graeme Turner

Australia is a post-colonial culture and so does not create its representational forms from whole cloth. Our novels are still novels, our films are still films, our poems are still poems; despite their 'Australianness', they are still in one sense determined by generic structures and readers' expectations articulated thousands of kilometres away, and often many years ago. The Australian utterance in any form—film, prose, videotape, speech—does not invent its own language but speaks an existing language with an audible and distinctive accent. To examine Australian television is to deal with specific industrial structures, sets of production practices, and repertoires of productions; it is also to talk about the complex processes of appropriation and transformation of foreign models that we can hear as the 'accent' of Australian television.

In 1985, Nick Roddick wrote a nicely appreciative piece on Australian TV for the British journal, *Sight and Sound*. Titled, 'Strewth! A Beginner's Guide to Australian TV',[1] it might easily have invoked the familiar colonialist myth of Australian culture as vulgar, populist, second-rate, and ultimately inferior. Instead, Roddick adopted a less conventional stance. While he recognised Australian TV's colonial dependencies, he also detected a freshness and richness not available in British TV. ('If there is one myth about Britain which has proved more tenacious than any other', he says, 'it is that we have the best television in the world.')[2] Unlike indigenous critics such as Phillip Adams and Richard Coleman, Roddick was able to admit the cultural legitimacy of, for instance, the SBS movie classics and a game show like *Perfect Match*. While the article makes a strong case for the originality of SBS programming, it also admires aspects of more mainstream Australian TV such as the 'quality soap', *A Country Practice*. For Roddick, Australian television—with its variety of textures and flavours—is 'new world television, unashamed, unbridled, magnificent'.[3] In such judgments, Roddick implicitly rejects the elitist view of popular television as bad art, as well as the more pragmatic, industry view which simply equates quality with ratings. What is notable in his piece is a sense of TV as a particular regime of pleasure that is as much dependent on its immediacy as its ability to stimulate reflection; a regime that is as likely to offer its viewers ritual or spectacle as drama or art.

This is not a point of view we often meet in general discussions of Australian television within the culture, nor is it a dominant point of view within academic discussions of the media. I want to develop it in order to do two things: to speculate on how such a view of TV might help us understand particular and important modes of television production and consumption; and secondly, to employ this understanding in an examination of a specific aspect of Australian television production. Roddick's piece is only a starting point, of course. A slightly more substantial argument, offering essentially the same kind of view of television, is presented in Adrian Martin's 'Stretch TV'.[4] Again, while it may mark the beginning rather than the end of an enquiry, Martin's piece is a provocative description of TV as a 'live' medium, and of its transgressive, unconventional possibilities.

Stretch TV

Adrian Martin outlines the category of stretch TV in the following way. First, he stresses the importance of television's formulas—the established sets of conventions which organise television productions and their reception by audiences:

> formula is simultaneously the saddest and happiest fact of popular television. What makes sitcoms like *Taxi* or *Cheers* so rich is the pattern of familiarities and predictabilities they set up from week to week—comically perverting and reversing our expectations quite as much as they fulfil them.[5]

'Formula', he goes on to say, 'is one of the elements which distin-
guishes TV from, say, the cinema, and gives it a specific richness as
a medium.' Importantly, Martin reminds us that there is a legitimate pleasure in the familiar, in developing the knowledge that
alerts us to the fact that Arthur Daley is about to 'drop Terry in it',
or that enables us to understand what Sir Humphrey really means
when he says, 'Yes Minister'. Having rescued the idea of formula
from its customary perjorative meaning, Martin nevertheless points
out that formula can also 'mean boredom and flatness':

> Geared to and structured around ad breaks, TV shows have to
> conform to a certain rhythm and a certain look which can
> become all too familiar. Which leaves viewers secretly wishing for
> a hiccup, a slip, a gaff somewhere along the way, a spanner to
> gum up this well-oiled institutional and industrial machine of
> popular TV.[6]

Some shows are wrongheaded enough to devote themselves entirely
to presenting such gaffes. *Foul-Ups, Bleeps and Blunders* incor-
porates the gaffes back into the slickness of popular TV, depriving
them of their subversive value by embalming them in the most rigid
and lifeless of formats. However, the shows Martin includes within
the category of stretch TV are those which not only maintain their
conventional generic structures and procedures, but also break
them, take risks, transgress what they have set up as their own
parameters. *The Young Ones, Hey Hey It's Saturday, Soap,
Moonlighting*, are shows where a complicated relationship is set
up between a formula that is, on the one hand, familiar, predictable and largely observed and, on the other hand, that formula's
deliberate subversion, the suggestion of a 'real multiplication of
possibilities'.

Stretch TV is the insertion of the possibility of anarchy, the
pairing of the familiar with a 'flagrant flaunting of the rules,
smashed conventions, fragmented surfaces'.[7] The 'produced' effect
of (particularly American) TV gives way before immediacy, contin-
gency. TV's immediacy, its 'liveness', its provisional status, even its
ephemerality, enables it to shock and surprise and scandalise. The
TV formula becomes a location for play, a licensed area set aside
for the exploitation of any opportunity to test the rigidity of its
boundaries. In shows such as *Moonlighting*, or *The Young Ones*,
the transgression of conventions, the break with the normal and the
predictable, is a kind of performance—a spectacle of pure TV.

What I am describing here could well be an essential property of
the medium, although it is a relatively minor aspect of the published
work in the field. Much TV analysis deploys quasi-aesthetic dis-

courses which derive essentially from cinema or literature (see the MacCabe/McArthur debates on realism, for example)[8] and which still inevitably, if implicitly, privilege the complete dramatic text or the filmic narrative as the preferred televisual form. However, the exploitation of the medium's potential for play turns TV away from the domain of the aesthetic and towards the more primitive modality of performance—spectacle, ritual and display.

Transgressive Texts

Martin's 'multiplication of possibilities' is of at least two kinds: one emphasises the variety of structuring principles behind television programming—narrative, spectacle, or even the performance of the technology itself (as in the *Australia Live* broadcast); the second, despite the common assumptions about the simplicity of the television message, lies in the range of social meanings generated by the one television text. A central tradition in TV research has argued that TV is entirely hegemonic, inevitably reproducing dominant views and attitudes to and for its audiences.[9] These days, however, it is increasingly widely recognised that television is a complex medium composed of many separate and competing signifying systems—lights, camera, sound, 'the talent', to name the most basic. In most instances, viewers have some choice as to how they compose what they see, which elements will dominate their reading. Broadcast TV is rich in its composition and its reception. Although the medium certainly does attempt to restrict the range of meanings generated by its texts it nevertheless, and persistently, produces 'more meanings than it can police'. As John Hartley points out,[10] the semiotic richness of the television message is rarely reducible to one single meaning received by every member of the viewing audience. Current affairs shows, for instance, live with the fact that they can screen a political interview and be accused of bias from opposite ends of the political spectrum. Such shows make use of the variety of viewing positions appropriate to any one message by conventionally representing unresolved conflicts in their material as open contradictions ('I guess that's the way it is, these days') which are only sealed over by the ideology of the program itself, or of its audience themselves.

Because of this 'semiotic excess', the multiplicity of possible meanings, much of what TV 'says' to its audiences can be quite contradictory or ambiguous—a fact which *necessitates* an active individual reading as members of the audience order and arrange what they see as 'their' meaning. The ingredients of luck and sportsmanship in *Sale of the Century* contradict the invocation of skill, talent and the importance of winning; calling *Mastermind* a 'game show' is to deny its specific format which is closer to that of the examination or interrogation; *Perfect Match* regularly oscillates between a reactionary sexism and a progressive representation of gender relations; the questions asked in, again, *Perfect Match*, negotiate the contradiction between discourses of difference and individuality, and those which draw on a range of established class, gender and subcultural codes in order to establish the contestant within a personality 'type'; TV advertising, generally, conflates consumerist images of lifestyle with opposing discourses of health and simplicity.

It would be wrong to assume that this mass of contradictions and ambiguities is necessarily confusing to the audience. It is not appropriate to approach TV with the hope of always constructing unitary meanings from its texts. There are many reasons for watching the one TV program, and any one viewer might watch *Perfect Match* for what seem to be entirely contradictory reasons. (They might watch the returnee segment to be embarrassed by the crassness and cruelty of the remarks, but then barrack just as cruelly during the selection sequences.) The ambiguity of *Perfect Match* is, in fact, its chief attraction. (This is at least true of the 1985–86 version, hosted by Greg Evans and Debbie Newsome or Tiffany Lamb; the changes in 1987 reduced the ambiguity and the ratings declined too.) The reason for this is that in ambiguity and contradiction we may find richness rather than confusion, a proliferation of possible meanings, a gradation of social/ideological positions and thus of possible uses to which audiences may choose to put a television text. John Hartley's 'Encouraging Signs' argues that if television attempts to control and limit its capacity for meaning to those meanings which are dominant, the continual production of semiotic excess is an encouraging sign of the uncertain tenure of any hegemonic meaning.[11] Hartley sees the leakage of ambiguity into the television message as a leakage from dominant social and political positions; it therefore holds out the possibility of resistance to the dominant. Of course, it is as well to remember that these ambiguities and these varied readings may well all serve the same ideological ends. Our active viewers may indeed be free to construct their own readings of television texts, but they are not therefore free of ideology or of their subjection to material, social conditions.

That important reservation aside, the distinctiveness of these transgressive, ambiguous, television texts lies in the degree to which they transgress their own conventions and thus invite a range of possibly contradictory responses from their audiences. The pleasure provided is notable because it depends on the relative freedom of the viewers, not their rigid positioning, before the television message. The regimes of pleasure governing such texts contain the familiar recognition of a formula as well as the exhilarating sense of its provisionality. And, ultimately, transgressive television works to minimise television's reflectiveness, its produced, static and unified aspects (its textuality, even), and its affinities with aesthetic forms like literature or film.

Transgressive Australian shows

This brings us to the second objective of this chapter, the application of this view of television to Australian television production. Transgressive television is well represented in the history of local production. It is crucial to the success of *In Melbourne Tonight*, *The Aunty Jack Show*, *The Naked Vicar*, *The Mavis Bramston Show*, *Number 96*, *The Norman Gunston Shows*, *Blankety Blanks*, *Perfect Match*, *Hey Hey Its Saturday*, the entire genre of *Tonight* shows, Clive Robertson's *Newsworld*—in fact, a significant proportion of the ratings successes and memorable moments of Australian TV. One could construct a history of Australian television from such shows; I want to briefly review some examples, beginning with that least transgressive of formats, the game show, and its current representative, *Perfect Match*.

Elsewhere I have described the discursive and structural ambiguity in *Perfect Match*[12]—for example, its apparent invocation of romance and young love competing with spectacles of failure and embarrassment for the viewer's interest. *Perfect Match* sets up a romantic game show format which it then subverts and parodies. The program's apparent object of uniting couples with a view to marriage is so rarely achieved, and so embarrassing when it is, that it clearly has little to do with the reason for the high ratings. Unlike most game shows, there are no clear winners on *Perfect Match*. Winning the weekend away is a far more equivocal achievement than winning a BMW—preceded as it is by the spectacle of the embarrassing clinch with a total stranger on national TV, and followed as it is by exposure to the analysis of one's behaviour, class and general desirability in the returnee's segment. To assume people watch *Perfect Match* purely for romantic reasons is to misread the parodic opening titles and to misunderstand how violently it oscillates between sentimentality and cynicism. The format is simply the frame for transgressive TV.

This is also the case with another game show, *Blankety Blanks*.

The format itself produces a static play on *double entendres* as the celebrity panel and the contestants try to fill in the blanks in the questions posed. However, in both its versions in Australia (the Graham Kennedy version in the 1970s and the Daryl Somers version in the 1980s) the game format was progressively subverted. Graham Kennedy often broke into long vaudeville-styled routines with Ugly Dave Grey; Kennedy himself was crucial to the show, using the panel of celebrities as the 'feeds' for his one-liners. Somers' version was even less interested in the game. Where Kennedy would at least complete the game so that each episode produced a winner, Somers eventually ceased even to worry about that. Questions were turned into performances as Somers adopted characters, mimicked famous personalities, and generally used the game as the motivation for a series of gags and sketches. By the end of its run, *Blankety Blanks* would rarely finish a contest, holding over a contestant for the next show even if it meant that only one answer had to be given.

Game shows are not the only members of this trangressive category. The success of *Number 96* derived from its parody of soap opera conventions and its studied and witty excessiveness more than from its attributes as conventional soap opera. *Number 96* was known for its aggressive Australianising of the soap opera format and also for breaking some of the restrictions on what should be seen on Australian TV—naked women, unashamed sex symbols like Abigail, and the first affectionate representation of a homosexual by Joe Hasham. However, it is probably in a format which Australian TV largely developed that the transgressive characteristics show themselves most consistently—the *Tonight* shows.

Originally modelled on such variety shows as the USA's *Steve Allen Show*, the early Australian *Tonight* shows were highly influenced by local, pre-TV vaudeville. Less chat-oriented in the beginning than later, shows such as those hosted by Bobby Limb and Dawn Lake depended on a succession of musical acts and sketches. *In Melbourne Tonight (IMT)* added some game segments to this format and then began to burlesque the advertising spots. With Dave Allen, Ray Taylor, Bob Rogers, and later Don Lane, talk and interviews became important—as in the US variety—but still we had impromptu performances, contests, games, the unexpected always threatening to happen. Dave Allen used to take dares from his audiences, which he would satisfy live; on one occasion he broke his ankle on a trampoline. 'Don's Wheel' was both a game and potentially fluid set-up for Don Lane and Bert Newton to feed off. The segment consisted of spinning a numbers wheel to select a prize for a viewer who was then called on the phone and asked a ridiculously simple question. This procedure would regularly take some twenty minutes of air-time and was used as a cue for sketches and extended ad-libbing from Bert and Don. Always risky, it produced some exhilarating moments of television.

The *Tonight* shows differed from their American models in similar ways to *Perfect Match's* departure from its American models: instead of taking the format seriously they used it as a set of conventions to attack and transgress. *Tonight* shows could produce moments of extreme confrontation in interviews, moments of inspired comedy, and some bizarre performances; they did this, however, through transcending or transgressing the formula—not by sticking to it. Graham Kennedy's *IMT* is perhaps the best example of a host and a show which was always trying to break out of its frame. As Sandra Hall has said, 'Kennedy raised expectations of the unexpected, augmenting what he had in his scripts with whatever he could grab out of the people and things around him'.[13] Even though the sketches were deliberately bad, the show was compelling viewing 'because of the suspense [Kennedy] was able to pump into it'.[14] Eventually, his transgressions were against the standards of the Broadcasting Control Board and he was prevented from broadcasting live.

One of Kennedy's writers at *IMT* was Ernie Carroll, now the producer of *Hey Hey It's Saturday* and the arm up Ossie Ostrich. Carroll's influence may well be a significant one, since Daryl Somers' use of television in his partnership with Carroll is reminiscent of Graham Kennedy. *Hey Hey It's Saturday* is true stretch TV. Originally based on a British children's show (which nevertheless commanded a large adult audience) *Tiswas*, *Hey Hey It's Saturday* started in childrens' viewing slots. Its development into a cult show for adults was acknowledged by its movement to a more prominent spot on Saturday night and by most of the reminders of the children's show—except for Ossie Ostrich—disappearing. *Hey Hey* uses the conventions of TV as its raw material; it parodies, inspects, and overturns them at every opportunity. Like *IMT*, it contains quasi-game show segments, such as the parody of talent shows, 'Red Faces'. In 'Red Faces', acts are expected to be bad, and a gong is available to curtail a really bad performance. When the occasional act turns out to be good there is some embarrassment— just as in *Perfect Match* when a couple return from their holiday 'in love'. The point of 'Red Faces' is to provide a spectacle of embarrassment, evidence of the power of television to seduce people onto its screens doing ridiculous things—just to be on TV.

Hey Hey encourages audience participation on regular fancy dress nights, turning the audience into content, and by moving the show from Melbourne occasionally. The audience has a more substantial, if indirect 'voice' in the running battle between the presenters, the guests, and the crazy misspelt messages superimposed on the screen throughout the show, commenting on the show. The privileged position of those on camera is further subverted through the disembodied voice of John Blackman whose comments override whatever else is on the soundtrack. It is hard to imagine what the running sheet must look like, such is the degree of flexibility and the number of competing discourses which threaten to hijack any one segment and take it into totally uncharted waters. Ellis's theory that TV is composed of segments rather than complete units is emphasised by *Hey Hey It's Saturday*.[15] The structure is provided by the naming of the various segments: 'Ad Nauseam' (a quiz show on TV ads), 'What Cheeses Me Off' (a complaints column), and 'Beat It' (a music quiz), serve to anchor the show for the viewer. The use of segment titles on the backdrops does at least remind the viewer what it is the show is supposed to be doing at the moment—even if it isn't. The use of segments, and the skill of a crew who appear to be able to adapt to new demands almost instantly, allows *Hey Hey* to use a relatively tame format as the basis for the regular production of the unexpected. It is playful, energetic, lively TV which uses the immediacy and flexibility of the medium as its benefit and its alibi.

None of these shows construct themselves as explicitly Australian; any 'accent' heard in these descriptions emerges from the recurrence of a pattern in the transformation of foreign models rather than through any direct construction of Australianness. This is not the case with Norman Gunston's shows, however. Almost entirely dependent upon their parody of Australian press and television conventions, the character and format of the Gunston shows has some claim to uniqueness. Certainly the most frequent response from his foreign guests was disbelief and bewilderment. Alternately cruel and pathetic, Gunston used the cultural cringe as camouflage, enabling the satirist it obscured to humiliate and expose. By pretending to be pathetic, he invited the contempt of the powerful; his pretence, however, was horribly familiar as it exposed the servility which underlay the Australian deference to opinions from outside. Inscribed into an alternative view of his character, though, was a nationalist avenging of cultural domination. So, when the Hollywood star, Warren Beatty, arrived for a triumphant tour of Australia he was asked by the little Aussie bleeder if he had ever considered getting a 'real job'. Gunston broke rules, frustrated expectations, and revealed the phony behind the facade on a regular basis. In Norman Gunston, the function of transgression in Australian television, and the myth of the iconoclastic Australian identity were combined and perfectly articulated.

Gunston's cultural specificity is exceptional, however, and few of
our television producers have spoken with such strong Australian
accents. The shows mentioned above nevertheless constitute a sug-
gestive list; they occupy positions of influence, and produce affectionate memories as key moments in the development of locally
produced Australian television. It is probably significant that the
programs which excite particular affection are those which were
based on, and outrageously transformed, more benign foreign
models: *Perfect Match* and the innocuous American show, *Blind
Date*, or *In Melbourne Tonight* and *The Steve Allen Show*. This
raises the possibility of political objectives being served by such
shows—along the lines suggested in John Hartley's article, for
instance, or as an articulation of post-colonial resistance to foreign
cultural domination. Certainly we need to know more about the
ideological and social functions of this kind of television; it requires
much more analysis than it has so far received.

The transgressive reader

Shows such as *Perfect Match* and *Hey Hey It's Saturday* (or, for
that matter, American shows such as *The Gong Show* or *Candid
Camera*) invade our private lives by turning them into television.
This is certainly a confirmation of the power of television, albeit,
and importantly, its particular power to inscribe itself into our
domestic everyday lives—not its power as a medium for the production of high art. It does seem, though, that the specific uses
audiences make of these shows vary even more than is the case with
realist narratives, which inevitably restrict the variety of positions
from which they can make sense. Where audiences experience
ambiguity or contradiction as a result of this reading potential, the
experience is as likely to be exhilarating as it is to be confusing.
Many programs thrive on their contradictions. So, it is arguable that
transgressive television shifts the balance of power away from the
TV producer, the performer, or the contestant, onto the viewer.
Most of the shows I have looked at ritually expose their performers/
victims to the power of TV. They thus place the viewer in an
especially privileged position. The compere, say, on *Perfect Match*,
will often recognise this, failing to comfort the contestant at all and
confining his role to that of a mediator between the audience and the
spectacle unfolding, rather than between the contestant and his or
her ordeal. In some cases, the show only exists for the viewer. The
performers can never experience the immediacy of *Hey Hey It's
Saturday*. The only position from which it can make sense, with

all its contributing discourses, is that of the viewer. The power of TV is indeed confirmed, but through the privileging of the power of the viewer.

Such a position echoes reorientations in the analyses of other representational forms: the recovery of the reader in literary theory, for example. The idea that a transgressive, rule-breaking text implies a politically resistant reader has quite a pedigree beyond television studies. It informs Belsey's notion of the interrogative text as the ideological alternative to the closed, authoritative realist text in literary fiction;[16] it motivates numerous appropriations of Bahktin's discussion of carnival in literary and television criticism (from Kristeva's incorporation of the notion into a feminist politics to the Curthoys and Docker chapter in this collection); assumptions about the ideological function of realism and the corresponding need for its deconstruction mark the MacCabe/MacArthur debates on the British TV series, *Days of Hope*.[17] While there are plenty of voices warning against reading an audience's ideology from the formal properties of the texts it consumes, transgressive texts, almost inevitably, continue to excite just such activity. So, the preceding remarks on transgressive television take their place in a long line of claims for new textual forms as signifiers of a resistance to dominant ideological systems: from the *nouvelle vague* films and their ambiguous endings, to American metafictions and their proposition of the fictiveness of reality, to the do-it-yourself kit of meanings provided by the contemporary music video clip. In television studies, the appeal of such claims is strengthened by two factors which are specific to the field of study; they supply another avenue of contradiction to stubbornly enduring assumptions of the unity of the television message,[18] and they suggest an alternative set of methodological strategies to narrative-based analysis.

There is a large body of culturalist analysis which focuses on the way TV 'smoothes over' gaps in ideology, naturalising existing social conditions through the resolution of narrative conflict, for example, or through the contestants' cashing in their education for the car and the prizes in *Sale of the Century*.[19] Recently, this emphasis has been shifting. John Fiske's chapter, 'Everyday Quizzes, Everyday Life', has a history which illustrates the movement; it originated in a discussion of quiz shows which interested itself in their unifying, naturalising function, but the later chapter charts patterns of resistance and ambiguity in order to construct a more complex, because more contradictory, account of the quiz show and its viewers. The pendulum of TV analysis is swinging back from the attempt to establish how television assists in the maintenance of the status quo, to the analysis of the specific plea-

sures it provides, how these specific pleasures might offer resistance
to ideological control—even to how television might facilitate social
change. Hodge and Tripp's recent *Children and Television*[20] con-
fronts the perennial question of the effect of TV on children and
proposes that children are not in fact the victims of TV at all. Their
description of the children as viewers has them relatively free to
'make over' the television message to their own needs, to read the
message through different sets of codes to those used by adults.
Ethnographic work on audiences also emphasises the danger of
assuming that the monolithic audience implied by ratings figures
actually exists.[21] As we have seen, even a show as apparently
formulaic as *Perfect Match* is not marked by much discursive
unity: in any one program, opposing discourses can be seen actively
competing for dominance and its attitude to existing social conditions can vary from the celebratory to the sceptical. Since the
message can no longer be assumed to be unified, assumptions about
what audiences might do with TV have to be re-examined.

Conclusion

To appreciate the usefulness of this theoretical shift is not to argue
that popular television is therefore never conservative, or that it is
never unified, or that it never rigidly positions its viewers. (TV
news, for instance, strikes me as a mode which aims very accurately
at such objectives, inscribing different reading positions while still
policing the ideological boundaries most effectively.) The argument
is rather that while certain forms of television may be marked by
their unity and their viewer positioning, it is not *ipso facto* a
property of the medium to be this way. We need to differentiate
between various modes of popular television; to assume that popularity only arises from the reproduction of existing conventions is
to be unable to explain the success of most of the shows I have
discussed in this chapter. It is also to ignore the strong evidence
of the different uses to which audiences will put the same TV
program—whether it is conventional or trangressive. Furthermore,
Horace Newcomb and Robert Alley's collection of American TV
producers, *The Producer's Medium*,[22] (together with our sense
of the roles played by Ernie Carroll, Graham Kennedy, Garry
McDonald and others in our industry), underlines the fact that
different producers use the medium differently too. What is clear is
that although the unity of television has only recently begun to drift
down the agenda of media and cultural studies, the ratings achieved
by trangressive programs have been telling us for years that TV does
not have to be simple or unified in order to be popular.

The importance of transgressive, 'live' TV to Australian audiences was underlined by its exploitation in the Bicentennial *Australia Live* telecast. A production of staggering technical achievement, with over 70 satellite crosses in four hours and mini-narratives taking us from Perth to Kalgoorlie to Antarctica, its highlights were nevertheless moments of subversion. Geoff Harvey took the camera on a manic plunge into an Italian wedding in Melbourne, Vince Sorrenti sampled and then threw away the culinary delights of Lygon Street in a parody of the gourmet, and Daryl Somers clearly had trouble taking the exercise seriously as he put his talents to work interviewing the cooks in the kitchens at Hamilton Island. Despite the high-tech production values, and the star presenters, the discourses of the show were as domestic as *Neighbours*. It was utterly appropriate that its most endearing, and perhaps most significant, moment came during an interview with an old couple in an 'outback' town. The old man, clearly second fiddle, was being beamed all over Australia (and further) but he didn't even bother turning on his hearing aid until his wife elbowed him in the ribs and said, 'Clive's talking to you!' (The interviewer, by satellite, was Clive James.) Despite all the technological wizardry, the celebrity hosts and presenters, that moment offered the most pleasure, and underlined how central a lack of respect for TV's conventions and formulas is within the history of Australian television production and its audience.

Notes

1   Nick Roddick, 'Strewth! A Beginner's Guide to Australian TV' *Sight and Sound*, Winter, 1985, pp.250–4.
2   Ibid., p.251.
3   Ibid., p.254.
4   Adrian Martin, 'Stretch TV' *XPress: Popular Culture*, 1:1, 1985, pp.22–3.
5   Ibid., p.22.
6   Ibid.
7   Ibid., p.23.
8   These are available in Tony Bennett et al. (eds) *Popular Film and Television* (London: BFI, 1981).
9   This is true of much of Stuart Hall's early work, for instance, and has occasionally resulted in a view of audiences that is very similar to that of the American effects' studies of the 1960s.
10 See John Hartley's 'Encouraging Signs: TV and the Power of Dirt, Speech and Scandalous Categories', *Australian Journal of Cultural Studies*, 1:2, 1983, pp.62–82.
11 Ibid.
12 Graeme Turner, '*Perfect Match*: Spectacle, Ambiguity, Popularity', *Australian Journal of Cultural Studies*, 4:2, 1986, pp.79–92. Some of the

points made in the present chapter derive from this more detailed study.

13 Sandra Hall, *Supertoy: 20 Years of Australian Television* (Melbourne: Sun, 1976), p.90.

14 Ibid.

15 John Ellis, *Visible Fictions* (London: Routledge and Kegan Paul, 1982).

16 Catherine Belsey, *Critical Practice*, (London: Methuen, 1980).

17 Cited above, in Bennett et al., *Popular Film and Television*.

18 For the Australian variant of an established international mode, see my 'Nostalgia for the Primitive: Wildlife Documentaries on TV', *Australian Journal of Cultural Studies*, 3:1, 1985, pp.62–71.

19 See John Fiske 'The Discourses of TV Quiz Shows, or School + Luck = Success + Sex', in the *Central States Speech Journal*, 34:3, pp.139–50.

20 R. Hodge and D. Tripp, *Children and Television* (Oxford: Polity Press, 1986).

21 The usual reference point is Dave Morley's *The Nationwide Audience*, (London: BFI, 1980).

22 Horace Newcomb and Robert Alley, *The Producer's Medium* New York: Oxford University Press, 1983.

4

Textual Innovation in the Australian Historical Mini-Series

Stuart Cunningham

In retrospect, the program that is generally regarded as the first Australian 'historical' mini-series, *Against the Wind*, can be seen to have pioneered many of the protocols of production and reception that have characterised this distinctive television drama format. Produced in 1978 for the Seven Network at, for the time, the considerable cost of $76 000 per episode, the program consisted of thirteen one-hour episodes and dealt, with critical historiographical insight, with the first decades of colonisation in Australia. *Against the Wind*—with its large number of episodes and its discrete as well as continuous episodic structure—tended to resemble earlier Australian 'historical' serials [such as the thirteen-episode *Luke's Kingdom* (1974–75)] more than the mini-series proper. However, its epic historical thematics and narrative coverage, its widely discussed 'revisionist' account of the historical record on early convictism, its promotion and reception as 'history' as well as drama, and its huge critical and ratings success all foreshadow the contours of the historical mini-series 'phenomenon' of the 1980s.

And quite a phenomenon it has become. Writing in 1987, Jane Freebury estimated that 50 mini-series had been made in Australia since the introduction of the 10BA tax legislation,[1] while only three were made before this.[2] This indicates something of the complex

of institutional preconditions and contexts for the establishment
of the mini-series at the high-budget end of film and television fin-
ancing in the 1980s in Australia.[3] These favourable conditions have
given us such memorable critical and ratings successes as *A Town
Like Alice* (1981), *1915* (1982), *The Dismissal, Waterfront* and
Power Without Glory (1983), *The Last Bastion, Bodyline* and
Eureka Stockade (1984), *Anzacs, The Dunera Boys* and *Cowra
Breakout* (1985), *A Fortunate Life* and *The Lancaster Miller
Affair* (1986), and *Vietnam* (1987).

However, it is not my purpose here to analyse these 'preconditions and contexts', nor to survey even a representative grouping
of this contemporary plethora of mini-series. Rather, I want to
be both more abstract and more particular than either of these
approaches would determine. I want to address the distinctiveness
of the mini-series as a televisual format and, woven into this, the
innovations and challenges that Australian historical mini-series
present in both their representations of national history and in their
expansion of the 'horizons of possibility' of televisual form. This
means that I will have cause to concentrate in detail on a small
number of 'limit-case' texts, thus moving from generic markers to
generic horizons, avowedly privileging what, in my opinion, are
the most exciting cases.

The mini-series format

What *is* a mini-series, and what makes it so interesting? The mini-
series is a quite recent addition to the established array of television
formats—news, current affairs, light entertainment, series and
serial drama, documentary, sport and so on. It is a veritable hybrid
—split between the series and serial drama formats, and between
documentary and dramatic modes. It can be understood to cover a
limited-run program of more than two and less than the thirteen-
part season or half-season block associated with continuing serial
or series programming, and whose episodes are not narratively
autonomous, like the series format. (Thus, strictly speaking, the
term 'mini-series' is a misnomer.) However, it is more akin to the
series format insofar as it moves to conclusive narrative resolution
across a limited number of episodes, unlike the serial, with its indefinitely (and what seems at times, infinitely) deferred denoue-
ments. Its 'hybridisation' of documentary and dramatic modes
also creates real definitional problems, perturbs many viewers and
commentators because of the ethical, legal and political imponder-
ables raised by its taste for 'impersonating history', but excites just

as much rapturous response for the risks and challenges it takes as it 'inscribes the document into experience'.[4]

The mini-series' hybrid status, as could be expected, poses further problems for general theories of televisual form. Commentators have thus sought family resemblances between cinematic forms and, especially, modes of promotion, and the mini-series. While there are indeed intriguing connections, the dramaturgical structures deployed in mini-series defy easy assimilation to a cinematic model. Finally, the approaches to issues and events taken up in the most interesting examples of the format move easily around traditional categories usually held to divide televisual material into 'entertainment' and 'information/education'. I want to look at these questions more closely now.

Australian historical mini-series

Taking perhaps the most evident aspect first, the Australian historical mini-series is 'quality', 'event' television. Its status is analogous to that of the 'art cinema' in relation to mainstream commercial cinema, albeit without the financial and promotional marginalisation typically experienced by art cinema. Historical mini-series are produced on regularly record-breaking budgets for television, are accompanied by major promotional campaigns, often as flag-carriers leading into new ratings periods, and in turn attract lavish spin-off campaigns and critical and ratings successes, all of which contribute to their placement as 'exceptional' television.

The mini-series' placement as 'quality' television has several interrelated levels of registration. It can be traced at an institutional level to the need for the major American commercial networks to inaugurate and market their own genre of up-market material in order to counteract the allegiances public television, cable and subscription services were soliciting from the demographically sensitive market sectors with high disposable incomes. It is evidenced by the diverse and high-profile 'circulation' of the mini-series as event in contiguous formats—from glossy presentations on production history (e.g. Brian Carroll, *The Making of a Fortunate Life*), novelisations (e.g. Sue Mackinnon's *Waterfront*), reprints of historical records (e.g. Paul Kelly's *The Unmaking of Gough* reprinted as *The Dismissal* upon the release of the mini-series by the same name), coffee-table 'records' of the series (e.g. Kristin Williamson's *The Last Bastion*), through to voluminous numbers of 'letters to the editor', historical reminiscence by actual protagonists, lavish and detailed critical reviews by more usually dyspeptic newspaper critics, and many educational packages produced for secondary students of history, media and social studies. Further, it is on display in the textual forms and protocols of production of the mini-series. With their high 'production values' —a fastidious attention to historical verisimilitude, 'epic' shooting schedules, the use of film rather than videotape as shooting stock, the highly publicised importation of theatrical workshopping techniques to prepare actors exhaustively for historical impersonation —mini-series bear direct comparison to other established zones of 'quality' such as the BBC and ABC classic serials or the Australian 'period' film of the mid- to late-1970s. It is this textual and production rhetoric of 'quality' that marks out a difference for the mini-series that now needs further analysis in terms of its modes of historical representation, its patterns of dramaturgical and narrative structure, and in terms of its inflection of the hybrid form of 'documentary-drama'.

Consider the relation of historical mini-series like *The Last Bastion*, *The Dismissal*, *Cowra Breakout* or *Vietnam* to other forms of Australian historical drama, such as the period film—*The Getting of Wisdom*, *The Irishman*, *The Mango Tree*, and so on—and television series—like *Rush*, *The Sullivans* and *Carson's Law*. These latter texts typically centre fictional characters who achieve a form of 'everyman' status such that they can be considered representative of a nation and its experiences (in youth, in war, in depression). Thus *The Sullivans* presents a 'typical' wartime Australian family. Crucially, these texts operate to set predominantly fictional narratives and characters' lives against the backdrop of historical events—wars, depressions. As Tom Ryan notes of the period film protagonist, however, these people do not influence the course of history to any extent: they are victims of, rather than participants in, historical events.[5] They achieve representative status precisely because of their historical anonymity.

In contrast, the historical mini-series often deals directly with actual historical events—the Eureka Stockade, the First and Second World Wars, the dismissal of the Whitlam government, the Kelly story, the Castle Hill rebellion—and offers accounts of those events. Moreover, it often deals with 'large' historical figures—Menzies, Curtin, Churchill, Roosevelt (*The Last Bastion*), Lalor (*Eureka Stockade*), Kelly (*The Last Outlaw*), Bradman, Jardine (*Bodyline*) —and still familiar politicians (*The Dismissal*). Rather than being victims of history, or in some cases actually attempting to evade historical change, these characters tend to be represented as the *makers* of history determining and directly influencing the course of events. In centring such figures and constructing accounts of the events in which they participated, the historical mini-series thus attempts to accede to 'history' in direct rather than mediated terms —as merely the backdrop for a narrative. In doing so, it operates in different conceptual terms to the period film. For insofar as the protagonist of the period film achieves a sort of 'everyman' status, the genre itself operates in a literary or mythical rather than an historical register. This point is underscored when one considers the reliance on literary adaptation in the period film—for example, *Picnic at Hanging Rock, The Getting of Wisdom, My Brilliant Career, We of the Never Never*—and the lack of it in the most pertinent instances of the historical mini-series. This, in turn, invites a rather different position for the viewer of the mini-series: as knowledgeable citizen, rather than distracted consumer. We shall return to this momentarily.

The period film tends also to reconstruct the past in nostalgic terms. It presents the past as a lost, desirable time, as a 'golden age' of lost ways and values. In contrast, the historical mini-series' representation of the past is not so much nostalgic as it is critical and interventionary. While the period film trades on this mythic representation of a national past, the historical mini-series frequently recreates Australia's past in less nostalgic terms. Thus it criticises the Australian's naivety (rather than innocence) in *The Last Bastion* and *The Dismissal* and presents lazy, prejudiced Australian soldiers as prison guards in *The Cowra Breakout. A Fortunate Life* is primarily an account of a young man's ability to *survive* a neglected childhood rather than an affectionate reminiscence of a difficult past.

Many mini-series, those produced by the Kennedy-Miller organisation especially, also promote a more radical 'multi-perspectivism' that effectively displaces the unreflective chauvinism that so much recent Australian media is prey to, and, in doing so, produce remarkably innovative *elliptical* approaches to major historical events in the nation's history. Thus almost half of *Cowra Breakout* is spent on the Japanese 'side', encouraging empathy with their point-of-view. The Japanese scenes contain Japanese dialogue and English subtitles—an extremely unusual departure from the conditions of intelligibility of commercial television. Similarly, *Bodyline*—while more conventionally reverting to a 'little Aussie battler' mode in its latter stages—constructs much of its account with reference to the point-of-view of Jardine (captain of the MCC tourists in 1932–33 and a convenient 'Lucifer' in Australian sports hagiographies), Edith, (Jardine's English sweetheart), and Fender (friend of Jardine and 'gentleman' cricketer). *The Dismissal* multiplies perspectives and points of narratorial authority with dizzying speed. *Vietnam,* like **Cowra Breakout**, insists on Vietnamese perspectives and shows them to be as fraught with division as Australian positions with regard to the war and the personal tensions it provoked.

Further, it is arguable that these mini-series take seriously the radical historiographical dictum that 'the past is only interesting politically because of something which touches us in the present'.[6] Thus, **The Last Bastion** mounts a case, *inter alia*, for a greater multilateralism in Australian foreign policy at a time, 1984, when the ANZUS alliance was in crisis over New Zealand's refusal to allow American nuclear warships into its harbours and America's consequent withdrawal from bilateral defence arrangements. This much is explicitly claimed for the series by one of its producers and scriptwriter, David Williamson.[7] Similarly, it is clear that both **Cowra Breakout** and **Vietnam** are major documents contributing to setting the emergent discourse of multi-culturalism on the national agenda. **The Dismissal** was deemed by the Ten Network to be a sufficient potential intervention in early 1980s politics to delay its broadcast twice until after the March 1983 federal election. It was held to be a unique, and uniquely courageous, staging so close to the event of the most destabilising contravention of constitutional convention in Australian, and probably Westminster, political history.[8]

Second, the historical mini-series presents us with innovative narrative and dramaturgical models when compared with established television formats. Consider the example of **Vietnam** as a model for some of these issues of textual structure raised by the historical mini-series.

Vietnam, a ten-hour Kennedy-Miller production broadcast on the Ten Network in early 1987, traces the personal, family and career histories of the (fictional) Goddard family—Douglas, Evelyn, Phil and Megan—from 1964 to 1972 as they intersect with the politics, historical figures and cultural movements across Australian (and Vietnamese) societies. The dramaturgical model on which the series is based is one of homology between what John Ellis in *Visible Fictions* described as the basic syntagmatic units of television programming—the sequence and the series.[9] Almost all sequences (material bounded by ad breaks) in **Vietnam** play out a kernel of contending scenes, characters, and perspectives: the generation gap, old teenagers–young teenagers, Canberra–Sydney, Australia–Vietnam, political process–family process, the resettlement village–the rest of Vietnam, Laurie and Le's house–the rest of Sydney and, subtending them all, the complex multiple perspectives offered by archival footage and dramatic reconstruction. These emerge, through accretion and repetition, as the series-long ingredients of dramatic and narrative tension. [The exceptions to this pattern are the breathtaking *temps suspendu* set-pieces that have become one of the 'signatures' of a Kennedy-Miller mini-series: the land mine, rape of Le, and murder of Lien's brother and aftermath sequences (Episode 1, sequences 14–15; 2:4–5; 3:2).[10] Compare the Test match sequences in **Bodyline** and the first episode sniper incident in **Cowra Breakout.**] Each sequence is marked off by the motif of the freeze frame and slow fade of colour, which makes a dramaturgical virtue of a televisual necessity, the ad break. Dramaturgical symmetries abound: Laurie escapes an explosion (1:14) then cops one (3:4); Le is raped by American soldiers (2:4–5) then emotionally 'raped' by Phil (4); Pascoe lectures on the absolute reciprocity of war (1:9) then embodies it (3); American soldiers rape Le and kill her father, the NLF murder Lien's brother, the South Vietnamese Regulars 'torture' Truong Long (3:2). Intermittently across the ten hours, the narrative re-centres around the trajectories of the central characters: Evelyn masters her 'hysterical' language (a trope for both her learning Italian and escaping the humiliations of her marriage) and Megan her sexual conduct while Phil practises his photographic career.

Historical movement—eight years from November 1964 to December 1972 across 50 sequences—also means the slow accretion or layering of perspectives such that when the family 'reforms' at the end (4:14), we have learnt to think of them historically. This is the opposite of dominant television dramaturgy in its series and serial formats: 'everything happens, nothing changes'.[11] To think of them, the 'central characters', historically is to decentre them in purely characterological terms. They gradually assume the status of markers of sectoral divisions within an historically delineated population itself undergoing irreversible change.

Characteristics of the historical mini-series

Historical reconstruction

All mini-series, and **Vietnam** is no exception, present themselves with a rhetoric of epic structuration, virtually all operate on the model of the nineteenth-century 'growth-to-maturity' novel, the *Bildungsroman*, and several of the best engage with formative historical events in a documentary-drama mode. What are the salient implications to be drawn from these shared formal characteristics?

Epic structure means extreme attenuation of narrative trajectory. A good deal of the criticism that mini-series attract focuses on this point—skeletal narratives 'padded out' to fit pre-determined program durations. However, if we consider both the usual length of the mini-series—eight to ten hours of viewing time—together with the propensity for historical mini-series to rework events whose 'narrative' consequences are already widely known, its dramaturgical cues for sustaining viewers' interest must lie outside narrative enigma. The commodious temporal format typically allows for a displacement of *event* by *causation* and *consequence*: the 'events' inscribed in titles such as *The Dismissal, Bodyline* and *Cowra Breakout* occur well into the second half of the respective series; in the case of *The Dismissal, The Last Bastion* and *Vietnam*, there is a pointed following-through of the political, social and public policy issues that are consequent on the events which are the series' *raison d'être*. In this sense, the historical mini-series offers an unparalleled upgrading of the terms within which historical information and argument is mediated through mainstream television. Consider, by comparison, that television's representations of history either trade on a comforting nostalgia or an event-led descriptiveness on the one hand, history as a lost Eden of traditional values (e.g. *The Sullivans*) or as a spectacle of otherness (e.g. *This Fabulous Century*); on the other, history as merely an indefinitely prolonged series of discrete phenomena (e.g. news and current affairs).

The 'pull', then, of narrative enigma is displaced in the historical mini-series by the fact that its plot and resolution has gained social currency before the text is screened. The series' initial prologue might announce its resolution (e.g. the early narration of *The Dismissal*), or the narrative may be familiar as social knowledge or as part of a canon of well-known literary texts (e.g. *Bodyline, The Dismissal, Eureka Stockade, The Challenge, A Town like Alice*). Regardless, the circulation of publicity around the screening of a mini-series guarantees such prior knowledge. As a consequence, a different viewing 'position' is invited. The central position conventionally occupied by suspense in televisual drama is replaced by an emphasis on the 'documentary look'[12]—the terms in which the viewer is situated in relation to the text's careful reconstruction of the past. The 'ambience' of this re-creation can become a central focus of the historical mini-series. This is not to suggest that there are never suspense structures. The known nature of the outcome of the plot, however, alters the function of suspense. One experiences a sense of pathos and tragedy in *The Dismissal because* of the knowledge that Whitlam will be sacked. Similarly, we attend to the *mode* of debate about Japanese honour in the Cowra internment camp *because* its consequences are foregiven.

Of course, much of this 'foregiven' status of the mini-series text has been ascribed by less sanguine critics to an all-pervading 'recognition-effect'[13] that secures a safely confirming viewing position. This criticism, however, overlooks or elides crucial aspects of audience composition and response. Not all audiences 'recognise' the historical material with the facility and smugness implied by such criticism. On the contrary, for younger audience sectors the historical mini-series may be an unparalleled means by which the 'document is inscribed into experience', if the number of educational packages produced to accompany mini-series into the classroom is any guide. Second, far from being lulled, many viewers regard mini-series as significant—verifiable or falsifiable—historical *arguments*, if the amount and nature of public correspondence generated around them is taken into account. Third, such a criticism smacks of a governing 'aesthetics of suspicion': the pleasure taken in the 'recognition-effect' need not necessarily be ideologically complicit in principle.

Multi-perspectivism

Perhaps the most crucial narratorial principle of the historical mini-series, however, is its multi-perpectivism. By this I mean the way in which the 'epic' length and structure of the mini-series both necessitates and makes possible a multiplication of authorising perspectives within a 'sprawling' narrative field characterised by the *Bildungsroman* format:

> Structurally, such narratives tend to sprawl. Although the focus is on one or two individuals, nevertheless, as part of an epic sweep, there is often a variety of stories and the accumulation of much social material, the latter often characterised by a painstaking accuracy of detail. The historical credentials of the form are often doubly secured; the elongated time scheme, as well as the extended social and even geographic dimensions and the narrative trajectory of the central figures, is frequently intermeshed with the narrative of more public events. Such narratives often require a 'slowing-down' of the main story. With the accumulation of parallel plots, tangential episodes, multiple themes and so on, the main narrative is frequently displaced. In the end, such a narrative may accumulate so much diverse material that it is difficult to bring it to a close. Endings are often not so much a climax as a 'point of let-up', where certain resolutions are achieved and the story is over.[14]

In the most interesting examples, there is a foregrounded 'battle' for enunciative authority where narrative order is put under considerable stress by contending claims on the historical record. The entrusting of narrative authority on the English 'side' for most of the first half of **Bodyline** was certainly a controversial displacement of enshrined Australian chauvinism. **The Dismissal's** radically complex mode of narration disseminates narrative authority across time and political combatants. Commentators have variously equated the 'line' the program takes with that of Fraser, Kerr or a left-Labor position of 'maintaining the rage'. Whatever else such differing readings suggest, they attest to the innovative multiperspectivism that certain historical mini-series produce.

Documentary-drama

A third general issue of the nature of the historical mini-series as a textual system concerns the vexed question of 'documentary-drama'. The BBC's banning of Peter Watkins' **The War Game** and the diplomatic crisis between Britain and Saudi Arabia over **The Death of a Princess** are two of the more explosive events which attest to the legal and political as well as textual volatility of the form.[15] This volatility should caution against attempts to 'define' the format; rather, it is more constructive to consider documentary-drama in the historical mini-series on a continuum between two sets of limiting markers. Toward the 'conservative' limit, one might situate mini-series like **1915**, which presents itself as a straight literary adaptation, is structured around fictional characters against a 'backdrop' of historical events, and which attempts little, if any, textual work integrating archival material into the dramatic reconstruction. Toward the 'innovative' limit might be found programs like **The Dismissal** and **Vietnam** which work from original screenplays and make complex use of mixtures of fictional and historical protagonists and archival and reconstructed diegetic material. Somewhere between the two are situated mini-series like **Power Without Glory** (derived from an innovative *roman-à-clef*) **Anzacs**, **The Last Outlaw** and **Against the Wind**—historical mini-series with original scripts written by experts on their respective subjects which attempt some measure of historical revisionism, but which are essentially 'straight' historical dramas; or **The Last Bastion** and **Bodyline**—with their original scripts, mainly historical protagonists and set piece mixtures of archive and drama.

   Consider the example, again, of **Vietnam**, which arguably best establishes a limit of textual innovation in integration of archival material and reconstructed drama. Most uses of archival footage in mini-series merely work to secure the 'recognition-effect', to 'authorise the fiction', or, to put it another way, to break down what the aesthetician Edward Bullough called the 'psychical distance' between textual field and audience.[16] *Vietnam*, however dramatises archival material extensively and in several ways, thereby achieving an unparalleled integration of archive and drama, thus shifting the usual relation of one to the other.

First, there are extended, inter-sequential integrations of archive and dramatisation/characterisation. Consider the start of the second episode, which moves from archival footage of an Easybeats concert to Megan and her girlfriends trying to 'crack it' as groupies after the show (2:1), after which the signifier 'Easybeats' is loosed from its diegetic moorings as 'Sorry' plays over Meg's flight in her father's car to Serge in Sydney (2:2). Drama comments on the archive, and archive comments on drama, as, for instance, Menzies' American firepower speech proceeds over Phil's training in the philosophy of absolute reciprocity in war (1:9), or as Lyndon Johnson's speech in Australia provides the aural cue for the extended sequence of Le's rape by the American platoon (2:4–5). Evelyn and Megan are stitched into the archival footage of one of the most momentous anti-war marches on 30 June, 1971, and, in turn, this is re-dramatised by Phil taking mug shots, ASIO-style, singling out his mother and sister from the demonstrators (4:8). Bill Peach and Paul Murphy play themselves as major figures in the 'original' highpoint of investigative journalism in Australia, *This Day Tonight*, when Serge, on the run as a draft resister, provocatively debates the Attorney-General Ivor Greenwood in a complex recreation of actual incidents in the history of the justly revered program. Reading the plethora of paradigmatic music of the period is more than a matter of mere texture, of nostalgic recognition effects: it cues the tone of many scenes and, sometimes, editing patterns; it *structures* desire —of characters and spectator alike, and even more. In sequence 3:4, an American soldier sings 'Light my fire', tells Phil the story of his wounded buddy singing the song to block out the pain, and then delivers the line as sexual invitation as he walks away with a Vietnamese prostitute. Or the music archive is politicised: as, for instance, *Bandstand* does vox pops on attitudes to Australian involvement in the war (1:9).

Second, there is a further level of inscription of the archive: the archive *as* characterisation and drama. Evelyn instances her nascent personal coming of age by 'quoting' the highly pertinent, for late 1966, rhetoric of cultural nationalism to no less a future champion of it than an attentive John Gorton, and Ainsley Gotto (2:6). Australian Minister of Defence Shane Paltridge has to stop munching his way through a thick sandwich as notorious war footage of the massacre of the innocents, the meat in the sandwich, is screened for him and Douglas as part of their Saigon briefing in January 1965, referencing the unforgettable Damien Parer rushes sequence in *Newsfront* (1:5). Veronica Lang, as Evelyn Goddard, replays her role from the film version of *Don's Party*, right down to dress style and gesture. Graeme Blundell (Miles Hagger) plays a composite of actual-historical [Bruce Petty penning memorable political satire from the period of his *Hearts and Minds* (1967), *Australian History* (1970), and *The Money Game* (1972)] and fictional-historical [Megan's seduction of Miles (4:1) is played out in the manner of an *Alvin Purple* scenario with the ages reversed] figures. In a marvellous cameo, Jim McLelland plays himself as the historical figure of fifteen years past (4:6). As can be seen, examples could be multiplied of *Vietnam's* pleasureful interplay of archive and drama.

Conclusion

Consideration of general characteristics of the Australian historical mini-series in this discussion has prevented extensive analysis of many outstanding examples, but it has suggested that such work is valuable: the mini-series offers a rich field for investigation of textual innovation in contemporary television. The format, and the uses to which it has been put in certain 'limit-case' series that have been cited regularly, might suggest a greater range of possibility for television than general accounts of it and its differences from cinema that are advanced in works such as John Ellis' *Visible Fictions*. Further, it has arguably given local, and international, audiences memorable innovatively conceived representations of major determinants of Australian history.

Notes

Many thanks to Arlene Lewis, whose formulations in 'The Australian Historical Mini-Series', BA (Hons) dissertation, Griffith University, 1986, I have followed at certain points. This chapter was written in 1987.

1   This legislation was passed during the period 1980–81, although significant tax shelter provisions for film investment had existed for three years before this. The history of the 10BA tax legislation and issues surrounding it are presented in an accessible form in Susan Dermody and Elizabeth Jacka, *The Screening of Australia Vol.I. Anatomy of a Film Industry* (Sydney: Currency Press, 1987), pp.211–16.
2   Jane Freebury, 'Film in Future', *Australian Society* (May 1987), p.14.
3   For more detailed accounts of the institutional history of the mini-series, see Paul Kerr, 'The Origins of the Mini-series', *Broadcast*, 12 March 1979, pp. 16–17; Paul Kerr, 'A Little Plot in Colorado', *Time Out*, 25–31 May

1979, pp.20–21; Bart Mills, 'Washington Behind Closed Doors', *Stills*, April–May 1984, pp.26–28; Harry Castleman and Walter Podrazik, *Watching TV: Four Decades of American Television* (New York: McGraw-Hill, 1982), pp.262–76; and, for Australian background as well as international antecedents, see Ewan Burnett, 'Mini-Series', *Cinema Papers* Nos.44/45 (April 1984), pp.32–6, and Albert Moran, *Images and Industry: Television Drama Production in Australia* (Sydney: Currency Press, 1985).

4   John Caughie, 'Progressive Television and Documentary Drama', in Tony Bennett et al. (eds), *Popular Television and Film* (Milton Keynes: Open University Press, 1981), p.346.

5   Tom Ryan, 'Historical Films' in Scott Murray (ed.), *The New Australian Cinema* (West Melbourne: Thomas Nelson, 1980), pp.122–5.

6   Colin MacCabe, 'Memory, Phantasy, Identity: Days of Hope and the Politics of the Past', in Tony Bennett et al. (eds), *Popular Television and Film*, p.317.

7   In an interview in the documentary *The Making of the Last Bastion*.

8   See, for more detail, Stuart Cunningham, '*The Dismissal* and Australian Television' in Stuart Cunningham et al. *The Dismissal: Perspectives* (North Ryde: Australian Film and Television School, 1984), pp.1–6.

9   John Ellis, *Visible Fictions. Cinema: Television: Video* (London: Routledge and Kegan Paul, 1982), Part II.

10 There are 4 episodes, with 16 sequences in Episode 1, 10 in Episodes 2 and 3, and 14 in Episode 4. A detailed breakdown and a more detailed analysis of *Vietnam* can be found in Stuart Cunningham, 'Jewel in the Crown', *Filmnews* 17, No.4 (May 1987), pp.8–9.

11 The title of Moran's chapter on soap opera, *Images and Industry*, Ch.10.

12 Caughie, 'Progressive Television and Documentary Drama', pp. 327–52.

13 See, for example, Jodi Brooks, 'Dismissing', New South Wales Institute of Technology *Media Papers*, No.19 (September 1983).

14 Albert Moran, *Images and Industry*, p.207.

15 See Andrew Goodwin et al. (eds), *Drama—Documentary* (BFI Dossier No.19) (London: British Film Institute, 1983), for accounts of these and other significant controversies around documentary-drama.

16 Edward Bullough, ' "Psychical Distance" as a function in Art and the Aesthetic Principle', quoted in Geoff Mayer, '*The Last Bastion*: History or Drama?', *Cinema Papers* No.50 (February–March 1985), p.39.

5

In Praise of *Prisoner*

Ann Curthoys and John Docker

The Festival of Light stated that *Prisoner* does a great disservice to the Department of Corrective Services: 'Staff appear no better than the prisoners. This program breaks down respect for law and order—especially young people still watching at 8.30 pm. It includes excessive violence and crude language.'[1]

One of Australia's most popular and long-running television serials, *Prisoner*, ceased production on 5 September 1986. During a run of almost eight years, the Grundy Organisation made in Melbourne 592 episodes for the Ten network. For the greater part of that time *Prisoner* maintained good ratings, and it won 21 major awards.[2] Yet it attracted little critical praise or attention. Believing *Prisoner* to be an outstanding achievement of the Australian commercial television industry, we argue that it should be accorded a secure and honourable place in Australian cultural history.

In terms of the history of television, *Prisoner*, set in 'Wentworth', a female prison, strikes us as remarkably distinctive. There's nothing else quite like it; there's certainly no overseas serial or series from which one can see it as deriving directly. Yet every cultural product has a history, antecedents, and contexts. We will begin with a discussion of the cultural contexts within which *Prisoner* was produced, move on to an analysis of *Prisoner* itself, and conclude with a discussion of its audience.

Prisoner's cultural context

Prisoner was devised in 1978, at a specific historical moment. Australia had had television for only a little over twenty years, and locally produced serials for only eleven. *Prisoner's* forebears include a variety of television forms—*serialisations* (in which a story is told from beginning to end over a fixed number of episodes), *series* (in which each episode is self-contained, though the central characters are continuous, and which has no ending, so that the series is able to be produced for as long as it attracts audiences), and *serials* themselves (in which a continuing story is told, as in a serialisation, but in which there is no 'end' and which therefore can, like a series, be produced for as long as audiences are held). To discover how it was that a serial like *Prisoner* was devised by Grundys in 1978, we need first to look briefly at the development of these televisual forms in Australia.[3]

The earliest serialisations watched by Australian audiences were of British origin, and were often based on a well-known novel. From the early 1960s locally made television serialisation appeared. It was pioneered and produced mainly by the ABC, sometimes in co-production with other local or overseas production agencies. Examples include *The Outcasts* (first shown in 1961), *Seven Little Australians* (1973) and *Ben Hall* (1975). In the mid to late 1970s, the Fraser era, the initiative in serialisation passed from the ABC to the commercials, a consequence of the financial starvation of the ABC by the Fraser government, the loss of key personnel and confidence within the ABC, and the ABC's relative lack of concern to respond to changes in popular demand. With this shift in the locus of innovation and energy went a shift in the form of the serialisation itself. As in the United States, it was by and large transformed into the mini-series, comparable to earlier serialisations in terms of television hours but screened over a shorter period. Pegasus Productions' *Against the Wind* (1977) signified the change, followed by such successes as *A Town Like Alice* (Alice Productions, 1981) and *The Dismissal* (Kennedy-Miller, 1983). The ABC continued to produce serialisations, but for a dwindling audience.

By contrast, the commercial stations had always dominated in the screening of locally made series. The major independent company here was Crawford Productions, whose pioneering *Consider Your Verdict* in 1961 was the first such series to attract large audiences. Crawfords followed up with the highly successful *Homicide* (1964) and its successors *Division 4* (1969) and *Matlock Police* (1971). Others also produced popular series, such as Norfolk International

Productions' *Skippy* (1968) and Sydney's ATN comedy, *My Name's McGooley—What's Yours?* (1966).

By the early to mid 1970s, however, series were losing ground to serials on commercial television stations. From the mid-1960s serials made overseas had been showing on Australian television: *Coronation Street* on the ABC from Britain, *Peyton Place* on the commercials from the US. Locally produced serials began in 1967 with the ABC's long-lived *Bellbird*, a fifteen-minute early evening program. The ABC followed up with *Certain Women*, shown in prime time, from 1970, but the first really successful prime-time Australian made serial was Cash-Harmon's *Number 96*, shown on the Ten Network for over six years from 1972. The Cash-Harmon company ceased production with the demise of *Number 96* in 1978. It was Crawfords who were most able to capitalise on the expanding audience for serials, its successes including *The Box* (first screening 1974), *The Sullivans* (1976) and *Cop Shop* (1977).

The reasons for the popularity of serials were similar to those for the popularity of earlier radio serials: characters and their relationships could change and develop over time in intricate ways; episodes could end with a 'cliff-hanger' and not with a resolution, and so invite audience return more strongly than in a series. With the additional power of the visual image, television serials could create in audiences a very high level indeed of interest in characters and story lines. As in the case of radio in the 1930s, 1940s, and 1950s, serials were often called 'soaps' or 'soap opera', a name based initially on the sponsorship of radio serials by companies making and selling soap, but later signifying serial drama which drew strongly on the forms of melodrama.

Crawfords' major competitor in the expanding field of television serial production was Grundys (and still is, though now we must add JNP, producers of *A Country Practice*). The Grundy Organisation, producer of *Prisoner*, had begun in 1959 as Reg Grundy Enterprises, a local producer of game and quiz shows for television. In the mid-1970s the company became Reg Grundy Productions and entered television drama serial production with *Class of 74* and *Class of 75*. Maintaining its emphasis on youth, the company embarked in 1976 on the highly successful *The Young Doctors* (which lasted nine years) and in 1977, *The Restless Years*. The inspiration for both *Young Doctors* and *Restless Years* had come from Reg Watson, in the senior ranks of Grundys, an Australian who had returned from England where he had worked for many years for ITV. Watson had been one of the originators of the long-running British serial, *Crossroads*. In the early 1960s there was no daily television serial in Britain, and Watson began discussing with

Lew Grade the possibility of establishing one. It was Watson who thought of locating the projected serial for ITV in a Midlands motel and who, as producer of the serial for ten years, had a great impact on its style and development. Watson had long had a philosophy of attempting to attract audiences, not please the critics. Of the *Young Doctors* (and it could have been any of his projects) he said, 'Are you trying to please the critics? The answer is no.'[4]

So far, we've looked at possible answers to the questions 'why a serial?' and 'why Grundys?' In 1978 Watson set out to devise his third serial in three years. But why set the serial in a women's prison? At this time there was considerable public attention, especially in New South Wales and Victoria, to prison issues generally and to the position of female prisoners in particular. Key events around this time were the Bathurst gaol riots, the Nagle Royal Commission into New South Wales' Prisons in 1976 and 1977, the founding of Women Behind Bars in 1975, and its eventually successful and very sustained public campaign for the release of Australia's longest-serving female prisoner, Sandra Willson. In 1978 *St. Theresa*, a low-budget discussion film about women in prison, was made in Sydney by Dany Torsch, with a script by Anne Summers and music by Margaret Roadknight.[5] The women's movement, prisoner action groups, and an atmosphere of public inquiry and media attention, together laid a basis for an interest in the lives of women in prison.

Watson and his team at Grundys began nine months of research for the new serial. Women in New South Wales and Victorian prisons were interviewed, as were prison officers and other people associated with women's prisons. The Nagle Report was studied closely, and later some of the actresses visited women's prisons. Watson was proud of the attention to detail: he told *TV Week* that even the prison bars were the same size as those inside. 'We've gone for realism', he said. The interviews with women prisoners formed the basis of many of the stories. Wentworth gaol was to be based on a combination of Silverwater (Mulawa) in Sydney and Fairlea in Melbourne and the rules and regulations depicted in the program were an amalgam of those operating in New South Wales and Victoria. Watson also urged the depiction of unpleasant prison officers and of lesbian relationships, on the grounds that everyone interviewed agreed these were part of the reality of prison life.[6] Ian Holmes, who took over from Reg Grundy as President of the Organisation in 1979, also insisted on the importance of re-search for the program and took notice of suggestions by prison reform groups.[7] Sandra Willson commented that the depiction of a halfway house for women in *Prisoner* related more to the plans of prison reformers than to actual provisions in New South Wales at that time (1981).[8]

When production began late in 1978, **Prisoner** was to show for one hour per week, but an early decision was made to increase the production schedule from one hour to two. Some key actors and actresses subsequently quit after the first six months, but the program survived and gathered strength.[9]

Yet if **Prisoner** draws on very contemporary, historically specific concerns it also draws on much wider and older cultural histories. Its concern with 'law and order' places it squarely within the arena of much popular culture, with its westerns, cop shows, detective novels and TV series, courtroom dramas, programs about prisons. 'Crime' is a staple of twentieth-century tabloid newspapers and radio and TV news, just as it was of the forerunners of the tabloids, in broadsheets and chapbooks. This interest in crime has often been attributed to the voracious appetite for the sensational and the morbid of popular audiences and readerships.

Mikhail Bakhtin, the early twentieth-century Russian critic recently rediscovered in cultural studies, offers, however, another explanation. He points to the narrative importance of crime in the uncovering of private activities: 'The criminal act is a moment of private life that becomes, as it were, involuntarily public'. Bakhtin writes of the 'enormous organisational significance' that crime, the criminal trial, and legal-criminal categories have in the history of the novel—and, we can add, in newspapers, film and television. Crime is that intersection where the personal and private become social and public: where private passions erupt into public knowledge, debate, contestation, and judgment. Hence its enduring cultural fascination.[10]

A further reason for the popularity of crime dramas is that through them can be explored the morality of a society's rules and regulations. This exploration is often pursued in crime dramas and indeed in much else in popular culture through the principle of 'inversion', the reversal of the usual and accepted in a society. In the last twenty years or so inversion, as cultural representation and practice in a variety of societies (traditional, in early modern Europe, and industrial) has received increasing attention from analysts of popular culture, and not least by Mikhail Bakhtin in his *Rabelais and His World*. In *The World Upside-Down*, Ian Donaldson has pointed out how much of seventeenth-century comic drama shows judges as incompetent, magistrates as fools, the rich as idiotic; and he traces such inversion back to broadsheet illustrations prevalent in early modern Europe of the normal world as upside-down, and to customs like carnival, festive periods and spaces where values of authority, status, hierarchy, power, in terms of class, gender and age, are mocked and flouted.[11]

We can also see the 'wise fool' (in various guises, the divine idiot, the innocent outsider, the trickster) as a carnivalesque figure who, outside of set festive periods and occasions, is licensed to 'play with' a society's ostensibly revered values and apparent certainties. And we can perceive a long female tradition of inversion and inversionary 'figures' in popular culture, from the 'unruly' or 'disorderly' woman of early modern Europe evoked by Natalie Davis in her essay, 'Women on Top', to the witch figures of English comedy discussed by Ian Donaldson, to the rebellious Maid Marions analysed by Peter Stallybrass in relation to Robin Hood ballads and festive activities.[12] In such 'wise witch' figures we are perhaps approaching the female equivalent of the male tradition of the trickster as outlaw, in figures like Robin Hood and Dick Turpin and Rob Roy.

Here is part, a strong part, of *Prisoner's* carnivalesque ancestry, carried through into Australian cultural history and developed and transformed in terms of a robust mythology, literature, and drama of inversion involving prisoners and authority, convict and officer, bush worker and squatter, bushranger and police. This Australian popular culture sees 'Australians', or at least 'true' Australians, as different from other Western peoples in supporting prisoners rather than their keepers, outlaws rather than the police. Australians are seen as anti-authoritarian, anti-police, pro-prisoner, deriving from images of ill-treated convicts, sadistic convict overseers, and 'Ned Kelly'. This view can take many forms, and become bound in with other historical discourses, of tensions between Irish and English, as in television series like *Ben Hall* and *Against the Wind*, or between Australians and English as in the Anzac myth in general, and in films like *Breaker Morant* and *Gallipoli*. It's particularly strongly affirmed in bushranger mythology.

But Australian attitudes to law and crime have been much more complex and ambivalent than this myth suggests. Robin Walker showed this historically in a close analysis of the public response to the police incapacity to capture the Ben Hall gang in the early 1860s.[13] In terms of modern Australia, we only have to think of the difficulties facing prison reform movements to realise that Australians are by no means universally or consistently pro-prisoner. There are in fact both pro- and anti-prisoner popular conceptions. Very often the conflict between the two is negotiated, both in public discussions and cultural representations, as a division between two kinds of prisoners—'hardened criminals' on the one hand, and social victims, prisoners whose circumstances have driven them into conflict with the law, on the other.[14]

If a modern audience inherits conflicting images of prisons and prisoners generally, so too does it construct conflicting images of female criminals and prisoners in particular. While one common image of women is that they are less violent than men, less a danger to society, another common one is that women who transgress, who end up in prison, are somehow more foul, more corrupt than men. They have, after all, broken social norms even more thoroughly than have their male counterparts. For a long time an image of the women convicts of the early nineteenth century was that they were worse than the men—more abandoned, profligate, degenerate.[15] They were slatternly, lazy, foul-mouthed, wandering around in a drunken stupor with their dresses half falling off. But just as there has been a conflict in popular consciousness between images of the early convicts as hardened criminals and as the starving stealers of handkerchiefs, so too Australian female convicts have also been seen as victims as well as exemplars of viciousness. Anne Summers' version of female convicts as pressed into prostitution to provide sexual services for the males—in which convicts and convict overseers are not very clearly distinguished—has had considerable impact on cultural depictions of female convicts in recent years, for example in *Journey Among Women* and *The Timeless Land*. In some ways it's as if George Arnold Wood's earlier version whereby all convicts were the victims rather than the perpetrators of a vicious social order, has now been reserved for female convicts only.[16]

Australian audiences don't, of course, receive only these kinds of conflicting images. There is also the whole Hollywood tradition. Without going into this in any detail here, we can point to those representations of women prisoners which depict them as brutishly lesbian and therefore terrifying. There are suggestions of lesbian rape or seduction of young girls, of leather and chains, of a deep viciousness of character, and of an extraordinary capacity for violence, all tolerated by the sadistic screws. The prisoners are seen as irremediable and unchangeable. In an episode of *Charlie's Angels* the main difficulty for the Angel concerned, who had to pose as a prisoner, was how to escape the terrifying lesbians in the gaol, and save the one good prisoner, young and confused, from a life of crime. Whereas in historical dramas and representations it's the issue of prostitution which is central, in modern dramas and representations that of lesbianism tends to be more important.

Before reaching *Prisoner*, another path has to be followed, the history and conventions of melodrama. In *The Melodramatic Imagination* Peter Brooks argues that tragedy as a form had lost its vitality by the end of the eighteenth century. But its prestige has lingered on in terms of a notion of the hierarchy of genres, where culture and particularly drama of 'quality' should be tragic, should be sombre and unhappy in its endings and give insight into the finally tragic nature of the universe. It's because of this hierarchy of genres that other forms, and especially melodrama, are so often denigrated and dismissed. Brooks argues that in melodrama characters relate in a way that people rarely do, confronting each other with their deepest feelings, beliefs, resentments, fears, anxieties. Indeed, says Brooks, melodrama is very close to the drama of psychoanalysis, the bringing to the surface of repressed feelings, states, and desires. It has affinities with dream and nightmare, and can be seen as a form of 'deep play', where attitudes, dreams and fears that aren't usually expressed in ordinary life can be represented and played with. In melodrama, every conversation is a confrontation, and this is one of the secrets of its fascination since it spread as a form (melodrama equalling drama plus music) at the beginning of the nineteenth century to England, the United States, and Australia, becoming enormously popular on the stage and then in this century, in Hollywood and, in serial form influenced by nineteenth century fiction, in radio and television.

Brooks argues that in melodrama virtue is tested to the very limit by evil (villain figures), evil being defeated, finally, by the forces of good in the universe. Yet, says Brooks, melodrama is consistent with the 'modern consciousness' in always being provisional in its dramatic solutions, and in featuring so much the strength of evil.

We can see melodrama as the most carnivalesque of modern forms. It burst onto the stages of Paris in the midst of the French Revolution, which licensed the speaking of words in popular theatre where this had been a right before only of the 'legitimate' upper-class theatre, with its privileging of tragedy and the high comedy of character, and its word-centred dramaturgy and narrow range of frozen gestures. Melodrama offered itself as a democratic form, open to all for attendance and 'reading'. It inherits the theatrical resourcefulness and visual and gestural expressiveness of pantomime and circus performance. It is carnivalesque in inviting the participation of the spectator in its drama of crisis for virtue, loss of name and identity, separation, and final (shaky) reunion; in its comic and farcical moments, recalling Bakhtin's notion of carnivalesque humour as questioning all values, including its own; and in its cosmology, its notion of fate and destiny as not necessarily tragic or closed. It recalls the early modern European social dramas of charivari and public square festivity, a public 'trial' of usually hidden attitudes, passions, actions. And it breaks with realism in its notion of character. Where realism demands that characters be well-rounded and psychologically believable in an everyday sense, and always explicable, melodrama denies that characters are 'rounded', are fixed. Rather it explores the way characters go through all sorts of transformations of 'identity', and in this sense melodrama is very like Bakhtin's evocation of folk motifs of metamorphosis, of crisis and rebirth.[17]

Melodrama was conceived in a time and spirit of social radicalism. From the very beginning it often featured the villain as a landowner or factory owner (a remarkable example is the 1832 English play *The Factory Lad*).[18] Melodrama, that is, doesn't have to be in the least embarrassed by its history, aesthetically or ideologically. It was not 'bestowed' from the top, and indeed has proved very influential on 'high' literature, as Brooks argues, for writers like Henry James, Dostoevsky, Conrad; it grew from illegality and the unofficial; it drew on popular forms and genres of all kinds, theatrical and literary. Melodrama is indeed a kind of 'meta-genre', allowing genres (romance, mystery, adventure, detective, horror, the tragic and the comic, even naturalism) to mix and confront each other. It can move easily between private and public worlds. Unfettered by the hierarchy of genres and exuberantly ignoring genre-purity, it can, aesthetically, do anything, and often does. In the terms that Bakhtin applied to the novel, melodrama allows many different 'languages' to speak and converse and contend and dispute and argue with each other. It is this flexible and lively cultural history, along with that of carnivalesque inversion, that *Prisoner* inherits and confidently and distinctively develops.

Prisoner as text

In the following discussion we focus on and use the ethnographic present for *Prisoner* in its 'middle' or 'classic' period, in the early 1980s, particularly 1983. We believe that the structuring relationships and conflicts evident then persist through the later changes in the cast of characters.

We can begin by noting that in *Prisoner* many of the ambiguities and conflicts so far touched upon appear. There is an ambiguity about the 'law' and the breaking of it, a concern with the relation of the moral and the legal and the powerful, and a distinction between 'hardened criminals' and the majority of ordinary prisoners. And there is an ambiguity surrounding the issue of lesbianism. The 'hardened criminals' are in fact rare—there might at any one time be only one, like the evil doctor, Kate, or later, Nola MacKenzie. But these characters are dramatically very important. They help establish a counterfoil to the troubled, confused, sometimes silly, but basically ordinary and sympathetically drawn majority of prisoners. Most of the inmates are in for things like petty theft, soliciting, involvement in the drug trade, and various kinds of fraud, forgery, or non-payment of debts. Few are inside for crimes of violence, and even those who are may fall into the social victim category. At times the drama shows how they came to be in prison, and the forces leading to recidivism. There's a strong element of seeing them as victims of social inequalities and misfortune, as people who never really had a chance. Once in prison their sentences are often made much longer because of their resistance to the repression of (particularly) the harsh screws. Some characters, especially the wayward granddaughter figures like Maxie or Bobby, are often in prison or return to prison because of their 'good', their selfless and loyal, actions (for example, Maxie, out of prison and living with her mother, covers up for her respectability-seeking sister, when brother-in-law robs the bank he works in).

Prisoner established plenty of room for dramatic conflict and tension. The first source is the pathos of the lives of many of the women. From time to time, various characters such as the long-term prisoners Bea Smith and Judy, express with painful clarity the experience of being locked up. On one occasion Judy was asked by another prisoner what she'd like to do if she were outside and Judy replied something like 'I don't know, just move around... just, you know, be *free*.' Bea at times contemplates the terrifying prospect of spending the rest of her life in prison, never able to have a sexual relationship, never really able to do anything, her enormous talents and energies doomed to remain wasted. At times we see old Lizzie contemplating dying in prison. Particularly important in this context is the character Hazel Kent. Hazel is not very clever, has got into trouble really through weakness and stupidity, and feels the loss of her children acutely. Hazel represents more than anyone else the plight of the ordinary woman who can't get her life together, can't take charge of her own destiny. Hazel is you and me, except that she's been unlucky and a bit silly. In terms of melodrama as 'meta-genre', the strand of narrative involving Hazel is in a naturalistic mode, harsh and relentless.

The second source of dramatic conflict arises from the relationship between the women. Since they are now away from their families, or have no family, or have through being in prison lost their family, they are outside the usual conception of women's lives. To a certain extent family-type relationships are formed between most of them. Lizzie, whom we presume is in her seventies and looks as old or older than anyone else regularly seen on television, is clearly a grandmother figure. But although Lizzie has a certain wisdom about human relationships, and is loving, concerned and kind, she's also a mischievous old lag rather like a child, liable to get herself into trouble. Bea Smith is in a certain sense her daughter, and a mother to the rest of the women. Bea has been a key character in the program since it began, and is in many ways a moral centre for the other prisoners. She is inside for the murder of her husband in an act of revenge, for supplying and thereby killing her daughter with drugs. Bea's main problem is a propensity to solve problems through violence: this is what got her into prison and what keeps her there. Although Bea generally mothers the women, she gets tired of this role at times, and wants to look after herself for a change, though never at their expense. And in this surrogate family, characters like Maxine and Doreen and Bobby are the granddaughters, with Judy as 'aunt' figure. These 'kinship' relationships, often remembered rather wistfully by ex-prisoners who are having a hard time of it alone on the outside, offer the possibility of close friendship, fierce loyalty, co-operation, genuine concern for each other: an image of *communitas*, inversionary since it is this community of 'good' prisoners, not those in authority, that the text continually invites us to sympathise and empathise with.

But the relationships between the women are by no means all of this supportive kind. Conflict and violence often erupt, and indeed the advertising for **Prisoner** tends to accentuate this side of it. A key conflict is the struggle between Bea and other dominant personalities, like the remarkable Nola MacKenzie, trying to topple her from her position as 'top dog'. The drama of **Prisoner** provides for continuous contrast between 'figures' like Nola and Bea Smith. Despite her propensity to use violence to get her own way or for purposes of revenge—she also kills Nola for trying to drive her insane over the memory of her dead daughter Debbie—Bea acts on moral principles that are the reverse of Nola's extreme individualism and selfishness. Bea possesses considerable wisdom about people and human relations which she uses for the benefit of the prisoners as a whole. Where 'hardened' criminals like Nola or Kate would lag to the screws, Bea practically never does: she believes in trust, loyalty, sharing between the prisoners; she dislikes and tries to counter and perhaps punish actions that are self-seeking and competitive at the expense of what she perceives as a family group. But if Bea is a moral centre in **Prisoner**, she's an unusual and complex one, in part, exerting her control through violence or the threat of it: she brands K for Killer on Nola's chest with a soldering iron.

Prisoner is complex in its treatment of the screws. These are a mixed lot, and from time to time we see aspects of their personal lives. They include Joan Ferguson (the Freak), who is hard, corrupt and extremely clever at avoiding detection though not suspicion from the other screws. At the other end of the spectrum is Meg Morris, who is more of a social worker, and indeed for a while became a parole officer but later returned to her original role. Meg, unlike Ferguson, or Vera Bennett (known as Vinegar Tits) before her, or on most occasions Colleen Powell, is aware that the women could make good with a bit of assistance such as skills, jobs, a place to live, caring family or friends. Meg's position is a little confused, for after all she is still a screw, as Bea and some of the other prisoners continually remind each other. But Meg is in fact a counterpart to Bea, a force for morality and commonsense. But whereas Bea is able most of the time to exert some kind of moral authority and crafty strategical leadership over the women, Meg is only able to have her point of view prevail in the administration of the prison when extreme authoritarian measures are seen to fail.

A third source of dramatic tension lies in the relationships between the prisoners and the screws, and beyond the screws, the Department. The screws know Bea has more direct control of the women than they do, and both use and resent this. Bea, on the other hand, knows that the screws and the Department really control everything that goes on, have the final sanctions of lock and key and gun and solitary confinement. The screws—for the prisoners —are always 'them', an alien force that controls, exploits, hurts and confines them. But *Prisoner* also explores differences between formal authority and real power; the screws, if they are to maintain order within the prison, have constantly to rework their strategies, and to take cognizance of Bea. Also, the struggle between the advocates of rigid discipline and of a more permissive, helping approach goes on and on, never really resolved, as each approach is alternately seen to result in further tension, restlessness, and disorder.

Prisoner seems to rest very little on conventional definitions of masculinity and femininity, beyond the basic point that sympathy generated for most of the women rests on the fact that they are women, and therefore not usually seen as violent or physically dangerous, and also seen often as cut off from their children. Many of the women are very strong characters indeed, active and independent. Figures like the Freak, Bea, Nola, and Marie Winters are most unusual in the characters of television drama. They are not substitute men, but active strong women. There have also been several gentle male figures—old Syd, the handyman who married Lizzie, Doreen's husband, and several young shy boys who enter the story via the halfway house. On the other hand there have been some hard violent male characters as well, such as the corrupt rapist screw Jock Stewart. Strength and gentleness are not distributed in

Prisoner on male–female grounds. The image of the powerful man and the weak or decorative woman is simply not there. Images of female strength are not uncommon in television drama; indeed they have proved extremely popular in characters such as *The Bionic Woman*, *Wonderwoman*, Steed's offsiders in *The Avengers*. But in all these cases strength and capability are intertwined with an emphasis on conventional female beauty.

The women in *Prisoner* are not in the least glamourised. They are dressed in crummy prison uniforms, or for those on remand usually in fairly ordinary clothes. Their faces suggest no make-up, and they range in bodily shape from skinny wizened old Lizzie to the big girls like Bea, Doreen, and Judy. *Prisoner* does not rely on notions of female beauty, nor on portraying the women as ugly. Their faces are shown as interesting, faces full of character, of signs of hardship and suffering, alternately soft and hard, happy and depressed, angry or bored. The sets more often than not are brick walls, a rudimentary laundry, a dull recreation room, a boring office or entry lobby. The appearance of *Prisoner* is varied to some extent by indoor and outdoor scenes set outside the prison but overall the look of *Prisoner* is spare, hard, and yet dynamic.

One objection to *Prisoner* we've heard is that it is voyeuristic, relying on images of caged and uniformed women, with a sexual suggestion of bondage. Further, it is felt to rely on images of violence between women, with soldering irons, knives, bashings and so on, which is something of a pornographic turn-on. The program positions the male viewer as someone who enjoys seeing women controlled and confined, and positions the female viewer as one who masochistically desires to be caged.

Certainly the advertising for *Prisoner* can be seen to display these elements. Early advertising also had suggestions of lesbianism, enhancing the idea of a turn-on. We ourselves did not watch it at all in its first year, for just this kind of reason, a suspicion that the whole thing was somehow anti-lesbian, and exploiting images of women in bondage. But *Prisoner* in fact regards lesbianism in a fairly complex and ambiguous way. Both Judy Bryant, ex-prisoner and manager of the halfway house, and Joan Ferguson have been established as lesbians. Judy Bryant is an extremely sympathetic character, whose lesbianism has been stressed less and less as time goes on. As far as we know she hasn't got off with anyone for ages. Ferguson's lesbianism, however, seems to be symbolised by her sinister black gloves, and to provide her with an extra dimension for threatening and controlling the women. *Prisoner* seems to suggest that lesbianism is OK among the women (though mainly in terms of an expressed identity than actual sex in prison) but not

OK among the officers, for it introduces the possibility of sexual harassment.

But apart from this, is *Prisoner* voyeuristic? We don't think so. The women are on the whole portrayed as fairly ordinary women, not violent sexual monsters in a cage. Their strong pro-children and anti-childbasher morality clearly establishes them outside this image. They are located in their society, they come and go, they usually suffer a denial of sexual relationships. Perhaps *Prisoner can* be read voyeuristically, but we are not convinced that it has to be, are not convinced that voyeurism is evident in its dramatic structures and visual appearance. The women are not held up as sexual objects, but as human, female, subjects.

Responses to *Prisoner*

Prisoner has undoubtedly been popular, only in its eighth year showing signs of falling ratings. Right from the beginning, on Monday, 26 February, 1979, in Sydney and Melbourne, *Prisoner* achieved and then maintained good solid ratings in its 8.30–9.30 timeslot. Its popularity has been measurable not only in the ratings but also in the continuing attention given to *Prisoner's* stars like Val Lehman (Bea), Sheila Florance (Lizzie), Maggie Kirkpatrick (Joan Ferguson) and Elspeth Ballantyne (Meg Morris), in *TV Week* and Logie awards, in the participation of *Prisoner* actresses in Telethons or in their well-publicised appearance in a performance in Pentridge Gaol.[19] As with all successful serials with long-running parts the stars of *Prisoner* have become popular favourites, and things they do that affect the show—like Lizzie leaving—can earn headlines in the tabloid press.

Popularity, however, is not necessarily accompanied by critical acclaim, instant or eventual. It might indeed be the fact of popularity itself which, either from the need for critics to assert their independence and toughness—to be *critics*—or from the application of high-culture criteria, gives many critics the irrits, as Bea might say. Dorothy Hobson has remarked of *Crossroads* that it is 'at the same time enormously popular and yet devastatingly criticised', and something similar, though in a milder vein, could be said of *Prisoner*.[20]

It hasn't been so much the academics as the journalists who have led the way. *TV Week's* John Michael Howson responded soon after *Prisoner* began with a hostile sneer, saying that it wasn't a drama at all, and it was so bad it was funny. Peter Dean of the *TV Times* was only a little more approving. *Prisoner* was, he felt, 'A slickly made tear-jerker that succeeds in showing a little of the torment endured by unhardened unfortunates thrust among harridans'. An American critic in the US *TV Guide*, with a weekly circulation of six million, was typical of those who opposed *Prisoner* for showing too seamy a side of life:

> Violence, homosexuality, humiliation and tough-talking female convicts. It's hard enough to believe that adult viewers really want a series that panders to the shabbiest, most sadistic tastes. It's much harder—in fact it's sickening—to think that in several large cities some stations don't mind if the kids watch too.[21]

The television reviewers for the *Sydney Morning Herald* have rarely (if ever) been kind to *Prisoner* either. Rayleene Harrison described it in *The Guide*, widely read on Monday mornings by the middle class and professionally trained, as lost in a 'myriad of second-class plots and truly unbelievable characters'. Then there was restaurateur Peter Simpson's view, offered in *The Guide's* 'My Choice' column: 'It's an insult to the intelligence—nothing but nasty people behaving nastily in a nasty situation'.[22]

In all this we can discern the operation of a double standard common to much cultural criticism: what is 'good' in 'high' culture becomes 'bad' in popular culture. What might be hailed in 'high' culture as admirable realism or touching pathos or a tragedy that questions the very depths and bases of human existence, is dismissed in popular culture as *too* realistic! Popular culture can't win: it's either regarded as mere light entertainment, or it's viewed with alarm and distaste as too grim. In comments like Peter Simpson's we hear the double standard speaking loud and clear: how different must *Macbeth* and *King Lear* and *Hamlet* be—nothing but nice people behaving nicely in nice situations.

Double standards are also evident in the comments of journalist Sandra Hall in her book *Turning On, Turning Off: Australian Television in the Eighties*. Here the fact that *Prisoner* depicts lesbianism earns it a hostile attack, in a way unlikely in criticism of 'high' culture:

> Sex is plainly an important part of its appeal, although it's sex of a kind which has nothing to do with sensuality. . .*Prisoner* is helped immeasurably by the fact that a large proportion of its cast is lesbian at least some of the time. The presentation of life in a women's prison is a mixture of a lesbian lonely hearts' club and *Tom Browne's Schooldays* gone ocker.[23]

Hall's is the kind of criticism, as was Marion Macdonald's in the *Sydney Morning Herald* and Nancy Banks-Smith's in the Eng-

lish *Guardian*, which likes to reveal the critic's wit and verbal play
at the expense of contemptible popular offerings—and at the expense, often of even the remotest accuracy of what actually happens in a program.[24] It wasn't just the lesbianism that annoyed
Sandra Hall, to the point where a very few characters' lesbianism
could become 'a large proportion of its cast'. It was also its general
grimness. As Hall put it, there is 'no light and shade, no humour,
no time for anything but belligerence. Consequently its characters
are not so much characters as laboratory animals, and the actors are
called on to produce just two emotions. They are only ever dour
or hysterical.'[25]

An exception to this hysterical chorus of dislike, disapproval and
contempt is Lesley Stern's essay 'The Australian Cereal: Home Grown
Television'. Written from within a post-structuralist approach
that owes much to Roland Barthes' *S/Z*, Stern's essay delights in
the very raggedness of *Prisoner*, its narrative discontinuities, its
play of contending and contradictory discourses, of identity and
difference, of unreconciled and unreconcilable oppositions, of res-
olutions that only beget new dramas requiring new solutions, all
without end; and in this view there is no single place, and so no
secure ideological stance, in which viewers can be confined and
inscribed.[26] Lesley Stern is anticipating here what the American
critic Robert C. Allen has argued of TV serials generally, that as
a form they are always refusing 'narrative closure' and are always
ambivalent in their cultural attitudes and meanings.[27]

Let's leave the critics (apart from the un-Stern) stewing in their
sourness and return to *Prisoner's* indubitable popularity. The
ratings have varied considerably according to city and age group,
proving most popular in Melbourne (where it is made) and with
13–17-year-olds irrespective of city. Clearly, then, in attempting
to ask why *Prisoner* gained popularity, we need to look at reasons for popularity within specific groups. In an earlier paper John
Docker suggested that the basis for *Prisoner's* popularity with
school children lies in its portrayal of a situation not so very different from that of school: the ethic about not dobbing, or lagging,
the ingenious strategies for circumventing formal authority, the
informal networks of knowledge and relationships, the getting of
things in or out of the institution that are not supposed to be there,
the use of humour, cheek and wit to resist authority and rules.[28]
Do the 13–17-year-olds enjoy *Prisoner* because they respond to
a portrayal of confinement and resistance not unrelated to their
own experience? Do they recognise their teachers as similar to *Prisoner's* screws, especially when those screws tell the women, in the
mornings on the way to the shower or later in the laundry, to get a

move on, hurry it up, no talking, why isn't everyone working in here, or when they confiscate various possessions of the prisoners or withdraw privileges. . .? Do kids see in the differences between officers like Vera Bennett and Joan Ferguson and Mrs Powell and Meg Morris recognisable differences between their own teachers? Do they sense that the teachers are not unified or undivided or free of conflict amongst themselves, like *Prisoner's* screws? But that all have a final power and authority and possible recourse to discipline and punishment, even the kindest and 'softest' of them? Do children see in the efforts of Bea to maintain her position as 'top dog' against various contenders dramas of attempted leadership and conflict among themselves?

Christine Curry and Christine O'Sullivan wrote in 1980 about the results of their research into the responses to certain programs, including *Prisoner*, of thirteen-year-old working-class school children in Sydney. They argued that children are not passive receivers of television but 'seek out aspects of commercial television as a consolidation and confirmation of their everyday lives'. The kids spend some part of each day at school talking about the TV they watched the night before, and using it subversively against the rule-bound culture and institutions of the school. Aggressive female teachers are nicknamed 'Vinegar Tits', after former tough screw Vera Bennett. Curry and O'Sullivan suggest that *Prisoner* expresses a higher level of social contradiction than does *Cop Shop* where audience faith in a repressive state apparatus is rarely challenged. One of them helped her class make a four-part serial called *Classroom*, based on *Prisoner*. As they put it, the 'similarity between gaol and school had not escaped the notice of the students and these generated a number of possibilities for simulations of both a narrative and a visual kind'.[29] Ethnographic research by Claire Thomas in Melbourne schools reveals similar appropriations of *Prisoner* amongst 'unruly (young) women'. For oppositional working-class girls, school is perceived as a hostile and repressive institution, likened to a prison:

> This school is like Wentworth Detention Centre. It is! It's like *'Prisoner'* on Telly! (T, 15).
> It's poxed! (—unknown).
> The teacher don't even care about us. (S, 14).
> Yeah, 'cos they're screws! (Chorus).[30]

It's clear also, from personal observation, and from several interviews with children printed in the *Sydney Morning Herald Guide*, that *Prisoner's* appeal is not confined to children of high school age. Can younger as well as older children see in the tricks and unrestrained language of old Lizzie, or the waywardness and mistakes of 'children' to Bea like Doreen or Maxie, the mistakes they make and the resistance they attempt to parental as well as school authority?

If *Prisoner* evokes school life, it refers to other kinds of institutional experience as well, for example, life in the highly undemocratic, authoritarian workplace—factory or office. *Prisoner* here presents contradictory images. Work in the laundry is revealed as tedious, unendingly repetitive, and the screws regularly visit to complain if work appears to be slacking. Yet the women often resist the oppression of a labour process that the prison 'management' forces on them by taking smokes, having fun, chatting, planning rituals like birthday celebrations, or being involved in dramas of various kinds that distract them from the boredom of the work. In offices, too, workers try to negotiate and resist the 'panoptic' discipline of managerial-level eyes always on them and the petty rules by creating their own social relations—of friendship, conversation, jokes and rituals like birthday celebrations (in the pub at lunchtime and cakes and presents at afternoon tea). But, as in *Prisoner*, such social relations are intersected and threatened by tensions and drama arising from conflicts of personalities and values. Do adults as well as children, then, see in the program the drama of power in different contexts, in the family, the school, the workplace—of how power is desired, and how it is resisted?

Notes

1 Australian Broadcasting Tribunal, *Public Inquiry Report, Licence Renewals*, Vol.1, 1985, p.179.
2 *Sun Herald*, 13 July 1986.
3 In the several paragraphs which follow we have drawn on Albert Moran, 'Television Drama Series: a Checklist of Titles and Production Companies', the Appendix to *Images and Industry: Television Drama Production* (Currency Press, Sydney, 1985).
4 Moran, *Images*, p.153; *TV Week*, 24 February 1979, p.8; Albert Moran, *Making a TV Series: The Bellamy Project* (Currency Press, Sydney 1982), pp.23–4; Dorothy Hobson, *Crossroads: The Drama of a Soap Opera* (Methuen, London, 1982), p.39.
5 *Womanspeak*, Vol.4, No.5, June–July 1979, p.24.
6 *TV Week*, 24 February 1979, p.8.
7 Interview with Ian Holmes, *Cinema Papers*, No.24, December–January, 1979–80, pp.613–15.
8 Sandra Willson, 'Prison, Prisoners and the Community' in S.K. Mukherjee and J. Scutt (eds), *Women and Crime*, (George Allen and Unwin, Sydney, 1981), pp.196, 199–200.

9   *TV Week*, 17 March 1979.

10 Mikhail Bakhtin, *The Dialogic Imagination*, ed. Michael Holquist (University of Texas, Austin, 1981), 'Forms of Time and Chronotope in the Novel', pp.111–29.

11 Ian Donaldson, *The World Upside-Down* (Oxford University Press, London, 1970), Chapter 1.

12 Peter Stallybrass, ' "Drunk with the cup of liberty": Robin Hood, the Carnivalesque, and the Rhetoric of Violence in Early Modern Europe', *Semiotica*, Vol.54,–1/2, 1985, pp.113–45; Natalie Davis, 'Women on Top', in *Society and Culture in Early Modern France* (Stanford University Press, Stanford, 1975).

13 Robin Walker, 'Bushranging in Fact and Legend', *Historical Studies*, No.42, April 1964.

14 For sympathy for escapees, as in the famous Simmonds and Newcombe case, see Les Newcombe, *Inside Out* (Angus and Robertson, Sydney, 1979); Jan Simmonds, *For Simmo* (Cassell, Melbourne, 1979).

15 For a discussion of historians' images of convict women, see Elizabeth Windschuttle, 'Women, Crime, and Punishment', in Mukherjee and Scutt, *Women and Crime*, pp.31–50.

16 Anne Summers, *Damned Whores and God's Police*, (Penguin, Ringwood, 1975).

17 Peter Brooks, *The Melodramatic Imagination* (Yale University Press, New Haven, 1976); Bakhtin, 'Forms of Time and Chronotope in the Novel', pp.111–21. See also John Docker, 'In Defence of Melodrama: Towards a Libertarian Aesthetic', *Australasian Drama Studies* 9, 1986 and 'Antipodean Literature: A World Upside Down?', *Overland*, pp.103, 1986.

18 See Michael R. Booth, ed., *The Magistrate and Other Nineteenth Century Plays* (Oxford University Press, London, 1974).

19 *TV Week*, 9 May 1981. This performance resulted in a one-hour special entitled 'Prisoner in Concert', shown on 7 May 1981 at 7.30 p.m. in Melbourne.

20 Hobson, *Crossroads*, p.36.

21 Quoted in *TV Week*, 14 June 1980.

22 *TV Week*, 3 March, 7 April 1979, 14 June 1980; *Sydney Morning Herald TV Guide*, 30 May and 6 June 1983.

23 Sandra Hall, *Turning On, Turning Off: Australian Television in the Eighties* (Cassell, Melbourne, 1981), p.41.

24 See Michael Poole, 'The State of TV Criticism', *The Listener*, 22 March 1984, on the tone that from early on dominated British TV reviewing: 'playful, top-heavy with "personality", aggressively non-specialist. Clive James inherited this tone and became its most accomplished exponent. . . Here is a man who knows full well that his real subject is not television but himself.' See also John Docker, 'The Culture Police: TV Criticism in Australia,' *Hermes*, 1987.

25 Hall, *Turning On, Turning Off*, p.42.

26 Susan Dermody, John Docker, and Drusilla Modjeska, eds, *Nellie Melba, Ginger Meggs and Friends* (Kibble Books, Melbourne, 1982). Stern's argument largely concerns the early **Prisoner**. See also Diane Powell, 'Soap', *Third Degree*, No.1, 1985 (Faculty of Humanities and Social Sciences, New South Wales Institute of Technology), drawing on the work of Tania Modleski.

27   See Robert C. Allen, 'On Reading Soaps: A Semiotic Primer', in E. Ann Kaplan, ed., *Regarding Television* (American Film Institute, Los Angeles, 1983), and *Speaking of Soap Operas* (University of North Carolina Press, Chapel Hill, 1985).

28   John Docker, ' "Unprecedented in History": Drama and the Dramatic in Television', *Australasian Drama Studies*, 2 April 1983, p.59.

29   Christine Curry and Christine O'Sullivan, *Teaching Television in Secondary Schools* (New South Wales Institute of Technology Media Papers, No.9, 1980).

30   Claire Thomas, 'Girls and Counter-School Culture', in David McCallum and Uldis Ozolins, eds, *Melbourne Working Papers 1980* (University of Melbourne, Department of Education, 1980), p.143. See also Patricia Palmer, *The Lively Audience: A Study of Children Around the TV Set* (Allen and Unwin, Sydney, 1986), and *Girls and Television* (New South Wales Ministry of Education, Sydney, 1986).

6

Everyday Quizzes, Everyday Life

John Fiske

A television weekday without a quiz show is almost inconceivable: quiz shows have become an essential part of the pleasures that television offers its working viewers, whether their work is performed in the home, in the school or in the waged work force. Their commercial attractions are obvious. For the producers of the goods and services to whose commodities quiz shows give star status, they provide a national shop window, and enable the producers to present themselves as 'sponsors' (i.e. generous, altruistic) rather than 'sellers' motivated by profit. The relationship between the sponsor and recipient appears to differ significantly from that between seller and buyer. The display (of both the goods and the 'goodwill' of the 'sponsors') is cheap—the cost of even the most expensive prize such as a $50 000 pair of cars on *Sale of the Century* is only a fraction of the cost of a five-day-a-week prime time commercial. For the distributors the advantages are equally obvious: the shows help to meet the Australian content requirements, they are cheap, consistently reach an audience that is both large enough and has the right demographics to be sold to advertisers, and occasionally become a prime time ratings success such as *Perfect Match* or *Sale of the Century*. *The Wheel of Fortune*, one of the solid, rather than spectacular, Australian shows, is currently a high-rating program in the United States used as a lead-in by NBC for its weeknight prime time. *Newsweek* (9 February 1987) revealed its economics for 1986:

the show cost $7 million to produce and generated $120 million in advertising revenue. The figures for Australian shows will of course be lower, but their profitability is comparable.

But quiz shows' attraction for producers and distributors cannot account for their popularity with viewers. In this chapter I wish to concentrate on their role in the popular culture of the viewer, and thus to explore the seeming paradox that a popular cultural commodity can serve the interests of both its producers and consumers, even when these interests contradict each other, as, necessarily, they will. In a capitalist consumer society, the cultural interests of viewers–consumers enter a complex, contestatory relationship with the economic interests of producers. Quiz shows, which appear to address the viewer so unequivocally as a consumer of commodities provide a good test case to explore the power of popular culture to use the commodities, both cultural and material, of capitalist industries for its own purposes.

Popular culture: the resistance of the subordinate

Some brief definitions are in order before we go any further. The social system, organised according to the economic needs of capitalism, provides the structure that determines our social experience and our social relations. Culture consists of the meanings that we make of social experience and of social relations, and the pleasures, or unpleasures, we find in them. Popular culture is the meanings/pleasures of subordinated groups in capitalism. These meanings are necessarily resistive, and need to be distinguished from those offered by mass-produced culture. Mass-produced culture, which has been so insightfully analysed and theorised by Marxists as different as those of the Frankfurt School and those of European semiotics, offers subordinated people a dominant sense of their subordination, that is, a sense that serves the interests of the dominant. Any pleasure in this sene is muted (and Marxism is notably weak in its ability to handle popular pleasure and consequently, as Hall[1] notes, it has tended to side-step the issue), and is limited to the pleasures of conformity and recognition. Popular culture, however, makes meanings of subordination that are those of the subordinate, and the pleasures involved are those of resisting, evading or scandalising the meanings proposed by the forces of domination. The experiences of the subordinate are diverse and dispersed, those of the dominant are centered and more singular: thus dominant meanings and pleasures are readily available to the sort of analysis that finds unified class (or gender or race) interests structured into and preferred by mass-produced texts. The meanings and pleasures of popular culture are multiple, transient and located finally in the diversity of social relations that constitute subordination, and which are experienced always in some form of resisting relationship to the forces of domination. They exist in the moments of reading, rather than in the structure of the text, and are thus less readily available for analysis. Textual analysis can identify those spaces or gaps where popular readings can be made, but it cannot, of itself, describe such readings in any concrete form.

Bourdieu's[2] productive theory of cultural capital traces the ways in which dominant culture (that of 'high' art and its institutions) serves to underpin and naturalise the class differences of capitalism. Culture and material wealth are equally and similarly unfairly distributed. This theory needs extending to include a notion of popular cultural capital that does not have its equivalent in due economic domain. Popular cultural capital consists of the discursive resources by which people can articulate *their* meanings of their subordination, but not their acceptance of it. It involves popular cultural competencies that, for instance, Brunsdon[3] finds in women soap opera fans and Grossberg[4] in rock fans, and that are the popular equivalent of the more validated and institutionally promoted discriminatory competencies of those who 'appreciate' highbrow, dominant art.

Theories of 'everyday life', such as those of de Certeau[5] explain the ordinary social practices of ordinary people as a series of tactical evasions or resistances of the order that society tries to organise them into. On one level this may involve social practices as simple as taking short cuts across the grass instead of keeping to the paths that architects have provided; on a more complex one it involves using the resources provided by the social order (which are the only ones available) in ways that detach them from the system that produced them and that enable them to be turned back against the interests of the producers.

De Certeau explains this contradictory use of social resources through a metaphor of war. He takes from Clausewitz the distinction between strategy and tactics: strategy is the means by which a large formally organised army seeks to secure its domination over an invaded people. Tactics are the practices by which the people resist and oppose strategy: tactics are guerilla warfare. The army is a metaphor for the social order, so strategy is the systematic exercise of power and control: tactics are everyday practices, not systematic, that exist only in their moments and contexts of resistance or appropriation. Strategy is language, tactics are utterances.

De Certeau uses language as a model to explain his theory. He argues that theories of language that stress *langue* over *parole* (Saussure) or *competance* over *performance*[6] (Chomsky) are theories that foreground language's strategic function as an agent of social control. *Parole* is an instance is *langue* at work. Theories that focus on the utterance, however, stress the tactical uses of language, the way in which its resources can be appropriated by, and used for the interests of, the weak. An utterance is the momentary, tactical language of the speaker, not an actualisation of the socially determined language system. The two ways of understanding the potential of the speech act are crucially different: an utterance is the resistive appropriation of the language system; *parole* is an exemplary, rule-abiding act that gives it a concrete realisation. As the linguistic system can be tactically appropriated, so can the economic. As tenants change the rented apartment and appropriate it by their transient acts and memories, so do speakers with their accents and turns of phrase make the 'landlord's language' temporarily theirs. Cooking, dwelling, walking in the city, shopping can all constitute tactical utterances that appropriate the products of the strong into the service of the weak. Enunciative appropriation is a metaphor, in de Certeau, for the tactics by which popular culture has instransigently resisted the disciplinary order over the centuries:

> Innumerable ways of playing and foiling the others game...characterize the subtle, stubborn, resistant activity of groups which, since they lack their own space, have to get along in a network of already established forces and representations. People have to make do with what they have. In these combatants' strategems, there is a certain art of placing one's blows, a pleasure in getting around the rules of a constraining space...Even the field of misfortune is refashioned by this combination of manipulation and enjoyment.[7]

Popular culture, then, negotiates the interface between mass produced culture, the product of the powerful, and everyday life, the practices of the weak.

Commodities as cultural capital: *The Wheel of Fortune* and *The Sale of the Century*

The Wheel of Fortune offers to its viewers mass cultural meanings of three social domains—those of language, luck and shopping. Metaphoric money is used as a semiotic currency which relates these domains to each other. The game is based upon the pencil and paper word game of *hangman* in which a word or phrase has to be guessed letter by letter. Guessing a letter correctly keeps the player in the game and gives him or her a spin of the wheel: but wrong guesses result in the turn passing to the next player. A large, garish roulette wheel is spun to enable players to accumulate money, which the winner of each round can then 'spend' on a variety of consumer goods.

The mass cultural meanings are quite clear—the reward for consumer knowledge, a little skill and luck is a spending spree in a temple of consumerism. The show culminates in the glorification of the market place, with the winners reduced to consumers and their desires displaced onto material commodities. The reduction of ordinary people to consumers in a market capitalist economy is reinforced and celebrated.

But such an account is only half the story, albeit a very important half. It cannot account for the show's role in popular culture, that is, why people *choose* to watch it, and choose they do. We know very little about the processes of popular discrimination, though we do know that they are crucial to popular pleasure. Studies of fans[8] have shown how firmly they draw the boundaries between texts they are fans of and those they are not, and how important are the meanings and pleasures of their fandom. At the other end of the process, the cultural industries produce 'repertoires'[9] of products (records, films, television shows) in the hope that one, at least, will be chosen and made popular by the public. It is popular choice that makes popular culture out of the resources provided by mass culture.

In **Wheel of Fortune** the word or phrase that has to be guessed is a cliché, a phrase in everyday oral currency. It can be a proverb or folk saying or a name of a popular text or object. It is, in de Certeau's terms, an utterance, drawn from the discursive practices of the subordinate: its roots lie in its everyday use, not in its status as a manifestation of *langue*. Utterances bear the social conditions of their use, and cannot exist without those conditions: *paroles* are examples of a controlling system and the theoretical and political difference between the two is crucial.

De Certeau also argues that consumption is a form of utterance. The commodity system, like the language system, works *strategically* to maintain power and order in the hands of the dominant. But both systems can be used *tactically*.

The strategy of the producers and distributors of commodities in late capitalism is clear and unarguable. The tactics of consumers, however, are much more problematic. Consumption is not a passive act: the word literally means eating—the transformation of an exterior substance into the health and well-being of the body. Consumption is the production of what the body needs from external resources. For de Certeau, commodity consumption is equally productive:

> To a rationalized, expansionist and at the same time centralized, clamorous, and spectacular production corresponds *another* production, called "consumption." The latter is devious, it is dispersed, but it insinuates itself everywhere, silently and almost invisibly, because it does not manifest itself through its own products, but rather through its *ways of using* the products imposed by a dominant economic order.[10]

Chambers,[11] for instance, argues that urban style, for many young people, at least, is a vernacular, oppositional series of statements that uses (often expensive) commodities to articulate their rejection of the dominant system. The expensively accessorised Harley Davidson of a Hell's Angel is hardly a sign of his incorporation into society: neither are the customised panel vans of other working class youths. Commodities are the only stylistic resources available and people have to make do with what they have: in this view cultural consumption cannot be adequately explained by economistic theories.

The differences between shopping in the **Wheel of Fortune**, or **Sale of the Century**, and ordinary economic shopping are vital. In quiz shows one 'earns' the money to spend by a native wit or everyday knowledge coupled with some luck: in 'real' shopping, the money is earned by subjecting oneself to the same economic system that produces the commodities. It is money earned on *their* terms. The symbolic money of quiz shows is not bound by the economic laws that govern social difference and subordination in capitalist societies: rather it is the product, and valorisation of an everyday knowledge and set of life skills which, by it, can be transformed directly into material goods or the pleasures of a holiday. This articulates openly the everyday ability of people to detach the pleasures and meanings of spending, from the pain and subjection of earning.

Gans[12] in his study of an Italian immigrant community in Boston has shown how the subcultural use of commodities cannot be adequately explained by theories of incorporation. Disposable income was spent on display, particularly on clothes and cars, which were used to express both community membership, and identity within that membership. The sense of self-esteem and identity that stylish commodities gave to the consumer, and the ferocity with which they were possessed and defended, showed that their use was the tactics of an alienated subculture, not the strategy of the dominant.

Commodities can constitute popular cultural capital, and, in quiz shows, their detachment from the restrictions of economic subjugation allow these tactical, vernacular meanings greater scope than in everyday life where the freedom and pleasure of spending is always, finally, held in check and contradicted by the subjugation involved in earning. As Silverstone[13] points out, popular culture works in the interstices and gaps of our governed and controlled society. It is essentially defensive, withholding itself from the control of the social order, sometimes playing along with it, yet always ready to seize an opportunity for a guerrilla strike, for a play of tactical resistance, always alert for moments of weakness that it can turn to its own advantage. De Certeau (1986) argues we need a new way of:

> thinking about everyday practices of consumers supposing from the start that they are of a tactical nature. Dwelling, moving about, speaking, reading, shopping, and cooking are activities that seem to correspond to the characteristics of tactical ruses and surprises: clever tricks of the 'weak' within the order established by the 'strong,' an art of putting one over on the adversary on his own turf, hunters' tricks, manoeuvrable, polymorph mobilities, jubilant, poetic and warlike discoveries.[14]

The 'bargain' is just such a 'trick', and 'bargain hunting' the guerrilla strike of the shopper. The bargain, the sale-priced item, is a sign of the producer's weakness, a sign of misjudging the market, that consumers had not behaved according to the rules he had predicated. So getting a bargain is exploiting a weakness in the system and turning it to one's own advantage, a perfect tactical moment. Nobody believes that the sponsors who give the prizes on quiz shows are acting altruistically: but the players' pleasure in winning the bargains on offer derives not from the knowledge that they are being used as publicity fodder (for no pleasure can be found in that) but in exploiting a gap in economic power, a gap which results from the producer's confession of his need to rely upon popular discrimination, but, despite huge sums of money spent on marketing, of his final inability to control and direct it to the extent that he would wish. The free prize, or one bought with symbolic money, is a symbolic recognition of consumer power.

In *Sale of the Century*, the bargains offered to the leader during the progress of the competition are excessive signs of this. Their 'real world' value is given, then their bargain price (which is about 10 percent of the 'real' value). The bargain price is, of course, to be paid for in metaphoric money which has been won by the contestant's wit, speed of response and everyday knowledge. But even the price of 5–8 metaphoric dollars may cost the buyer his or her lead in the competition, so Tony Barber, the host, will often increase the temptation by adding $100–$300 real money to the bargain, and simultaneously decrease the metaphoric money needed to buy it. Such 'bargaining' is a dialogue between the powerful and the weak, and in the game world of the quiz shows, the weak can only win: the bargain bought is an economic victory, the bargain resisted maintains the contestant's lead in the competition.

Similarly, when a simplified version of **Wheel of Fortune** is played in shopping malls, the metaphoric money required to play consists of receipts for goods already bought in the mall: the prizes are vouchers for more goods from the shops in the mall. Using a receipt as money is a carnivalesque inversion, a momentary freedom from the normality of economic subjection.

Bakhtin's[15] theory of the carnivalesque has similarities with de Certeau's of the everyday. Both depend centrally on the belief that the social experiences and pleasure of ordinary people constitute a powerful oppositional force to social control and discipline. For Bakhtin carnival was a licensed moment of freedom from the control of everyday life, when repressed pleasures (usually those of consumption and the body) could be enjoyed to excess and when normal social relations (and the power inherent in them) were temporarily inverted. The sense of fun, excitement, almost ecstasy with which commodities are greeted by contestants and studio audiences in shows like **The New Price is Right** exhibits all the excessiveness of the carnivalesque. It may be debatable whether the carnival acts as a safety-valve, that is, by releasing pent-up frustrations in a harmless, licensed moment of freedom it makes it easier to exert social control subsequently: or whether, by articulating and giving public expression to the disruptive forces of the people, it confirms and validates their existence. But at the least the need for carnival is evidence of the popular forces that are ordinarily repressed, and the excessiveness of their expression evidences their strength.

Economics is the domain in which ordinary people feel their social subjection most acutely and painfully: everyday life is full of the experience of 'not being able to afford'. The orgasmic excitement of temporary liberation from this subjection is evidence of the acuteness with which it is felt. The dominant ideology teaches us that money works socially to reward and encourage talent and hard work: quiz shows demonstrate the opposing 'truth', that the social distribution of money is a prime means of exerting social control. Quiz shows are thus in touch with everyday life, where lack of money is not understood in terms of lack of talent or hard work, but rather in terms of lack of power.

The meanings of luck in quiz shows serve similar functions to those of money-as-social-power. Our dominant ideology proposes that we should understand our society as a meritocracy, that is, as a society where everyone has equal opportunity to succeed and where individual talent and hard work will 'naturally' result in social success. This, of course, is a remarkably comfortable belief for the dominant classes, because it proposes that those with social power possess it because of their natural talent, and equally, those lower down the social structure are there because of their natural lack of talent. Social and class differences are thus displaced onto individual differences, and the (apparently) natural differences of ability between individuals are used to underwrite the social and economic differences between classes.

In Australian society there is also a powerful myth of egalitarianism which appears to contradict the ideology of meritocracy. Egalitarianism produces the often noted (and sometimes deplored) desire to cut down 'tall poppies', to refuse to admit that there are major differences of merit between individuals, and thus to refuse to accept the class distinctions based upon them. This egalitarianism is essentially a bottom-up myth, it works most actively amongst the socially subordinated to produce meanings of their subordination that are often aggressively hostile to the ones proposed by meritocracy. For meritocracy proposes that the socially subordinated are so because of their own lack of merit: egalitarianism denies this, and the social meanings of luck are used to mediate the contradiction. For luck offers egalitarian meanings of social difference—'you got where you did, mate, because you were luckier than me, not because you were better', and its corollary, 'I'm no better than you, mate, just luckier'. Expressing absolute poverty as being 'down on one's luck' may be as politically reactionary as implying that it is deserved, but at least it allows the socially disadvantaged a measure of self-esteem that the ideology of meritocracy refuses.

It is not surprising then, that luck plays an important role in Australian quiz shows: it enables the winners to escape the charge of being 'tall poppies' and provides the losers with non-meritocratic meanings of losing. It is, of course, closely connected to the prominence given to gambling in Australian culture at large, for gambling provides both a means of overcoming economic and class subjugation and a mythological way of explaining it. So the British *Sale of the Century* differs from the Australian one in two respects: it has no lucky 'pick a personality' section and the 'bargains' scattered throughout the contest are open to all the players, not just the one in the lead. The lucky section means that the winner need not be the contestant who answers most questions, but the luckiest.

Similarly, the Australian practice of restricting the purchase of bargains to the leader is an enactment of egalitarianism, for the money/points spent on the bargain will bring the leader back to, and often behind, the other contestants.

Perfect Match: sexuality as pleasure

Perfect Match, the ratings hit of Australian television in the mid-1980s, shows many of the features that we have been discussing, in particular it allows everyday experiences and knowledges a public articulation in implicit and sometimes explicit opposition to the strategies of social control.

The game involves the choice of a date of the opposite sex from three people that the chooser can hear but not see. Each program has two choosing games, with the genders of chooser and dates reversed in the second. The 'winner' is the date who is chosen, who is then sent with the chooser on a date, usually a weekend on a tropical island or a luxury resort. The two 'choosing' games are separated by a segment in which a previous pair of winners return to the show and tell how successful, or otherwise, their date was. There is also a computer on the show which selects scientifically the perfect match for each chooser as a point of comparison with her or his actual choice.

The domain in which *Perfect Match* operates is that of sexuality. Foucault[16] has shown us how the sexuality of the body has become a prime site for the exercise of social power. Nineteenth-century capitalist patriarchy used its power to define the norms (and abnormalities) of sexuality as a way of defining the norms of individual and social behaviour and being. Thus women's sexuality was confined to the requirements of the patriarchal family, and her sexual pleasure was displaced by the notion of duty (to her husband's sexuality, and to produce children). Sexuality that overspilled this control was constituted as a problem, and a whole range of medical/psychiatric discourses was developed to contain and cure it. Similarly, homosexuality or masturbation by young people was constituted as a problem or sickness. The effect of this was that only the sexual pleasure and desires of the heterosexual male were 'normal' and 'natural' and thus, unlike those of the female, they could be allowed expression outside the family. This power to define normality in terms of the interests of a particular social category is social control at its most typical. It is all the more effective because what it appears to be doing is defining what is natural, not class/gender specific: there was therefore little experience of contradiction when women, for instance, accepted this definition and vigorously promoted it in the name of family morality. It is by such discursive means that, to use Foucault's[17] phrase, 'men [*sic*] govern themselves and others'.

This patriarchal definition of sexuality was mapped onto the emerging product of capitalist industralisation—the nuclear family. Lovell,[18] for instance, has shown how during the nineteenth century, men established the public sphere, the world of work, economics and politics as theirs, whereas women were constructed as mothers–nurturers with the nuclear family. The move from traditional agrarian communities to rootless industrial cities made the family, and not the community, the centre of social life, and consequently 'naturalised' the gender roles within it. Society then developed a literary genre, the romance, that taught women that their sexual and social fulfilment was to be found in their wife–mother role within this new nuclear family.

The dominant ideology leaves many traces of its nineteenth-century origins, though the challenges to it are more frequent and significant. **Perfect Match** is one of those challenges. In general it defines sexuality as a source of pleasure for both genders, and does not grant its 'moral' use within the family the ideological status of the 'natural' and therefore the 'right'. In other words, it extends to women the definition of sexuality that had previously been reserved for men.

Women and men alternate the roles of chooser and dates, and there is no preference that women choose by different criteria or for different ends than men. For both, the choice is of a suitable partner for a weekend of (probably sexual) pleasure. Patriarchally constructed differences between masculine and feminine sexuality are denied by the structure of the show and patriarchal privilege is discounted.

Sexuality is understood as the source of equally valid pleasure for both genders, not, more 'responsibly', as the basis for a long-term, hopefully marital, relationship, with the gender power differential inevitably inherent in it. The politics of pleasure are egalitarian to the core.

This challenge to patriarchal power and social discipline is explicit in the structure of the game and implicit in the title sequence which establishes the discourse of the show and the reading relations we are invited to adopt towards it. The sequence takes the most conventional signs of conventional romance—soft focus, pinks and pale blues, hearts, sentimental music, dewy eyed expressions—and combines them so excessively that they become parodic or satirical. The disciplined, strategic meanings of sexuality are there, but the excess produces an overspill of meaning that is available for tactical, resistant purposes. The excess allows the sequence to undercut what it apparently celebrates. The struggle to liberate the meanings of women's sexuality from the control of men has been a major enterprise of the feminist movement. *Perfect Match* goes further, it offers and invites tactical resistances to the social control of sexuality for both genders. The romance is a disciplinary genre that controls masculine wildness and cruelty to the same extent as feminine suffering and subjugation.

Of course, the tactical resistances to sexual discipline are limited, at least in terms of their representation on the show. For its sexuality is confined to that between heterosexual, unmarried and conventionally (i.e. patriarchally) good-looking young people. A few older women and men appear on the show, otherwise the players are young, urban, employed, financially secure enough to have an active and satisfying social and sporting life, trendily and not cheaply dressed and coiffured, and sexually attractive. This does not mean, of course, that the meanings and pleasures of the show are confined to those with similar social characteristics, for characters on television are embodiments of ideological values, not iconic representations of real people. For instance, the challenge to patriarchal definitions of feminine sexuality may be mounted (indeed, may be *most effectively* mounted) by the restricted class of women represented on the show, but that does not mean that other women are excluded from the meanings and pleasures the challenge can offer.

The opposition between conventional sexual morality as a social strategy and the everyday tactics of experiencing sexual pleasure despite it becomes explicit in the way that the show 'plays' with the knowledge of, or insight into, people. The chooser selects his or her date from three people who each answer three questions that she/he asks. She/he can only hear them: the studio audience and the home viewers can see them as well. The chooser has to work with restricted information, with language and paralinguistic elements such as tone, accent, volume and so on. The language that gives this information is, of course, that of the utterance (the concrete here and now appropriation of the language system for the purposes of its user) it is not a '*parole*' seen as an actualisation of *langue*. Language is used not to convey social, common meanings inherent in it as a system, but the unique, transitory meanings of its speaker. The art of using and understanding language like this is an everyday art, quite different from the linguistic arts taught in school and validated as the 'proper' use of language. The players' use of language here, and their use of commodities in other shows, are both tactical appropriations of strategic systems.

And this everyday knowledge, of course, is one that the studio audience and home viewers share also, only they can add to it the visual languages of dress and the body. There is high viewer participation in the process of choice, and viewer choices are actively (and often vocally) compared or contrasted to the actual choice. These viewer and actual choices are in their turn compared to the 'scientific' choice of the computer which spells out its 'perfect match': if the actual choice coincides, that is if everyday knowledge and scientific knowledge come to the same conclusion, the doubly validated couple are each given an extra prize.

The couple then go away on their date, usually a weekend holiday, and half the couples return to a later show to tell of their experiences. This is the centre of each show and one of the most popular segments, particularly when, as is often the case, the match has turned out to be less than perfect. In it the everyday knowledge, and, to a lesser extent, the scientific knowledge, that informed the choice of date is set against actual everyday experience. The couple return to the studio, and, on a split screen, we see (as do they) a replay of the comments that each of them made about the other in a 'private' interview immediately after the date. They then answer more questions together 'live' in the studio. The question that is never directly asked, but to which everyone tries to infer the answer, is whether they actually had sex together or not.

The appeal of this segment is strongest when the couple did not get on well together. Part of this appeal may trace back, for those viewers who made a different choice, to the validation of *their* everyday knowledge—'I knew they weren't right for each other; she/he should have chosen X'—but I suspect that the appeal rests more strongly on the validation of everyday experience against the disciplinary system. Sexuality is, above all else, a system of discipline, that is a system by which people govern themselves and others. The discipline of sexuality, its social strategy, for young single people is that it should be used, despite its temporary pleasures, as training for marriage. The teenage magazines are full of the problems of how to find and keep the good date, and how to identify, and dump, the bad one. The evaluative system of good and bad is always, finally, the disciplinary one of long-term, responsible mutual satisfaction that is a miniaturisation of marriage. Sexuality is disciplined into the social concept of 'the couple' and the resulting contract is a social one, not one concerned solely (and 'irresponsibly') with immediate everyday pleasure. This discipline is so strong because its social dimension is masked and displaced onto the individual, so that when the couple 'uncouples' the process is frequently experienced in terms of guilt and failure. The most powerful discipline of all is one whose disruption results not in a sense of freedom, but of guilt.

The less than perfect couples, who good humouredly tell of their failures to match, who make public and enjoyable experiences that are normally private and agonising, who can laugh at and validate experiences that we are taught should be ones of guilt and self-criticism, are refusing the discipline of sexuality.

Conclusion

The Australian pride in egalitarianism and the concommitant disrespect for authority means that here the tactics of everyday life may well be more explicit and oppositional than in more conformist societies. These tactics are integral parts of everyday Australian life and have become defining parts of the national character. They include those by which beach-goers have steadily increased the beach areas within which they take off more clothes than society wishes them to, or, to take another example, the practice of 'proletarian shopping' by which young people appropriate shopping malls for their own purposes, consuming space and images, but not commodities.[19] The colourful, often obscene, always changing Australian vernacular language is a series of enunciative appropriations of the English mother tongue and is used with a pleasurable defiance of accepted linguistic norms. It is scandalous, tactical, everyday language. For a typical Australian, discipline offers a challenge not a guideline for behaviour.

It is not surprising, then, that the United States equivalents of *Perfect Match*, the *Love Connection* and the *Dating Game*, build in fewer signs that sexuality is a field of contestation between social strategy and tactical pleasure. Neither involves the romance as a disciplinary genre, neither uses a computer to oppose the scientific to the everyday. The dates do not extend overnight or for a weekend, and the players are far more likely to mention their desire for a long-term relationship. Typical everyday practices, from women refusing to wear bikini tops on beaches, to jay walkers taking *their* route through the city traffic, to the widespread fitting of radar detectors in cars, to graffitists making other people's walls speak their language, all are everyday tactics that produce the popular pleasures of opposing social strategies.

Quiz shows, such as *Perfect Match, Sale of the Century, Wheel of Fortune*, are made into popular culture because they negotiate the opposition between the strategic systems (of language, of knowledge, of commodities, of sexuality) and of the everyday tactical appropriateness of them. They contain the forces of power and those of resistance in carnivalesque instability. They are such *fun* because they show the strategies of the strong at their moments of vulnerability to the guerrilla attacks of the weak. The mass-produced culture that informs and distributes them can only be made into popular culture by its appropriation, by the activity of the people who use it as part of the tactics of everyday life.

Notes

Quiz shows have not been well served by academics, but the following references are examples of some of the more accessible work:
Davies, J. (1983) '*Sale of the Century*—Sign of the Decade', *Australian Journal of Screen Theory* 13/14 pp.21–42.

1   S. Hall, 'On Postmodernism and Articulation: An Interview with Stuart Hall', (L. Grossberg, ed.) *Journal of Communication Inquiry*, 10:2, pp.45–60.
2   P. Bourdieu, 'The Aristocracy of Culture', *Media, Culture and Society* 2, pp.225–54.
3   C. Brunsdon, '*Crossroads*: Notes on Soap Opera', *Screen*, 22:4, pp.32–7.
4   L. Grossberg, Another Boring Day in Paradise: Rock and Roll and the Empowerment of Everyday Life,' *Popular Music* 4, pp.225–57.
5   M. de Certeau, *The Practice of Everyday Life* (Berkeley: University of California Press, 1986).
6   For readers unfamiliar with any terms, see Tim O'Sullivan, John Hartley, Danny Saunders and John Fiske, *Key Concepts in Communication* (London: Methuen, 1983).
7   de Certeau, *The Practice of Everyday Life*, p.18.
8   See J. Radway, *Reading the Romance: Feminism and the Representation of Women in Popular Culture* (Chapel Hill: University of North Carolina Press, 1984,); and L. Grossberg, 'Another Boring Day in Paradise, pp.225–57.
9   N. Garnham, 'Concepts of Culture: Public Policy and the Cultural Industries', *Cultural Studies*, 1:1, pp.23–37.
10 de Certeau, *The Practice of Everyday Life*, pp.xii–xiii.
11 I. Chambers, *Popular Culture: The Metropolitan Experience* (London: Methuen, 1986).
12 H. Gans, *The Urban Villagers* (New York: The Free Press, 1962).
13 de Certeau, *The Practice of Everyday Life*, pp.39–40.
14 Ibid.
15 M. Bakhtin, *Rabelais and his World* (Cambridge: Massachusetts Institute of Technology Press, 1968).
16 M. Foucault, *The History of Sexuality* (Harmondsworth: Penguin, 1978).
17 M. Foucault, 'Nietzsche, Genealogy, History', in P. Bouchard (ed.)

Language, Counter-Memory, Practice: Selected Essays and Interviews by Michel Foucault (Oxford: Blackwell, 1977).

18 T. Lovell, 'Writing Like a Woman: a Question of Politics', in F. Barker et al. (eds) *The Politics of Theory 8* (Colchester: University of Essex, 1983).

19 J. Fiske, R. Hodge and G. Turner, *Myths of Oz: Readings in Australian Popular Culture* (Sydney: Allen and Unwin, 1987).

7

Television Documentary

Dugald Williamson

In this chapter I consider TV documentary from the point of view of the representational processes which it employs. The main reason for addressing this topic is that TV documentary has received less attention in media studies than have genres such as TV drama, drama-documentary and news and yet, like these others, it raises the issue of realism.[1]

There are many dimensions to this issue, which cannot all be dealt with here. A dominant, empiricist notion of realism is that the text represents a given reality and simply 'reveals' its meaning. A variant of this notion is that the media distort what they show: this claim is still often based on the assumption that language (including audio-visual language) ought to record reality directly and neutrally, and simply treats certain texts as failed representations. Now, in relation to TV documentary, while shades of this naive idea of realism may often be encountered in the arenas of production, publicity or reception (for instance, in claims that a documentary is objective, hard-hitting, factual), this is only part of the picture. Normally, it is thought that documentary is not strictly limited to presenting facts, and that in contrast to the news, for instance, it editorialises: it provides the opportunity for interpretation, communication of ideas, persuasion, controversy, or the addition of an artistic to a journalistic purpose.[2] However, if one consults a typical script-writing manual like Willis and D'Arienzo's *Writing Scripts for Television, Radio and Film*,[3] one could be forgiven for thinking that there is something in the ether called 'the documentary idea'. A certain kind of attention is paid to the 'language' of the media, but it is as if motivated individuals simply happen to have ideas, and the correct use of scripting, filming and editing techniques will allow these to be realised, and the inner significance of events, objects or relationships to be explored.

The idea of inspiration which lingers here is ultimately an impractical one. A TV documentary is an assemblage of materials—ideas, topics, data, interpretations, and other texts including films and tapes—which do not necessarily originate with, nor fit neatly under the control of, those individuals who make the program. Arguably, to document a subject means to employ particular formats of knowledge, and these formats bring their own ways of posing questions, of opening and even closing avenues of enquiry, and so have an influence on the kinds of ideas one 'has'. The usual advice given by instruction books is to steer a course through the issues by investing the materials with dramatic and emotional values and so build up 'human interest'. In general, one is advised to focus on the psychological experience of individuals and, frequently, to draw out a sense of conflict within or between these individuals as 'characters' in the program, in a form of portrayal with which everyone supposedly can identify.[4] However, such advice raises the vexed question of what it means to make psychological characterisation the central means of documenting cultural, historical or political events. To interrogate what I have begun by calling the 'representational processes' of TV documentary, means to go against the grain of the notion that a process like psychological characterisation provides a neutral reflection of reality or natural register of social or historical meaning. Such a process, along with forms of narrative, involves a definite set of techniques including medium-specific codes (camera angles, editing, sound-image relations, etc.). These techniques of representation produce particular types of meaning (this is the sense of the term 'signification' as opposed to 'reflection') through their own operation, and so have definite effects upon what is represented.

These effects, if not merely 'transparent', are not automatic or intrinsic to a technological system either, but depend on social uses of the techniques, on trainings and institutionalised practices including the work of production and of viewing. Let me briefly follow up the issues raised by instruction manuals and the approaches they advocate.

It is still difficult to make connections in and around media studies between, on the one hand, orthodox publications which disseminate information about the techniques and rules preferred in the television (and film) industry, and, on the other, methodologies which focus, heterodoxly, the ideological or social uses of those techniques.[5] In relation to TV documentary (as well as many other genres), manuals, handbooks and training tapes usually naturalise a system of rules and conventions grounded in certain institutional practices. Explicitly or implicitly, they justify those techniques and practices as appropriate to the supposedly intrinsic nature of the technological medium, and the potential it contains for 'communication' between autonomous subjects with assumed psychological interests, needs and thresholds of impatience. It is supposed that to break main-stream technical rules disturbs the natural equilibrium of the viewer. The technological determinism implicit in such manuals and in the popular aesthetic of realism—that is, the notion that a technology dictates a way of using it and a form of visual literacy—can go with the apparently opposed humanist notion that the technology liber-ates people's consciousness, extending the power of the eye to see, and hence the mind to know the world, in a form of expression freed from distorting personal interests and ideologies.

Now, while not dealing explicitly with production manuals or venues, in this chapter I analyse a 'product' which clearly embodies a number of standard technical procedures. The aims of the reading are to illustrate the role of techniques in producing meaning within TV documentary, and to indicate the porosity of those techniques to surrounding social knowledges and representations. The example chosen belongs to the sub-genre of art documentary, and is treated as neither exceptional nor completely representative, but is used to indicate a method of analysis which would need to be applied flexibly to differentiate between various kinds of documentary. A sweeping critique of realism in TV documentary is not implied here, as if all the forms and effects of realism could be apprehended at a glance. On the contrary, the following discussion would provide evidence for an argument that the term 'TV documentary' covers heteroge-neous types of program which use technical devices in various ways, exploit many generic forms (biography, autobiography, historical narrative, interview, travelogue, etc.), and mobilise diverse discip-linary—and popularised—organisations of knowledge (literature, fine arts, history, sociology, politics, psychology, psychoanalysis, etc.). A rhetorical method of analysis of the kind indicated below may help to recognise the institutional nature of various represent-ational techniques and conventions, while allowing debate to occur on their uses, effects and limits.

An art-documentary: remembering the Heidelberg School

The Rough and the Smooth is a documentary on what is commonly referred to as the Heidelberg School of Australian painting in the late nineteenth century.[6] From a realist point of view, the texts or documents which it brings together—paintings, photographs, newspaper reports, diaries, letters, etc.—would be thought of as given 'traces' of the artists' time, traces which are brought to life as one recaptures the individual and social experience assumed to have given them original form. The idea of the document as a trace is oversimplified and may be revised by attending to those conventional methods by which the paintings and other materials are deployed now, in and around the documentary, as sets of signs within the recounting of artistic and cultural history. Accordingly, I shall outline some of the frameworks which this program uses to document—and which help shape an audience's expectations about—the artist's life, art history and national culture. These frameworks are part of the process by which a popular conception of past events is constructed. These events do not contain some essential meaning, which we recognise intuitively by looking into the images of a past which tradition somehow naturally preserves. Instead, their significance is selected and constructed by an ensemble of cultural rituals and representational forms which, through their present use, organise *how* we remember a cultural past.[7]

I shall deal with two major conventional influences on the present example: the life-history of the artist, and a humanist idea of cultural history which co-operates with that individualising schema; both of which involve some form of narrative patterning. A detour through these forms of biography and cultural history needs to be made, in order to establish their relevance for studying a television text like **The Rough and the Smooth**.

Biography, as a textual form, comprises a group of techniques and criteria whose major effect is to individualise their subject. By treating biography as a mechanism of individualisation, I emphasise that a biography does not represent some naturally intelligible, individual life-experience, but that on the contrary, it involves a generic, discursive patterning of materials. This discursive patterning determines what we count as individual experience within the biographic genre, and shapes the significance, including the sense of unity, which we attach to an order of events in the life being portrayed.

Two general points can be made here. First, there are cultural pre-conditions for biographic representations, and not every individual has a biography. These pre-conditions are that a social group must attach a certain importance to the idea of individuality and also to particular categories of individuality. Generally speaking, modern artists can have their life-stories told because they are placed within a cultural category where individuality is striven for, expected and valorised. The representation of the artist by which the text under discussion is influenced, draws on deeply embedded notions that the artist is the author (that is, unique point of origin) of texts, and that he or she is endowed with special gifts of insight, mysterious talent, freedom from or the ability to transcend the constraints of convention, 'antenna-like' sensitivity to the truth about the epoch in which they live, and so on. On the other hand, the persons who produce art materials do not have popular biographies: this is not because their lives inherently have less individual shape or meaning, but because there is (generally speaking) no cultural construction of 'the life' of the artisan or technician, as there is for the artist in terms of uniqueness or transcendence of the social. It is not surprising, in this context, that the kind of knowledge of art produced in TV documentary is built around life-histories of artists, rather than detailed analysis of other institutional agents, funding policies or marketing structures.

The second general point is that there are several biographical sub-genres, and a sub-genre such as the life of the artist marks a particular configuration of narrative, thematic and characterological elements. In the historical work, *Legend, Myth and Magic in the Image of the Artist*,[8] Ernst Kris and Otto Kurz analyse the construction of the artist as a 'culture hero' in the Classical and Renaissance periods.[9] They are concerned not with the empirical verifiability of accounts of individuals' experience, but with the way in which artists' lives are recounted according to a pattern, which is revealed especially in a style of anecdote. It is the general principle rather than the fine detail of their analysis which is of interest here, especially the identification of thematised narrative sequences which recur across many different stories about artists' lives. It is possible to trace certain regularities in post-Romantic representations of the artist, just as Kris and Kurz do for earlier periods. Modern biographies of artists tend to include such features as the individual's precocious display of talent (an event identified in their own materials by Kris and Kurz); an urge for self-expression and the possible familial or cultural repression of this urge; resistance to the pressures of aesthetic conformity; alienation from society; absorption of creative influences; maturation of creative powers and vision which also renovates cultural tradition; and other overlapping narrative and thematic details. The textualised figure of the artist *as* individual is not forged out of some unique quality of his or her experience, but is built up by the very reiteration of generic, biographical terms.

To link these comments to the present example: *The Rough and the Smooth* draws upon a popularised narrative of the painters of the Heidelberg School in Australian art, which broadly conforms to post-Romantic ways of recounting the artist's life, while introducing local inflections. This particular program does not reproduce every detail of the 'popularised memory' of this era of painting, and its formative role in national culture, but in 'documenting' art history it marshals—and builds upon—discursive representations with which audiences are already more or less familiar. The popular account referred to here has been widely circulated in the teaching of art history, in exhibitions and publicity, and in books on Australian art and artists. Some common features of the institutionalised stories about the Heidelberg School artists (including Tom Roberts, Arthur Streeton, Frederick McCubbin and Charles Conder) are as follows:

- The youth, displaying signs of talent, aspires to become a painter, often in the face of vocational constraints.
- The young artist encounters obstacles, especially old-fashioned trainings and conventionality.
- He (and the artists discussed in this context are generally men) undertakes a journey, perhaps to Europe, and a chance encounter brings knowledge of new techniques, leading to experimentation.
- Having broken with convention, the artist develops a style in which technical skills are mediated and deepened by a new perception of Australian life, people and landscapes, to whose meaning he is especially attuned. (Frequently, it is said that the essence of Australian landscape is realised in the imaginative representation of light.)
- The artist achieves public recognition and /or notoriety. Different subsequent developments may occur: continued growth; compromise between creative and economic demands; deracination and nostalgia, etc.

The artists are individuated by stories which play upon the possibilities of this schema, and by the work of characterological codes. The latter include the mythic representation of the bush as the setting for the psychological formation and expression of Australian character. In popular accounts of the Heidelberg School, the celebration of mateship, implicit in this myth, is combined with a romantic geography of the bush as the site for the artist's communion with nature and creative exploration, and for the spontaneous yet culturally symptomatic growth of an aesthetic community. These things might be viewed as part of a *fin-de-siècle* fashion in Europe, Britain and Australia for cultivating aesthetic schools and life-styles, an activity strictly confined to *côteries*, rather than the encapsulation of some essential feature of national culture, but that is another story.

The second general point to make, by way of background to *The Rough and the Smooth*, is that the individual biography is frequently combined with and runs parallel to a more general narrative concerning the growth of cultural and national identity. The major convention to note in this broader narrative is that the history of the culture or nation is constructed, at least in part, on a model derived from the biography of the individual human subject. The culture or nation is thus represented as having evolved through stages of early, formative experience including, in this case, a colonial lack of independent identity; the discovery of diverse elements of new identity; and the synthesis of these elements into a distinctive and self-conscious sense of national character.

A relation of mutual support exists between the story in which the artist's vision is realised and the story in which national, cultural identity is forged. So, for example, in *The Rough and the Smooth* it is suggested, in sociological terms, that artistic subjectivity has been shaped by historical and cultural forces: at the same time, it is thought that the artist 'sees' and responds to what history and national culture were already becoming. This is the general idea that art must grow out of a specific reality, yet transcends it to reveal the essential form or spirit of human history. This difficult ambiguity informs familiar ways of speaking about the artist as being true to, and being the authentic voice of, his or her time. It underlies a stock of commonplaces such as the claim that the artist must fully realise his or her own self in order also to be truly representative. In *The Rough and the Smooth* Tom Roberts is thought to discover the proper form of his own art when he achieves a style which 'changes the way Australians looked at their country'. Style is understood not merely as personal or conventional manner, but as the expressive intensity of a particular individual in a particular time and place, who fathoms the experience of his or her age.

This identification of cultural and subjective histories can be referred to as a structure of 'humanist' cultural history. The conflation of individual biography and cultural history is supported by the shifting role played by the concept of creative origin. The idea that language and art have an organic origin in experience can be attached to the category of culture (cf. nation, people, spirit of the age) which influences the consciousness of the individual. Equally and simultaneously, the origin can be identified with the self of the artist, shaped by history, yet realising it in all the precious indeterminacy of experience; such that the artistic expression of his or her experience gives universal human significance to the particular historical moment.[10]

This detour through biographic and cultural representations has been taken in order to emphasise that a documentary does not devise single-handedly its materials and ways of organising them, but integrates and reworks a potentially wide array of textual and cultural sources. Of course the ideas isolated here are not the only ones used in writing about the Heidelberg School: it is sometimes argued, for example, that this work reflected a conservative *class* consciousness rather than an essentially human, that is class-less, vision.[11] The key point is that the television documentary is articulated to particular, adjoining textual representations, however shifting these may be, and that it adopts a certain position within a field of cultural representations.

This conventional portrayal is affected by the complex technical processes of TV. I turn now to this aspect of the documentary. The way in which **The Rough and the Smooth** assembles various kinds of texts (paintings, sketches, photographs, letters, pamphlets, posters, books, newspaper articles, etc.) indicates some established principles of composition, such as continuity of story and narration, psychological characterisation, and sound/image unification.

The general continuity of the voice-over narration derives in this case from the systems of authorial appreciation of texts and artists' biography already discussed, integrated with contextual elements of cultural and social history (for example, reference to social developments such as the growth of cities, and changing lifestyles). Within the presentation of any particular phase of an artist's work, events are connected narratively, that is, in chronological and apparently causal order, and the paintings are linked to the context of individual production in a way which allows cross-reference to other painters. Segments on the various individuals are edited into an overall sequence according to a general principle of alternation. That is, the text juxtaposes episodes of different lives to sustain an effect of approximate simultaneity between them, in those episodes, rather than telling each individual's story without interruption. The transitions between such segments are frequently secured by evoking some spatial or temporal relation between the subjects: this is the principle of linking elements by establishing that meanwhile, in another place, another event is occurring which fits into the greater design unfolded in the story. Transitions are also consolidated by producing analogies between the subjects, that is, verbal or visual comparisons —and indeed contrasts—which provide the cue to shift attention to another figure. Analogies are constructed by narrating similar actions and speech, as well as by including signs of communication between the subjects in the story. Such analogies are important in this text, since Roberts and Conder are presented as two complementary figures in the cultural period, but also as embodying different directions, an unresolved tension between the intense search for a nationalist vision and the romantic identification with Europe, between the 'rough' and the 'smooth' of Australian character. So, for instance, the pun which connects the sequence of images on Conder's death in Paris to another sequence on Roberts has a binding but contrastive effect. A first-person quotation from Conder's own hand, about 'the Tree of Life', is read elegiacally over a painting of women in a forest. To make the transition back to Roberts, the narrator says: 'Life went on for the rest of the world', over a photograph of Roberts tending his suburban garden, resuming his work in Australia, continually needing to link art to practical matters, subsequently to take commissions, and so on. The cues for the technical process of editing are provided by certain habits of writing and reading. Here, these are poetic, since the pun foregrounds the conceptual or paradigmatic link between the elements (life/death) and plays off the metaphoric and literal levels of meaning; and narrative, where one element is linked to what happens after and perhaps because of, or despite, what has occurred. Such editing patterns thus call into play, and through their own continuities confirm, different ways of resolving biographic narratives.

On the question of sound/image relations, let me specify further how the sound-track carries the narration of individual and cultural developments. The narration in fact comprises several devices. It includes the already mentioned voice-over of the narrator who addresses the viewer directly, relates the historical events in the past tense, refers to participants in the third person, and cites materials from the period. This is a conventional form of narration in historical documentary, which synthesises various sources and points of view, and so approximates to (though need never claim completely to attain) omniscience. There are at least two other kinds of speech which, although assigned to characters who participated in the situation, still partly function as narration, as means of 'telling' the events, indirectly, to the viewer. There are statements by the main protagonists, spoken by different readers for the program, which offer identification with an individual point of view. These create the sense of a more direct access to the 'interior' of the character, precisely because of the contrast between third and first person, and the element of dramatic elocution in the first-person statements. This form of speech helps to naturalise the culturally constructed popular memory through a simulacrum of personal memory, created within a system of psychological characterisation. Also there are comments by contemporaries, about the main protagonists. These various positions of speech involve varying shades of performance (low-key for the direct, more expressive for the indirect narration).

They provide the means by which the text anchors the images, linking them to the progress and experience of the individual artists, in accordance with the biographic narrative interwoven with the broader history.

The system of narration here ties into a more general framework of reading texts in terms of their relation to an authorial personality, explaining the genesis of art-works by grouping them with other texts which bear the same name and are assumed to signify authorial intentions, hopes, desires or moods. Such author-centred processes of citation and reading rely on the idea that a more or less uniform principle of expression runs across the many texts and endeavours linked to an author's name.[12]

The images, in general, play the role of supporting the sound-track, providing it with a visual field of reference. In a documentary like this one, images are rarely, if ever, presented unaccompanied by sound-track information about them and cues for reading them: to do so might begin to pose the problem of by what criteria we read the flow of images.

In *The Rough and the Smooth*, a range of devices for producing and organising images supports the construction of the painters as characters. These devices include camera angle, scale and movement, and editing of images and sounds. Five tactics may be noted here:

1 Paintings and photographs are re-presented by methods similar to those conventionally used in filming persons. An example is the use of close-ups of pictures of the artists' faces to invite a characterological reading of physiognomy and attitude, in relation to the narration of speech and thought on the sound-track.

2 The images of the artists are presented in relation to particular environments by various kinds of composition and editing (cuts, cross-dissolves, etc.) which convey meanings by association or analogy. For instance, the re-presented elements of a landscape painting, or of a painting of an interior setting such as the gaiety of forms in a cabaret, are used to signify something of the character of the painter, by evoking how he might have perceived a setting or lived a cultural moment.

3 The techniques of camera angle, scale and movement are used to alter the original spatial relations within paintings, re-composing them in the television image and in relation to the information carried on the sound-track. The program frequently uses the art-documentary convention of framing and/or panning across the surface of a painting inside its original borders, which has the effect of investing elements of the still picture with a life-like

independence, especially through the imaginary sense of movement transferred onto objects from the movement of the camera.
An example of this is the editing together of a series of panning
shots, in contrary directions, over the surface of 'The breakaway',
whose forms (stockman and sheep) thus seem to echo with movement through a landscape: shots which coincide with the voice-
over statement that Roberts changed the way Australians looked
at their country.

4 Shots of the paintings frequently are edited into sequences in a
mode of dramatisation analogous to the organisation of signs
within a televisual (and cinematic) system of psychological point
of view. That is, these shots answer to others (such as photographs of the painters) which establish the sign of a look—albeit
the look of an imaginary or ideal character—and so can be read
as either the objects or projections of the artist's vision. This
technique suggests the 'inspirational' gaze in relation to its
original objects. The effect can be observed in the cross-dissolve
from the eyes of Tom Roberts to the shots of 'The breakaway',
or in the view of the painting 'Bourke Street, Melbourne', where
the camera angles and movement suggest Roberts's real-life view
from his office which is referred to by the voice-over.

5 Music and sound effects are combined with the images, to create
a mood or to intensify the effect of the real, that is, to intensify
the imaginary presence of past or absent scenes evoked in the
image. So, for example, sound effects evoking the action of the
riders and animals are brought up over the images of 'The breakaway'.

Within the network of image and sound relations, the paintings
and other materials are constructed as manifestations of the artists'
experience of their age. The scenes shown in the images are offered
as influences on and emanations from an ideal point of view, namely
the artist's mediating consciousness with which we are invited to
identify.

This text allows a general point to be underlined, which concerns
the unification of sound and image, and the technical way in which
expectations are continually created and satisfied as sound and image
anticipate and answer each other. This interrelation is never a purely
mechanical and self-contained process, but co-operates with potentially diverse frameworks of ideas and cultural expectations. In this
typical art documentary, the sound-track recurrently sets up a way
of reading the paintings as an expression of the character or sen-
sibility of the artist. Simultaneously, images of the paintings are presented as a kind of evidence, to suggest that authorial qualities are

waiting to be read off from them. So, for example, the narrator suggests that the Coogee Beach paintings reflect the different personalities of their painters:

> Conder's picture shows his quiet visual humour and flair for decorative stylisation, while Roberts' version, strong and realistic, is in keeping with the character of the man.

As these words are spoken, the image-track shows the paintings to which they refer. We are invited, through the contrast, to see these manifestations of individuality as the intrinsic properties of the works. What makes such a reading possible, since no image of an art-work announces its own meaning? The kind of meaning created here is not an isolated effect of connecting sound to image. The presentation of the image calls into play a habit of reading a work's stylistic features as expressing the authorial personality. Only if one employs this technique of reading here does the image confirm the truth of what is said on the sound-track. In other words, the text invites the viewer to employ a well-established form of interpretive commentary. This is a way of interpreting a text as if its organisation of signs were a vehicle to express a deeper meaning, usually guaranteed by authorial experience. Supposedly, this meaning simply needs to be recovered from the text and everything in the text works to confirm the existence of that original meaning. This habit of 'mining' the text for an immanent meaning influences the kind of relation which commentary on a sound-track will have to paintings shown on an image-track in a conventional art documentary. Moreover, once activated, this mode of interpretive commentary is consolidated by the technical unification of sound and image, as an apparently natural way of producing textual meanings. Sound/image unification, which can take various forms (for example, sound anticipating image, or vice versa), is no automatic guarantee of coherent meaning, as criticism of its 'realist' closure of meaning sometimes implies. It is a definite technique for securing meaning, but can be informed by many different ways of interpreting data and drawing inferences.[13]

In relation to this rhetorical analysis of techniques and conventions, one might keep in mind the use of this kind of text within educational settings as well as its role as general, relatively 'serious' entertainment on broadcast TV. Documentary techniques and methods have differential functions, including a role in the teaching of modes of reading, aesthetic appreciation and particular knowledges of art. More could be said about how this text works, and many other types and uses of documentary might be mentioned. However, this example must serve to illustrate the argument that 'documenting' a subject is not a matter of 'representing' given events, objects, individuals or cultural developments, in the realist sense of this term. Television documentaries employ specific representational techniques, and through these techniques, far from capturing some given reality with an innocent eye, they bring into play methodologies for 'reading' documents and so making sense of situations. The plausibility of a television documentary, as it constructs particular kinds of meaning and knowledge of its topic, is relative to an audience's familiarity with, or critical attitude towards, the technical conventions employed. It is also relative to an audience's interest in the discursive categories activated in the text, and the degree to which these are accepted and accorded explanatory status.

Notes

1 This is not to overlook the important work found in, for example, N. Garnham, 'TV Documentary and Ideology', *Screen Reader 1*, 1977, pp.55–61; S. Heath and G. Skirrow, 'Television, a world in action', *Screen*, 18/2, 1977, 7–59, and N. King, 'Current Affairs Television: social problems and the problem of representation', *Australian Journal of Screen Theory*, 13/14, 1983, 43–58, on current affairs documentary; and D. Vaughan, *Television Documentary Usage* (London: British Film Institute, 1976).

2 Cf. E. Willis, *Writing Television and Radio Programs* (New York: Holt, Rinehart and Winston, Inc., 1967), ch.12; and E. Willis and C. D'Arienzo, *Writing Scripts for Television, Radio and Film* (New York: Holt, Rinehart and Winston, 1981), pp.64–85.

3 Willis and D'Arienzo, *Writing Scripts*, pp.64–85.

4 Cf. R. Hilliard, *Writing for Television and Radio* (New York: Hastings House, 1962), pp.129–63; W. Miller, *Screenwriting for Narrative Film and Television* (New York: Hastings House, 1980), especially pp.217–20 on non-fiction film; Willis, *Writing Television*, pp.243–8; and Willis and D'Arienzo, *Writing Scripts*, pp.64–85.

5 Examples of the kind of production or script-writing guides referred to here include (in addition to those already cited on TV documentary) D. Davis, *The Grammar of Television Production* (London: Barrie and Jenkins, published under the auspices of the Society of Film and Television Arts, 1974, 3rd edition); some of the instructional videotapes produced by the Australian Film, Television and Radio School, such as *Approaches to Interviewing*, introduced by Bryon Quigley and *Interview Techniques*, with Stuart Littlemore; and the BBC *On Camera* training tapes (1984). See T. Pateman, 'Ideological Criticism of Television Technical Manuals', *Screen Education*, (1974) 12, 37–45, for a critical discussion of the uses of techniques recommended by manuals and handbooks and the ideological dimension of technical 'objectives'.

6 *The Rough and the Smooth* was broadcast on the ABC's 'Australian Impact' series, 20 November 1984.

7   Cf. K. Tribe, 'History and the Production of Memories', *Screen* Vol.18, No.4, Winter 1977/78 (also published in T. Bennett, S. Boyd-Bowman, C. Mercer and J. Woollacott (eds) *Popular Television and Film* (London: British Film Institute, 1981), pp.319–26) for a discussion of textual and political constructions of memory, in terms opposed to the empiricist assumption that the text re-presents or discovers an immanent meaning of past events. Of course, the documents themselves of a past period have already been organised within certain contexts and uses of knowledge, and come to the present as palimpsests, with a history of uses and readings. On the 'popular memory' debate, see T. Bennett, S. Boyd-Bowman, C, Mercer and J. Woollacott (eds) *Popular Television and Film* (London: British Film Institute, 1981), Part IV.

8   E. Kris and O. Kurz, *Legend, Myth and Magic in the Image of the Artist* (New York: Yale University Press, 1979).

9   I am grateful to Jeffrey Minson for bringing this book to my attention.

10 A more detailed study might consider the Hegelian element in this familiar kind of historicisation of art and culture. It could also analyse other texts which give accounts of the Heidelberg School and Australian cultural history by combining biographic and historical representations of the kind being discussed. One example of the kind of text with which *The Rough and The Smooth* overlaps, within a general framework of recollection, is the pictorial history, *Australian Impressionist Painters*, by William Splatt and Susan Bruce. In this kind of book the combination of artists' biography and cultural history generates an account of the Heidelberg School which includes conventional elements such as the following:

a   Social and historical developments begin to create a spirit of national identity, which shapes the consciousness and aspiration of the young artists.

b   The teaching of young painters is dominated by an academic, conventional view of art, and Australian painting remains under the sway of inappropriate European ideas of form. These problems mark the need for a distinctive local aesthetic form, and for a break from a colonial mentality.

c   The negative factors are contrasted with the young painters' display of talent, their search for new directions, and the positive influence of mediating figures, especially Louis Buvelot.

d   The stages of individual development are realised. Talent burgeons, and the artists grow away from imposed convention and taste, towards an authentically individual style which is true to the specifically Australian subject and historical moment.

e   The artistic movement fades, original style becomes convention, the artists' lives diverge. The key principle of understanding art and art history is still the idea that they express the authorial experience of self and of the age, an experience which continues yet changes through time.

A 'deconstruction' of the traditional narrative of the Heidelberg School, and the role of artists as characters within a national history, is contained in the video Australian Fragments, produced by Ross Harley, at Griffith University, Brisbane, 1982; and another critical view, in relation to work by McCubbin, is given in the film **Serious Undertakings** of which a release script has appeared: H. Grace and E. Addiss, **Serious Undertakings**:

Release Script, *Framework*, 1984, 24, 128–41.

11 See, for example, I. Burn, 'Beating about the Bush: The Landscapes of the Heidelberg School', in A. Bradley and T. Smith (eds) *Australian Art and Architecture* (Melbourne: Oxford University Press, 1980).

12 Cf. M. Foucault, 'What is an Author?', in D. Bouchard (ed.) *Language, Counter-Memory, Practice* (Ithaca, New York: Cornell University Press, 1977).

13 There is a contrast between my account of narration and sound/image relations, techniques for *organising* discourses (*types* of knowledge) and that developed in C. MacCabe, 'Realism and the Cinema: Notes on some Brechtian Theses', *Screen*, 1974, 15/2, 7–27; and C. McArthur, *Television and History* (London: British Film Institute, 1978), ch.5, where narration and image-trace are treated as discourses in their own right, ranking other discourses (in the sense of individual's speeches), and imposing themselves ideologically as transparent and true; although there is no room to develop this contrast here.

Videotapes

Approaches to Interviewing n.d. Instruction tape produced by the Australian Film, Television and Radio School, presented by Bryon Quigley.

Australian Fragments (1982) Videotape produced by Ross Harley, at Griffith University, Brisbane.

Interview Techniques n.d. Instruction tape produced by the Australian Film, Television and Radio School, presented by Stuart Littlemore.

On Camera (1984). A set of four tapes produced for the Education and Training Division of BBC Enterprises, London.

The Rough and the Smooth: The Story of Tom Roberts and Charles Conder (1983) Art documentary broadcast in the ABC 'Australian Impact' series, 20th November, 1984. Produced by Film Australia, in collaboration with the Friends of the Art Gallery of South Australia. Written and directed by David Muir.

8

Publicising Progress: Science on Australian Television

Philip Bell and Kathe Boehringer

Scientific/technological 'progress'

Science, technological change, inventions, medical research, bio-logical/environmental controversies ('test-tube' babies, pollution, etc.) are the subject of continuous media attention. The visibility of modern technology, the easy recruitment of 'medical miracle' stories (e.g. heart or bone-marrow transplants) to 'human interest' genres, and the drama of high technology (e.g. space exploration) mean that 'science and technology' is one of the most commonly presented areas of socially significant television. *Beyond 2000*—the promised future surpassing the limits of contemporary science and technology —this is the typical form of Australian televisualised science in the 1980s. And what does a random night's program offer by way of an advertisement for the future? Perhaps less than the awesome spectacle of science which is suggested by the computerised format and digitalised music that introduces such a program. Here is the menu of *Beyond 2000* for 23 June 1987:

1   a new treatment for drug addicts;
2   the powers of ginseng;
3   Seoul's Olympic running track;
4   a new approach to projecting TV images using laser.

Applied technology, human social problems solved, sports technology, media innovations—an agenda in which science is shown in its application to psychological/medical, sports and communications fields. In short, science which has implications for the assumed television audience and which inflects the agenda of popular TV towards the most concrete, short-term issues in science and technology where the celebration of human control of the social and physical environment can be displayed.

In this paper we shall examine, from a critical perspective, how science and technology are generally made known through the rhetoric of programs such as *Beyond* (previously *Towards*) *2000* and *Quantum*. We will argue that such programs translate into the vernacular idiom of television the more abstract discourses of science to produce a limited, present-minded and instrumental view of the world in which the equation of technology with progress is made, divorced from any human political context. First, however, let us describe more fully what sorts of 'stories' and meanings characterise Australian science magazine programs:

> Good evening. Well the idea of human beings roaring through the sky Buck Rogers style has long been the stuff of dreams. But on TOWARDS 2000 tonight we'll see just how close to reality those dreams are as Iain Finlay reports from the U.S.
> The parched plains of India and satellite technology would seem to be literally poles apart, but there's a growing dependence on satellites to provide knowledge vital for survival for that subcontinent. And the manufacture of radio-active isotopes for medicine. A life-saving process from a highly contentious area.
> They're three of the reports on TOWARDS 2000 tonight.[1]

The ABC's *Towards 2000* brought scientific and technological advances, innovations and controversies to an assumed 'mass' audience. In this quoted introduction, it promises (on behalf of technology) to close the gap between 'dreams' and 'reality' through a future of satellites and radioactive isotopes. 'Knowledge' of formally-defined, scientific domains (agriculture, aeronautics, medicine, computers and communications) is ubiquitous on television and in the daily press. But what sort of 'knowledge' do the media conceptualise and circulate, and how is this 'knowledge' contextualised and formatted within the media? As the quoted example shows, these questions are closely related. Its item on the possibility of individual flight epitomises some of the most obvious tendencies in uncritical, infantile, open-mouthed, 'gee-whiz', television:

CREDITS

DATELINE:
MICHIGAN, USA

ASSIGNMENT:
UP, UP AND AWAY

REPORTER:
IAIN FINLAY

Archive footage of old flying machine (Nickelodeon music)

FINLAY in studio

(Insert hang-gliding film)

I'm sure at some stage or another everyone has seen some of these old movies on early attempts at individual flight. Well, over the years probably the closest we've come to flying like a bird has been hang-gliding. But although it's a beautiful way to fly, you're still dependent on the wind. With ultralight aircraft, however, you've got the power to go where you want to go, but you're surrounded by a great deal of paraphernalia, and also, you need an airstrip.

ILLUS. Buck Rogers

CUT to man wearing rocket backpack

Well, Buck Rogers had one answer with his strap-on rocket belt which could whisk him to wherever he wanted to go. The nearest we've come to that idea is the sort of rocket backpack which was seen at fairs and showgrounds quite a bit over the last few years.

Clip from James Bond movie

And they've come a long way since those first flights. But although James Bond used one to escape a tricky situation in one of his movies, this sort of rocket backpack, the kind of flying that everyone dreams about, has never really come to fruition, except for experimental flights and show-biz exhibitions like the flight at the opening of the Los Angeles Olympics. The main drawback has been fuel and the limited range of the machine. They've only been able to carry enough fuel for a few minutes flight.

With something so spectacular and exciting it's been a major disappointment to many prospective emulators of Buck Rogers that this has prevented them from becoming more widely available. Well, there was a sequence in the latest *Star Wars* movie, *The Return of the Jedi*, which showed an amazing flying machine, somewhat different from these, that you rode like a motorbike, and it zoomed through the trees about five or six metres above the ground. Well, if you saw that movie and thought of it as an exciting bit of future fantasy, well think again because it's here already.

CUT to flying machine demo

IF/VO

This is the 'wasp', an incredibly compact one-person flying machine that's being built by a company in Michigan in the United States. Built under a contract for the United States army it can fly at speeds of up to a hundred kilometres an hour for as long as 30 minutes. And fly, as you can see, below tree-top level, or as high as 3000 metres. It can fly close to buildings and cliffs and reach areas that would be impossible for helicopters. It can take off and land in an area of less than half a square metre. It's powered by a 270 kilo-thrust mini fan-jet engine that weighs only 110 kilos, and it carries 68 kilos of fuel. The operator just stands on the small platform, starts up the motor and flies. In the air, it's controlled simply by shifting your body weight and leaning in the direction you want to go. Forwards, backwards, sideways—hovering or rotating on its own axis. At the moment its development is tightly controlled by the United States army. But if its military tests continue to be as startlingly successful as they have been to date, there's little doubt that widespread civilian use of such a fantastic flying machine won't be too far off.[2]

The rhetoric focuses on technology overcoming impediments (duration and range of alternative machines) in the development of an unquestioned *advance* (one that 'you' are assumed to be keen on, and capable of, sharing). The new machine is not just fantasy but an incredibly compact reality, whose technical specifications attest to its utility while giving viewers enough hard information to be convincing. Of course, the machine is being developed by the US Army, but the report optimistically asserts that it will have 'civilian use' (as though this were the inevitable consequence of such technological 'progress'). At the risk of emphasising the obvious, the following points might be noted concerning this rather banal example:

1 It is enthusiastically positive about technology.
2 It relates technology to 'us', the viewer *directly*—addressing the viewer directly, colloquially.
3 Science-fiction (fantasy) is the model for presenting 'real' technological developments.
4 The economic/political (in this case military) context of the innovation is not examined. The detailed consideration of the *costs* of, or alternatives to, its development are not canvassed.
5 The existence of the 'wasp' is unquestionably seen as socially desirable, although no reasons are advanced for this.
6 The reporter's enthusiasm for the invention is spoken of in words which effectively advertise 'the future' in glowing terms —it must be better than the present *because* of technology (a curiously circular argument). One implication of this is that science is value-free (see below).

More generally, of course, the item presents as 'factual' (true) the details of the physically real (photographable) invention. The facts about the machine are those of a closed technological discourse into which questions of *social value* do not intrude. The scientificity of the program emphasises *observable demonstration* and *technical detail*—unquestionable factuality.

Not all science–technology reporting is as naive as this example. However, this *Towards 2000* report is by no means unique. In surveying the general field of televised science and technology, Gardner and Young[3] point to a number of similar, common characteristics.

Gardner and Young's critique of televisual science

We have on the one hand a firmly-established and highly-regarded set of conventions for the presentation of science—conventions which are expository, narrative and fundamentally celebratory, purveying culture to an audience of passive consumers who regard a spectacle. On the other hand, we have developments in science which are fundamentally reconstituting aspects of life, including conception, birth, behavioural control, work, education, sexuality, leisure, consumption, bodily repair, senescence, death and the recycling of human organs. There is an alarming inconsistency between the mode of presentation and the significance of these issues. We want to argue that it is an urgent priority for television to alter its approach to these matters in fundamental ways:

– to move from science as cultural consumption to science as critique;

– from the content of science as progress to an analysis of the constitution of science, technology and medicine, of their labour processes and of their articulations with other practices;

– from the 'impact' of science to the process of constitution of its research programme, opening up to public scrutiny and prioritisation the origination of issues, facts and artifacts.[4]

Gardner and Young illustrate the 'fundamentally celebratory' presentation of science as a spectacle of progress which television audiences merely consume, by referring to British programs such as *Horizon*, and *Man Alive*. They point out that science is presented as an isolated domain of *factual* knowledge, divorced from socio/histoical determinations. Facts are value-free, even theoretically neutral units of knowledge. Hence, 'scientific' and 'factual' have become virtually synonymous in popular discourse; both are beyond critique. 'Facts' being the *content* of science, the media may focus almost exclusively on the *drama of their discovery* or on their *personal/social effects*.

As with all other domains of social knowledge, mediated science is presented by 'neutral' experts who access and quote 'experts'. The journalist is the digester/packager of the complexities of scientific processes and knowledge. This frequently means that the reporter assumes an almost reverential attitude to technology—whether military or medical—as the two Australian examples below attest.

In one of its earliest programs, ABC's *Towards 2000* visited the US Boeing factory and reported on missile research and development. The reporter commented that the gleaming instrument along which he ran his reverent hand was 'really quite a clever little toy', and referred to its warhead as 'the real business area'.[5] The reporter sought to convey his own awe at the sophistication of the weapon's technology, ignoring its purpose.

The 'miracle' of microsurgery reported on in the same program[6] perhaps typifies the ways by which journalists may present 'progress' from the dual positions of awe-struck, ordinary viewer and journalist/expert granted access to the inner sanctum of medical research. The scientist–surgeon as hero and the viewer as vicarious beneficiary are brought together by the hushed tones of the reporter:

TOWARDS 2000 Introduction and Items on Microsurgery (29/8/84)

STUDIO INTRODUCTION	Good evening. Tonight on *Towards 2000* we look at two very different sources of producing electrical energy. In the west of England hot rocks beneath the earth's surface are providing a challenge to scientists to produce electrical power in vast quantities, whilst in Russia, super-heated air is now supplying power stations with a long sought after efficiency. In England we take a flight on board a new agricultural aircraft, whilst back home in Australia we look at the miracle of microsurgery, a field in which Australia is now world leader. These are some of the reports on *Towards 2000* tonight.

1st Item on English Agricultural Aeroplane

2nd Item on Microsurgery

OPENING MUSIC—'Für Elise'

OPENING CREDITS	DATELINE SYDNEY ASSIGNMENT: THE MIRACLE OF MICRO-SURGERY REPORTER: CARMEL TRAVERS
OPENING SHOT: Child in highchair, young girl sitting beside him. Widens to include Travers *CT*	These two little children — the result of a medical miracle, the miracle of microsurgery. If there'd only been one, it might have been dismissed as a miracle of the more biblical kind, but two, and a medical milestone has been reached, because the father of these children was sterile like many men in Australia.
MUSIC OVER	It has taken little more than a decade for the scale and skill of microsurgery

Cut to Operating Theatre	to advance from the rejoining of severed parts to the reorganisation of the body's tiniest internal components.
CT/VO	
CUT to teenage boy playing 'Für Elise' on piano	In 1968 medical history was made when the severed index finger of Jason Todd, then a 2-year-old child, was reattached to his hand. Such operations now, though less exacting, are almost routine. Today's challenges to microsurgeons could almost be described as invisible mending.
CT/VO	
CUT to Operating Theatre	What we're about to witness is the most complex of all microsurgical operations. . . It's the reversal of a congenital or birth defect which has rendered this patient sterile. Sterility affects up to about 5% of all males. And so the fact that this operation has now been developed by the Microsearch Foundation in Sydney, is a source of great encouragement to most males who until now would have had little hope of reversing their sterility.
CT (in theatre with mask and gown)	
VIVALDI MUSIC OVER	To the soothing strains of the 'Vivaldi' this microsurgery team led by Dr Earl Owen, the acknowledged pioneer of microsurgery, prepares to operate. This team is the first in the world to have conducted a series of successful operations correcting congenital male sterility.
CT/VO	
ILLUSTRATION of a testicle and a tube	The sterility is basically caused by a blockage, often a congenital defect in which connection is obstructed between the epididimus, where sperm develop, and the vas, the tube through which the sperm travel. To correct this problem the surgeon must bypass the obstruction.
More detailed illustration of 'it'	The surgeon selects a higher tubule of the epididimus to join to the inner

core of the vas. The outer muscle layer of the vas is also stitched to the epididimus. In this, most fastidious of all operations, the microsurgeon is attaching one tube, which is twice the width of a human hair, to another, which is just half a hair's breadth. It's like painting a masterpiece on a grain of rice.

DR OWEN (peering into microscope)

What makes this operation a little more difficult than the others in microsurgery, is the size of the tubes we're joining. We're joining the inside bore of the vas which will admit two human hairs, to a tube which is so small, it's the inner lining of the epididimus, a tube which will not even admit one hair. And so this—um—technological challenge, that's only recently been overcome.

MUSIC

CU of testicle

CUT to surgeon CT/VO

Operating under an optically perfect microscope, the surgeon and his assistant manipulate their surgical instruments with just the slightest movement of the fingertips.

CUT to surgeon CT/VO

The magnified image is at all times displayed on a video monitor for all operating room staff to see. To the naked eye, the microsurgeon's needle and thread is practically invisible. But for the operation to be successful, an obsessive attention to detail is essential.

Op. in CU

OWEN (into microscope):

The success rate of that in our hands over the first 100 patients is producing a 60 per cent appearance of sperms now, in the male's ejaculate six months to a year after the operation—60 per cent—but—um—unfortunately only 20 per cent of the patients in the series have as yet fathered children. But 20

Children noises and clapping
CUT to two children and
mother
CT/VO

Carol, now aged four, was conceived eighteen months after her father's operation. Daniel followed three years later, and a third child is planned.

CUT to outside
Microsurgery Centre. Owen
walks in with CT
CT/VO

With such success behind him where does Earl Owen and his team go from here? Back to the Microsearch Foundation in Sydney's Surry Hills for further experimentation.

CUT to Operating Theatre

CU arm
CU hand

The re-attachment of amputated parts—this arm and hand was wrenched off in a concrete mixer—has brought the Microsearch Foundation international notoriety. But other developments like the design of a surgeon's chair, a microscope, and the microsurgical instruments have also come out of the Foundation.

CUT to theatre
CT in theatre

CU of instruments

Every second is precious when restoring the lost blood flow of a severed hand or limb. The nerves and tendons must also be rejoined, and with the refinement of the surgeon's skill's has also come the refinement of the delicate instruments required for that operation. These two, developed by Dr Earl Owen, have more than doubled the operating speed of the microsurgeon. This is a needle holder with retracting scissors and these, the micro-forceps. Now these two instruments alone have completely replaced this entire box of surgical instruments.

CU of box

They enable the microsurgeon to perform almost any function in every speciality.

per cent is an enormous advance on previous techniques which had little to no success at all.

CT (pulling a hair from her head)

So now, to see the instruments at work, Dr Owen will repair this. So there's no blood, no human tissue, just an opportunity for you to enjoy the craftsman at work.

MUSIC—Vivaldi
CT (handing hair to Owen)

The micro-instruments, gold-plated to cut down light reflection, are held in the fingertips like a pen. The combination of functions eliminates the need for surgeons to put down and pick up the instruments.

OWEN (explaining):

...so that it slightly swells and—a—it will hold a stitch. Human tissue of course is..has circulation going through it in every part, and—a—it is much easier to put the tissue into supple living tissue.

MUSIC
CT/VO (CU of Op.):

Just as a hair is rejoined, so too is a nerve.

CU of patient

In this patient, a stroke had paralysed one side of her face. A reconstruction of the network of facial nerves gradually restored this woman's smile...to this.

DIAGRAM of face
Photo smiling face
CUT to operating theatre

In the future, the microsurgeon will likely lead medicine to previously untouchable territory. Already clinical trials on foetal primates have proved successful. As this operation to correct a hernia on a rhesus monkey foetus shows. Throughout the operation, only the hand and arm of the foetus is removed from the uterus. Once the hernia is repaired, the foetus recovers inside the best intensive care ward possible. Three months later this foetus was born, showing no obvious scarring from the operation. Foetal surgery on humans may be some years away, though Earl Owen is convinced intra-uterine microsurgery is the best method of correcting such congenital problems as spinabifida and diaphragmatic hernia.

MUSIC-'Für Elise'   Just sixteen years ago Jason Todd's
                             amputated index finger made history.
CT/VO: What had previously seemed impos-
CUT to boy at piano   sible, was achieved.
CUT to monkey's hand

END[7]

Gardner and Young point to the pace and circular presentation of science in programs which set up a problem that is 'solved' by science/technology. This effects a *closure* (e.g. the impossible is achieved) as complete as that of the most formulaic private detective genre, conveying a sense of inevitability. In the presence of such a closed *story*, the viewer can only marvel at the ease with which scientific progress meshes with the conventions of television magazine stories. Science, argue Gardner and Young, is seen as authoritative, non-controversial, positive and value-free in such genres. Science programs are almost invariably about 'progress' (or the 'fight' to overcome a natural obstacle) and thus optimistically ignore *real* social/historical determinations.

For example, while the high visibility of scientists on science programs seems unproblematic, it is important to remember that researchers and institutions need to attract funds, and to promote themselves as leaders in their respective fields. Their need for publicity, for that positive image which counts for so much in the modern bureaucratic state, renders them vulnerable to sensationalistic and simplistic reporting. Newsworthiness is crucial in gaining access to the media in the field of science as in other domains. Hence, the privileged access that is given to (some) institutional spokespersons who reinforce the view that science is an exciting, progressive inevitability, constitutes a form of 'subsidised' news in which the state—and privately funded science industry—trades its newsworthiness for media publicity. The media, therefore, are not merely non-analytical and uncritical where 'science' is concerned; they are sometimes little more than publicity machines for the science and technology institutions, relying on the press releases of the 'industry'. Although isolated items of social concern occasionally find a voice (e.g. environmentalism, natural versus 'high tech' medicine), these are drowned by the incessant buzz and hum of publicising progress.

The *institutional* aspects of scientific and technological development are generally ignored and the bureaucratic structures, corporate –economic and political context overlooked. Science is *scientists* at work; and although in the real world, bureaucracy may inhibit the activity of such individuals, it is never seen as a *condition* of the modern technological State. The result is programs which offer no terms for understanding science as a conflict-ridden, historically complex set of processes. Indeed, 'science' seems to be utterly independent of history:

> *Horizon* increasingly attempts to address questions which go beyond the exposition of the content of science but does so in an uncritical fashion. In a programme about sugar production in Brazil we are told (three times) that 'Brazil has plenty of cheap labour', which is roughly equivalent to saying that Pakistan has lots of thin people. In a programme on Mexican oil *Horizon* manages to state in conclusion that 'Nobody wants the oil to distort the Mexican economy or the happier aspects of the Mexican way of life' and cuts to ole singers with guitars and sombreros. These examples are drawn from a large collection to indicate just how careless of other aspects of its context science programmes can be. The division of labour operates here as in other spheres so that it precludes access to the totality of relations which make up any whole. *Horizon* does science alternating with environment; *Tomorrow's World* does new technologies in a 'gee whiz' way; *The Risk Business* does a combination of 'gee whiz' technology and retooling in the 'national interest'; *Mari Alive* tells 'stories of folk' on the receiving end—the sociological and human interest aspects; *The Money Programme* deals with the economics of it all; *Open Secret* catches out individuals and companies who have abused (otherwise neutral?) science and technology.[8]

Gardner and Young recommend a three-fold change in media representations of science, technology and medicine:

1 'What forces evoke and constitute the kind of questions, frameworks and specific priorities of science?'[9]
2 'The labour process: What are the relations of production of science, technology and medicine?'[10]
3 The articulation of how science is *connected* with the rest of society, and especially with social issues of political significance such as race, gender and environmental conflict and debate.

They see the need for a thorough critique of the *sources* of scientific questions and models, and of the funding and bureaucratic/economic determinations of science and technology. They recommend opening up the media to allow conflicting analyses of the 'origination of new facts, antifacts, and procedures', for '[a]s things now stand, we are faced with them at the point of impact when they are so highly developed and/or capitalised that it is difficult to believe that any real democratic process is possible'.[11]

This critique sees scientific reporting as, in effect, mystifying and ideological in so far as it ignores or displaces the analysis of the material production of socially determined and significant knowledge by focusing on the epiphenomena of science/technology as echoes of an unchangeable, progressive development in modern capitalist societies. Other critics of media 'scientism' have developed these arguments to conclude that it has 'become an integral part of the cultural hegemony of the mass media', 'a legitimating ideology of advanced capitalism' which acts as a 'compensatory response to the breakdown of consensus in the social and political system'.[12]

Science fictions as ideology

Dunn's argument rests on a notion of 'scientism' as perceiving social reality through the lens of narrowly technical criteria, bound to positivist conceptions of value-free knowledge and efficiency: '. . . [S]cientism represents a closed universe of discourse, where alternatives to societal arrangements are automatically dismissed by restricting definitions of reality to the existing factual order. . .' where '. . . the domination of people is inseparable from and justified by the "management of things"'.[13] Thus, *political* questions, questions of *value*, become subsumed to merely technical matters of 'scientific expertise'. (Here we might emphasise that 'scientific' includes the *social* sciences, economics and sociology, not merely the physical sciences appropriate to the technologies of the military or the electronic media.)

Dunn repeats many of the arguments we have canvassed from Gardner and Young. However, his examples are primarily from the *fictional* programs of television (*Superman, The Six Million Dollar Man, The Bionic Woman*, etc.) rather than the news and news magazine genres we have considered. Dunn links scientism as a cultural force to the arguments of critical theory and its Frankfurt School antecedents, asserting that, like electronic mass culture in general, scientism is an aspect of 'the degradation of knowledge and experience which has resulted from "instrumental rationality" and which has turned the individual into a passive spectator of a reified social existence'.[14] Action dramas, for example, focus on technical control as the means of human survival (e.g. science fiction), and 'technical solutions. . . become linked to the political and moral authority of major institutions, most notably the State'.[15] Dunn argues that this is a recent development, replacing the image of science as an evil, uncontrollable, destructive force against which 'humanity' fought. Generally, he suggests:

> Beginning in the sixties, television replaced the evil imagery of the 'Frankenstein' monster with an essentially favourable image of science as an institutionalised enterprise supporting the general welfare and promoting social justice'.[16]

Though not universal (e.g. the British program *Dr Who*), the professional or expert serving a bureaucratic team has generally replaced the eccentric individual scientist. Dunn sees this as symptomatic of a dominant representation of science as a necessary and benign value in 'social integration and control'.

Dunn's approach is a useful corrective to that of Gardner and Young which utilises an essentially political economy critique. Although Gardner and Young are on firm ground in criticising the media's ahistorical treatment of science, a treatment which suppresses the emergence of state-organised science and technological development as the leading productive force of advanced capitalism, it is doubtful whether identifying television's prevailing modes of representation as 'ideological' goes far enough. While Gardner and Young maintain that television erroneously and mystifyingly represents science as existing in an internal–external dichotomy with society rather than correctly canvassing science 'as constituted by and constitutive of social relations',[17] Dunn's view is that contemporary television portrays science (particularly in fictional programs) as 'fully integrated into contemporary social reality'. He claims that:

> Significantly, scientism has been thoroughly incorporated into television dramatizations of the perennial battle in popular culture between the forces of good and evil. The imagery of control and domination has become central to television dramas featuring violent struggles against crime, subversion and immorality, and the eventual official triumph over enemies of society. More importantly, as *technical control becomes the focal point of human action and survival in these programs, technical solutions simultaneously become linked to the political and moral authority of major institutions, most notably the State.* This institution uses scientistic rationales both to preserve social order and to strengthen its own ideological supremacy.[18]

On the Gardner and Young view of television's mode of representation, science appears as a 'natural' phenomenon rather than as a central institution of capitalism; on the Dunn view, science appears both as an institution and as 'institutionally controlled and benign . . . defined by and embodied in official agencies of protection and control'. Do these differing viewpoints result from looking at different genres, i.e. non-fiction as opposed to fiction programs? Is one view 'right' and the other 'wrong'? Can these two views be reconciled?

It is our view that Dunn's contention that media representations of science privilege technical control as a value and pre-suppose the extension of control techniques to all aspects of society, is more persuasive. His charge is not, as in Gardner and Young, that the media merely mystify the real social relations which exist between classes in contemporary conditions. It approximates instead to the critical theory view that *it is no less than a condition of modernity* that the political system is no longer oriented toward the achievement of some substantive notion of 'the good' but rather toward the solution of what are seen as merely 'technical' problems. Government activity increasingly orients itself toward administratively soluble technical problems; the presumptive domain of politics—questions of value—conveniently disappear, freeing the political realm to get on with the job of administering economic growth and development, the 'life process of society'.[19] On this analysis, then, the Gardner and Young recommendation that science broadcasting be less closed, to represent science not as 'above the battle of competing interest groups and classes' fails to take seriously that science and the attendant notion of scientific 'progress' are not simply constitutive of the social relations of contemporary capitalism but occupy a privileged position within the vastly changed circumstances of a society which is more 'administered' than capitalist.

Contrary to the view that most news is 'bad news', science/technology/medicine furnishes an abundance of 'good news'—space conquests, robots relieving human drudgery, new hearts for sick children (the subsequent deaths of whom are as under-reported as the successful transplants are over-reported). The critical examination of science and technology is rare in the contemporary media. In its place are disaster stories (science gone wrong or 'mad') or analyses which contrast the stereotype of inevitable scientific progress with its occasional exceptional mis-application, exceptions which 'prove the rule' of scientific progress itself.

Awe-inspiring 'good news' overwhelms news or analysis which allow readers/viewers to understand and to judge the desirability of the 'progressive' connotations which accrue to technological 'developments'. Who would question the medical priorities which give rise to heroic items such as: 'Artificial Heart Man Sets Record'[20] which relates the joy of the family and friends of the man who has survived for 112 days with 'a mechanical heart beating in his breast'? Yet heart transplant and artificial heart programs must compete with other medical options for resources. Even on grounds of economics, criticism of these programs could be advanced. But the media largely ignore the costs, even the success (or failure) rates of many such 'advances' for the more popular optimism of (young) lives 'saved'.

Notes

Since this piece was written, a comprehensive, nontheoretical account of the relationships between science, technology and the press has been published in the USA: Dorothy Nelkin, *Selling Science: How the Press Covers Science and Technology* (New York: W.H. Freeman and Co., 1987).

1 *Towards 2000*, ABC-TV, 19 September 1984.
2 Ibid.
3 C. Gardner and R. Young, 'Science on television: a critique', in T. Bennett et al (eds), *Popular Television and Film* (London: BFI/Open University Press, 1981). pp.171–196.
4 Ibid, p.174.
5 John O'Hara, quoted in *National Times*, 5 September 1981.
6 *Towards 2000*, ABC-TV, 29 August 1984.
7 Ibid.
8 Gardner and Young (1981), p.175–6.
9 Ibid, p.190.
10 Ibid.
11 Ibid, p.191.
12 R.G. Dunn, 'Science, technology and bureaucratic domination: television and the ideology of scientism', in *Media, Culture and Society*, 1979, 1(4), p.352.
13 Ibid, p.344.
14 Ibid, p.345. The reference to Horkheimer and Adorno in this quotation is M. Horkheimer and T.W. Adorno, *The Dialectic of Enlightenment* (New York: Seabury Press, 1972).
15 Ibid.
16 Ibid.
17 Gardner and Young (1981), p.174.
18 Dunn (1979), p.345
19 H. Arendt, *The Human Condition* (Chicago: University of Chicago Press, 1958).
20 *Daily Telegraph*, 19 March 1985, p.13.

9

Soaps and Ads: Flow and Segmentation

John Tulloch

Commercial TV drama works as part of a defined syntagmatic space[1]: in relation to the sequential flow of genres as channels seek to deliver audiences from one program to the next; and in relation to its segmentation by advertisements as channels seek to deliver audiences to advertisers. Traditionally media critics have taken this economic determination of program flow to suggest that the effects of TV flow and segmentation are clear cut and conservative. Thus Budd, Craig and Steinman argue that commercials tend to close off the problems opened up by drama: 'commercials respond fairly directly to the problems, desires and fantasies articulated in the program's narrative by promising gratification through products'.[2] However, as Fiske argues, the audience effect of the interrupted flow of advertisements and drama is not simply and reductively economic: 'many more viewers gain pleasure from advertisements than buy the products being promoted'.[3]

Recently, theorists have looked for an 'excessive' and progressive potential in what Hartley[4] calls the 'structural marginality' of television (the sequenced relationship between its different genres, and between its programs and its 'gaps', like advertisements, promos, and so on). Modleski[5] has taken this analysis of TV segmentation and flow perhaps furthest, in arguing for a space for play between sequenced genres (quiz/soap; soap/advertisement). This, she suggests, 'decenters' conventional narrative closures, even though the subject matter (the climactic success of the quiz show, the resolution of trivial chores in advertisements) may seem conservative. The antithesis between the commercial's resolution of daily problems (the saggy nappies and carpet stains) and soap opera's *lack* of resolution of the 'large problems of human existence' (love, death, dying) in fact:

> embodies a deep truth about the way women function in (or, more accurately, around) culture: as both moral and spiritual guides and household drudges, moving back and forth between the extremes, but obviously finding them difficult to reconcile.[6]

Flitterman, too, emphasises the nexus of interruption and flow, the continuity *and* conflict between soaps and commercials: 'To the soap opera's conventional and consistent fare of illegitimacy, rivalry, false parentage, adultery, secrecy and betrayal, the commercial offers the happy family, the good mother, the affectionate companion and the conscientious housewife'.[7] On the one hand, advertisements work as a central part of capitalism's 'equation of material consumption with well-being';[8] on the other, they operate in a play between genres that makes women's pleasure narratively 'off-centre' and arguably critical of dominant patriarchal modes.

Hartley has argued for a critical analysis which both accounts *for* these television areas of excess and marginality and brings them *to* account, since otherwise 'both capitalism and popular consciousness continue to develop and change *unaccountably* in the margins of television'.[9] Yet much of this recent work has been very general as well as empirically vague, relying on notions of the textual positioning of subjects which takes no account of either recent ethnographic approaches to audience readings or to production practices within specific institutional structures. Elsewhere[10] I have adopted an ethnographic approach to a particular audience—the elderly—to argue that old people carve out their pleasures as a kind of guerilla activity against the rejection of their preferences by television programmers. They mobilise television's segmentation and flow to select out from different genres (whether quiz shows, advertisements, soaps, or cop shows) a particular space for 'older people', so that their pleasure is a '*bricolage*' (or collage) of generic appropriation. In this chapter I want to examine segmentation and flow in terms of particular production practices.

Soaps and ads: normative margins

Allen[11] has pointed out that the transition from radio to television soap operas has led to the removal of the authoritative narrator.

This, together with a greater dispersal of narrative perspectives (as soaps got longer and characters proliferated), led to the opening up of the soap opera text to 'normative daring'—to a greater range of values and norms. Current soap operas are able to 'accommodate a far greater range of "negotiated" readings than other, more normatively dominant forms of fictive narratives' and hence are opposed to the 'perspectival determinacy of its commercial messages'.[12] However, the possibility of 'normative daring' that Allen raises will also depend on production practices within the specific institutional structures of commercial television. A channel like ATN7, which has traditionally regarded itself as a 'halfway house' between the ABC and other commercials, may experiment with a more socially 'nutritious' soap as long as it is backed by conventional material.

> Our image comes closer to the ABC than the other commercial
> stations. This can help us. People can come out of the ABC and
> perhaps be slightly more inclined to come to Channel 7 than they
> would be to Channels 9 or 10. *Sons and Daughters* is . . .
> predictable. . . traditional soap opera. . . Like everyone knows
> the finale. . . of *Punch and Judy*. . . *A Country Practice*
> contributes something different. . . more nutritious.[13]

This particular institutional space for *A Country Practice* allows it to take more 'normative risks' than *Sons and Daughters*, and I have described elsewhere[14] how this can flow through into political contradictions in the making of the show itself. Here I want to look at how this institutional space and political ambiguity bears on the sequenced relationship between the program and the 'gaps' within it.

The ratings success of *A Country Practice* depends on its broad audience demographics; but different episodes will adopt a varying age-focus, in order to keep specific age and gender groups 'hooked' to the show. The episode, 'A Touch of Class' started life targeting a middle-aged female audience, when executive producer James Davern suggested at a plotting conference 'a kind of *Romeo and Juliet* story that will attract the mums'. Writer David Allen, however, had broader intentions: 'It was the migrant woman story, with her son and the daughter of the rich factory owner who was doing the exploiting. What's interesting is that the *Romeo and Juliet* idea came first, and the exploitation came afterwards.' Allen had a clear sense of the institutional space ACP operated in, going 'as far as it can as a popular piece of commercial dramatic fiction in at least acknowledging that social problems exist'.[15]

In 'A Touch of Class' the problem of exploitation is bluntly stated by the migrant boy, Lorenzo Belotti to his Alfa-driving girlfriend,

Ashleigh Lyall, who thinks Mrs Belotti's tenosynovitis can be cured by taking a few day's rest:

Lorenzo:	It's always the same with people like you. You look at all this (*indicating shirts strewn around the entire room*) and you still don't understand. My mother can't afford to take a few days' rest. Let me spell it out to you. My mother sits here for fourteen hours a day. They pay her for the number of uniforms she completes. But this *generous* employer deducts the payments on the machine, which my mother must have or she can't do the work anyway. In the end it works out she makes about a dollar an hour. She gets four hours' sleep. She keeps that up for *seven days a week*. She's got to. If she doesn't make a quota, then there's nothing. Now her hands have seized up on her, and the only treatment that will cure her is if she stops sewing, Ashleigh. Here, look. (*Handing her a shirt*) Do you know how many of these she has to sew before she makes her one dollar an hour?

(*ASHLEIGH looks at the label on the shirt and realises the employer is her father.*)

The power of capital over migrant labour is clearly stated in the episode by the threat of Jimmie Lyall to move his clothing factory to the Philippines to secure even cheaper labour. At the end, this is what happens, and so what David Allen calls ACP's 'often easy solution' is avoided, and Ashleigh and Lorenzo are separated. Indeed, the problem of class exploitation is generalised beyond that of an individual capitalist, when one of the 'good' doctors among the leading characters relates it to his own affluent, medical background: 'talking about cutting costs and capital gains'. The normatively marginal is brought to the serial's centre, ready (as we will see later) to be woven into ensuing story lines.

Script editor Michael Brindley told us that the executive producer didn't like this ending, but it stayed in. As writers and senior production personnel with varying political persuasions come and go, the space for 'negotiated' reading expands or shrinks, and in ACP more radical intentions can lead to production problems.[16] The point to emphasise here is that it is the relationship between the interruption/flow nature of television and both audience *and* production agents, which opens the way to this potential for negotiation.

The sequence I will examine from 'A Touch of Class' occurs at the beginning of the first episode, when Ashleigh and Lorenzo meet after their respective private and state schools have debated 'rural unemployment in Australia'. Encouraged by her friends to pick up the good-looking Italian, Ashleigh engages him in conversation.

Ashleigh:	Congratulations. You cut me to pieces —I will never again open my mouth on rural unemployment.
Lorenzo:	I thought you did pretty well—for a woman.
Ashleigh:	You're new around here, aren't you?
Lorenzo:	Pretty new.
Ashleigh:	Funny, I haven't noticed you before.
Lorenzo:	No reason why you should
Ashleigh:	Well—you do stand out.
Lorenzo:	'Cause I'm Italian?
Ashleigh:	No, not just that. I guess you'll have the advantage tomorrow. We're debating Australia—as a multi-cultural society.
Lorenzo:	Maybe it is. Personally I'm from Venetia, a Venetian—and given the choice between Venice and Wandin Valley. . . .
Ashleigh:	Oh, no contest?
Lorenzo:	Here's my bus. Your friends are waiting for you
Ashleigh:	Let them. I've got a car if you'd like a lift.
Lorenzo:	No, I'm all right.
Ashleigh:	It's an Italian car—an Alfa-Romeo.

Lorenzo: I'm sure it's very beautiful—but no
                                           thank you.

At the plot level, this is the first move in a narrative that will bring
Lorenzo and Ashleigh together, only to emphasise their class in-
compatibility, and final separation. But this seduction performance
by Ashleigh in front of her friends is also contained within a
discourse about 'Australianness'. Lorenzo is a 'spunk', a beautiful
Italian whom, like her equally beautiful Italian car, Ashleigh wants
to possess. 'Italianness' is conceived here as an exotic national
product, an export which, together with other foreign cultures,
make up Australia's 'multi-cultural society'. As such, Ashleigh's
discourse equates with those of a number of advertisements that
went to air during 'A Touch of Class'. I will look at some of these,
before turning to the actual sequencing of advertisements at this
narrative moment.

(a) A Kraft Cheese advertisement represents the chaos of multi-
culturalism at an international cheese-fest where male Italian excit-
ability is exposed to blonde Nordic female cool, and American cheese
'know-how' argues with Swiss 'mountain flavour': 'When it comes
to traditional tastes, no two countries see eye to eye.' But this
advertisement's little drama closes with the warring multi-cultural
community facing camera, and, to the familiar call of 'Say cheese',
smiling their reply: 'Kraft'. As the voice over announces, 'Happily,
there's a traditional taste everyone agrees on, Kraft Traditional
Cheese.'

(b) In a Papa Guiseppi Pizza advertisement, the happy community is already in place, preparing for the family mealtime:

If you need a helping hand,
Remember all the love's a-cooking,
And that's why everybody loves their Papa.

The final frame, over which 'why everybody loves their Papa' is
repeated, is of the mother and three children at table, clustered
around the husband. The 'helping hands' that prepare for this finale
include the mother's. But the opening shot of hands are Papa
Guiseppi's, professionally crafting the pizza according to traditional
skills. These hands provide *both* an Italian food that is authentically
traditional (*crafting* hands, as in a Grierson documentary), *and* a
'fast-food' that is modern ('frozen/fresh'). There is a narrative ambiguity of hands in this advertisement: the hands that prepare the
pizza also seem to be those of the family itself, and so, as in the
Kraft Cheese advertisement, the traditional makers are also the

consumers. The 'authentic' exotica of other cultures and the commodity plenitude of 'Australianness' are one.

(c)   In an Impulse Exotique body spray advertisement, 'foreignness' signifies oriental charm and sexuality, and its narrative is played out between Asian female (*her* red sportscar reproducing Ashleigh's) and Australian male. So here foreignness and Australianness come together in a different way, emphasising the sexual (rather than familial) merging of cultures. Nevertheless, in both the food and the body spray commercials, fulfilment lies in the blending of the Australian with the foreign, as multi-culturalism is commoditised.

The significant difference between food and body spray advertisements is one that Flitterman ascribes to an equivalent difference between day and prime-time advertisements, between *services* (with the emphasis on the home, and the qualities attributed to the consumer-as-producer) and *goods* (with an emphasis on beauty independent of domestic surroundings, and the quality ascribed to the perfumed commodity). Flitterman, though, overemphasises the distinction between prime and daytime advertisements: ads focusing on cosmetic improvement of housewives (such as Limits weight-watching biscuits) and advertisements emphasising the sexually sophisticated independent woman are both common during this prime-time show. More significantly, what is occurring here is a build up (by way of a *series* of narrative closures) of different characteristics of 'femininity' in the advertisements.

An important target of prime-time dramas like *A Country Practice* is the housewife, whether careered or not. As Robert Allen notes, modern advertisements 'reflect the accretion of "model qualities"' to the traditional domesticated representation of the housewife: 'woman as mother, nurse, cook, housekeeper, shopper, compassionate spouse, *and* sex object, *and* competent professional person.'[17] The *series* of advertisements shown during 'A Touch of Class' represent women, literally, in all of these roles: mother (mother and daughter in Ripper Carpet Stain Remover advertisement), nurse (as district nurse in Gemini car advertisement), cook (in Sharp microwave advertisement), shopper (Westpac), housekeeper (Cold Power washing powder), compassionate spouse (Aim toothpaste), sex object (Impulse Exotique, Razzamataz stockings), and competent professional person (MacDonalds). In addition, she is (multiculturally) 'foreign' (Kraft Cheese, Impulse Exotique). The 'model' woman constructed out of this *accretion* of advertisements is *both* working *and* has leisure time, whether at business (MacDonalds advertisement which cuts from office to beach) or at home (Sharp Microwave

for the women who wants time 'to do the thing *I* want', as she goes
to the elegant living-room piano).

(**d**) In this context of *model accretion* the multi-cultural food
advertisements have the *same* inscribed audience (in the 'all-purpose'
woman) as the labour-saving advertisments; for instance, the Sharp
Microwave and the Elnapress commercials. But in this latter case,
the 'traditional' is signified by 'frills' and 'fiddly collars and cuffs',
rather than by 'authentically' crafted food:

> These women hate ironing, and they're doing something about it.
> They hate the boredom, the waste of time. They hate ironing
> jeans and frills and fiddly collars and cuffs. So join them. Throw
> away old-fashioned ironing and move up to Elnapress—so easy,
> so quick, so professional. Elnapress cuts your ironing time in
> half. Elnapress will change the way you iron. It will change your
> way of life.

Together these 'domestic' advertisements construct a world which
loses nothing, but has it all faster. It is traditional, but professional,
quick but authentic: 'frozen/fresh'; and consequently a world of fast
work pace *and* leisured time. Each commercial anchors its message
in the assured consensus of *community*: of traditional cultures, of
family, and—in the Elnapress advertisement—in a 'feminist' col-
lectivity of women. Elnapress invokes a 'liberationist' theme, as the
women, monumentally lit, stride aggressively forward, and one
of them (by way of a traditionally *male* sport, hammer throwing)
hurls the sign of their oppression, the iron, straight at us. These
are women in action—shot heroically from below, and marching
through the smoke of change to the 'hurrahs' of the people. They
'hate' their oppression and are 'doing something about it' (as the
male voice over tells us). 'So join them...and change your way of
life': from one way of doing the ironing to another.

The 'current' liberationist accent supports the 'new' technology
slant of the advertisement, just as the traditional crafts slant matches
the 'authentic' culture of the food advertisements. But the differences are superficial. Fundamentally the advertisements are similar
in their synthesis of traditional quality and time-saving modernity,
and in their unproblematic emphasis on community and consensus
in the resolution of problems and conflict. In their accretion of
model audience qualities the advertisements parallel the broad
demographic search of the drama that contains them. But there are
also significant differences between the soap and the advertisements.

In the Elnapress advertisement there is a foregrounded shot of a
woman's hand holding up a collar for close inspection. There is an

almost identical shot in 'A Touch of Class', but here the discursive *field* of the image is quite different. In the Elnapress shot, the voice over announces 'change your way of life'. In 'A Touch of Class', the accompanying voice is Lorenzo's, telling Ashleigh of her father's exploitation of his mother, as Ashleigh sees her father's factory label inside the collar. The Elnapress shot establishes the consensus of traditional (frills) and modern (ironing). The 'Touch of Class' shot explores the exploitative *dependence* of modern Australian capitalism on the traditional skills of women and foreigners. Unlike the heroically abstracted domestic background of the Elnapress advertisement, Mrs Belotti's living room is depressed, cluttered and crowded with the dozens of shirts she must sew and iron. The consensus of cultures, families and genders of the advertisements gives way here to conflict. Mrs Belotti cannot 'change her way of life', because of a *system* of exploitation which is Australia-wide, and world-wide.

Consequently, in 'A Touch of Class' the cultural stereotypes which the opening scene sets up are more than the 'characteristic situation' of advertisements, the '30-second struggle against the forces of evil'[18] which the narrative quickly resolves. Here they are lures to draw in the mass audience, to 'hook' them before confronting them with less resolvable issues and areas of normative risk. As Michael Brindley said about *A Country Practice*:

> To begin with, you present the stereotype. By doing that, you hope to engage the audience's interest, and then for the next two hours you steadily undermine that stereotype, and in the end turn it right over... I'm concerned to say to the audience that... often whole structures have to change before a problem is alleviated.[19]

So, in 'A Touch of Class', the stereotypes of the 'beautiful Italian', the 'excitable Italian' and the 'pasta-eating Italian' are all quickly introduced. But the pasta-eating 'family mealtime' scene contrasts remarkably with the Papa Guiseppi advertisement. Here Mrs Belotti tells Lorenzo (who is proud of Ashleigh's debating skill),

Mrs Berlotti:	What sort of school teach women to argue with men!
Lorenzo:	Didn't you ever argue with my father?
Mrs Berlotti:	*Never.* That misery I bear in silence until I can bear no more.
Lorenzo:	My father was a *disgraziato*.
Mrs Berlotti:	We don't talk about it. Maybe I was a bad woman for running away. I can

	take no more of the beating, the drink- ing, the playing the cards all night. Now we don't talk about it. You wake me midnight, remember.
Lorenzo:	You need more sleep than that.
Mrs Berlotti:	When the machine is paid for I sleep like a baby, till then...

(*Mrs Belotti screams as her injured hands give way lifting the heavy pasta pan, and the boiling water pours over her.*)

The melodramatic resolution of the scene destroys the happy family mealtime of the Papa Guiseppi advertisement, and here it is the *absent* father (as Italian husband, as Australian employer) who is signified. Moreover, he is signified as 'villain'. The 'helping hands' of the pizza advertisement become the callused, scalded hands of this migrant woman, as a world of patriarchal (Italian) and capitalist (Australian) exploitation is revealed by way of the 'pasta-eating' stereotype.

This *A Country Practice* episode *links* and systematises the extremes of soap representation that Modleski refers to, between the 'large problems of human existence' and the daily chores. 'A Touch of Class' makes the 'foreign' stereotype work to expose a woman's daily labour as an *effect* of, and contributor to, those 'large' problems—here given a clear economic dimension. Mrs Belotti's exploitation and 'bounded knowledgeability' is marked both in class terms (it is her labour which pays for Ashleigh's car, house and clothes), and ethnic/gender terms (as she seeks to reproduce her own culture's patriarchal codes in her son).

All of this is in embryo in the first sequence between Lorenzo and Ashleigh: in the contrasts of culture (his 'Venezia' versus her Australian multi-culturalism), class (his school bus, her Alfa), and gender (her collection of beautiful Italian commodities, his 'Not bad for a woman'). Already the currency of 'Australianness-as-multi-culturalism' (the commoditisation of foreign exotica by the Australian rich) has been 'seeded'.

Soaps and ads: 'Australianness'

At this point in the on-air transmission, the drama was dislocated by the first commercial break, and the following three advertisements immediately picked up the theme of 'Australianness', establishing a continuity between drama and advertisements. So far I have been comparing the fictional and ideological closures of advertisements screened during 'A Touch of Class' with the construction of multi-culturalism within the drama. But, as Philip Drummond has argued, we should also be concerned with the process in which drama and advertisements *become* narrative, a shift (as he puts it) from the analysis of 'structure' to 'structuration'.[20] In doing this I want to examine the way in which the relationship between narrative deferral and resolution (or plenitude) that Modleski and Flitterman discuss is inflected by way of its *particular* institutional and production setting.

(a) The first advertisement was a 'promo': an advertisement controlling television flow, and primarily located there (at the beginning of the first sequence of commercials) to deliver the audience from one program genre to another on the same channel. The promo was for an upcoming documentary on ATN7, 'Mutiny on the Western Front'. This purported to be a *history*, which was authenticated by its sepia tone, and presented as a narrative progression, beginning with the naive face of a young volunteer, through a series of actuality sequences (joining up, departure, sailing to battle, the horror of shells and mud, skulls and corpses), and ending with the worldly resistance and cynicism of mutiny. The soundtrack carried authenticating voices from the period reading the mutiny charges, and was preluded by the hit Eric Bogle song, 'The Band Played Waltzing Matilda', which, as most of the Australian audience would know, is about the naivety of the youthful swaggie's enlistment, followed by maiming and obscurity. The narrator retold the myth of young Anzacs: 'between 1914 and 1918, 330 thousand young Australians volunteered, one in five died, representing the highest losses of anyone in war. . . . Fatigued and horrified by the human carnage, 7 battalions were forced into open rebellion.' The dominant myth is of an active and freedom-loving Australia, offering naively and generously of its youth overseas, but (betrayed by politicians) becoming worldly-wise, its high physical skill, individualism and endurance blending with a certain irony and resistance.

One current signifier of this cultural stereotype of 'Australian-ness', of ironic resistance and courage during the First World War, is the star image of Paul Hogan. In the Australian mini-series *Anzacs*, for instance, Hogan plays the lounging older bystander to the eager young recruits, until the speech of a conniving politician sends him on his way.

Politician: If you had one speck of shame, you'd join up.

Hogan: I am going to join up—gonna join your outfit.

Politician:	My outfit?
Hogan:	Yeah, B-company—be here when they go and be here when they come back.

The recruits laugh, and prepare to leave. Hogan casually joins them.

Recruit:	Joining us are you?
Hogan:	I might as well. When it comes to a choice between facing the guns and facing old windbags like him, I'll take the guns every time.

(b) It is this 'Anzac' Hogan star image that would provide many Australians with foreknowledge of how to 'read' the second commercial, the Hogan Australian Tourism Commission advertisement. Allan Johnston of Mojo Australia, who designed this advertisement, said 'We were trying to portray a typical, easy going, dry, Australian... He's the one who insults Prime Ministers... fairly irreverent about authority. He is what an Australian... *should* look like.'[21] Hogan is appropriated for this task *because* the inter-textuality (across advertisements, comedy shows and television drama), together form an aggregate image of 'Australianness'. Nevertheless, this is made to work in the Tourism advertisement in particular ways, according to its specific inflection of the semiotics of image and sound as these are inserted within the segmentation and flow of a block of commercials.

(i) Image: As the advertisement sequencing cuts from the 'Mutiny' to the 'Tourism' commercial, there is an immediate contrast, from the sepia still photo of sullen soldiers to the colourful moving shot of an exotic swimming pool, from Europe to Australia, from hell to paradise. The advertisement's narrative fills out that paradise as the 'Lucky Country', the goal since the Second World War of so many Mrs Belottis from southern Europe, and, after the First World War, home for the returning soldiers. But now the threat which the narrative addresses is not war but unemployment. And *this* threat, we learn, is easily effaced by nothing more strenuous than voyeurism: tourists gazing at Australian nature in the same way that we, in the advertisement, are encouraged to gaze at the women serving Hogan.

All narrative action in the advertisement is of women leading to the recumbent male beside a swimming pool, Paul Hogan. The camera initially closes in, following a diving, then swimming woman. It picks up a waitress who moves as the camera reaches her, then follows the wet swimmer again, her thighs and legs visible behind Hogan, crossing the thighs and legs of the waitress, whom the camera finally follows to Hogan, who is reclining on a pool bed.

Hogan: G'day. I suppose you think I'm just laying around takin' a holiday. Well, don't be fooled by the surroundings. I'm actually working flat out for our mighty nation. You see, when you give yourself an Aussie holiday, you give the Aussie economy a boost.

(*Waitress arrives to serve Hogan an exotic drink.*)

Hogan: Ah, thanks, love—see, I just provided a job.

(*CU of Hogan head and shoulders, bottom and legs of departing waitress behind him.*)

(*Cut to ECU of Hogan.*)

Hogan: Now, there's not one of us can deny. . .

(*Orange/yellow of Hogan's craggy chest/hair dissolves to orange cliffs/ yellow grass of rugged Australian landscape.*)

Hogan: That this is the greatest country in the world. But not many of us has actually seen it.

(*Series of shots of river, mountain, lakeside, cliff pool and underwater coral views, as Hogan says 'There's so many different Aussie holidays you could fill a book. And that's what we've done. Cut back to Hogan showing the 'Australian Made Holidays' book.*)

Hogan: There's another bloke working flat out for his country.

(*Cut to prostrate bearded figure in the middle of the pool on a rubber mattress.*)

Hogan: Keep up the good work son.

(*Cuts between Hogan and man.*)

Hogan: Workaholic!

(*Ironic kookaburra call.*)

Hogan: Yeah, it's a tough job, but someone has to do it.

(*Camera pulls back to opening wideshot of pool, but now with fore-grounded floating man in place of the diving woman.*)

Virtually all camera movement, physical movement and eyelines in this advertisement are from women to men; while the male, Hogan, looks out at us inviting us into this world of beautiful people. The males relate, not to women, but to nature—to the economy, as the rugged texture and colour tones of Hogan *invade* the Australian landscape, peopling it, and subjecting *it* to a camera gaze that in the first sequence was directed at the bodies of women. Of course, the first two sequences are not really separate. Women here *are* nature. The waitress is directly associated with exotic nature (flowers in her hair and on the bushes behind her; the orange drink); whereas Hogan's prop is cultural (the Australian holidays book establishing an *economy*, of tourism). As we switch our gaze from women in the first sequence to nature in the second, voyeurism becomes economically productive. It becomes 'tourism'.[22] The sexual potency of the first part gives way to the economic potency of the second, providing (in both sequences) jobs. We might consider here the significance of the fact that the drink that is put in Hogan's hand is not his usual can of beer. Beer would have established very different resonances. The orange cocktail signifies the service that woman/nature offers to man/Australian economy. The drink is both functional (providing jobs) and symbolic (exotic: it is the exotic Australian landscape that will provide jobs).

(ii) Sound: The dominant sounds in the advertisement are Hogan's voice-over and music (various inflections of 'Waltzing Matilda'). Theo van Leeuwen notes that:

In the first place the music says something about the essence of Australia, and it says two different things about it. It says something about Australian people—and you see Hogan; and it says something about Australian landscape—and you see the landscape. It is also relevant to consider in what kind of mode the music is woven into the text as a whole. . . In the first sequence the music is backgrounded, it underscores what is already more dominantly signified by the image of Hogan and by what he says. In the second sequence the music becomes a major interpretive factor, like a commentary. . . establishing the landscape's grandeur and also cementing the whole sequence together, because the music track is continuous while the images are chopped up. . . In the first sequence we might have expected the legato march or procession-type rhythm typical of a national 'anthem', using quite 'serious', 'strong' string or brass instruments. But here there is a quirky, 'silly' sort of old-fashioned dance rhythm, emphasised as a light staccato on a vibraphone-like instrument, with pizzicato strings used ironically. This means all it means because 'Waltzing Matilda' *is* 'Waltzing Matilda', otherwise it would just seem an unexceptional piece of light music. In the second sequence you go into another aspect of Australia—the grandeur of the landscape, legato with full orchestral strings. The female voices—that type of 'heavenly choir' of very cohesive female voices without words quite common in popular music—establishes an admixture of mystery, the *Hanging Rock* type aspect of the landscape.[23]

As van Leeuwen says, in both sequences there is quite a close synchrony between the musical rhythm and the actions of people or camera. In the first sequence the women's movement is choreographed to the ironic beat, as they 'dance' around and towards Hogan. In the second sequence the music *establishes* the editing rhythm, as we cut to a variety of 'exotic' Australian locations. Subordinated to Hogan by the various semiotics of image and sound in the first sequence, the women give nature coherence in the second sequence, establishing the unity of its grandeur, and mixing that with mystery (the puzzle, the *hermeneutic* of woman, of nature, of tourism). The whole, of course, is still dominantly contained within Hogan's 'tourism' voice-over ('there's so many different Aussie holidays, you'd fill a book—and that's just what we've done').

In this Tourism advertisement, the good is still the young, beautiful and egalitarian Australia (profit is a matter of universal voyeurism, not class labour). This young Australia will easily defeat the new evil: unemployment and a shrinking economy. But history has had its effect; the good is no longer naive, but worldly wise and ironic. The sound track of the first sequence introduces a 'laughing' kookaburra together with the ironic, pizzicato 'Waltzing Matilda'. This gives way in the second sequence to the heroic, fully orchestrated 'Waltzing Matilda', consonant with the majestic landscape, before swelling heroics *and* ironic kookaburra combine for the final sequence. The final 'point' of the advertisement is clinched by music, as Australia's unofficial anthem rises in scale and volume (a call to collective action, as is common in national anthems).[24] But the visual it accompanies is of a prostrate man in an exotic swimming pool; a sound/image conjunction which synthesises the two earlier ('ironic' and 'heroic') sequences, and at the same time establishes beyond all doubt that national 'victory' lies in leisure.

Several layers of communication—camera, sound, music, framing, gesture, setting and performance—collude in this advertisement to construct 'what an Australian *should* look like'. Hogan is recognisably Russel Ward's typical Australian: 'ever willing to "have a go"', but willing 'to be content with a task done in a way that is "near enough"... usually taciturn rather than talkative, one who endures stoically.'[25] The cultural joke in this advertisement relies on audience competence in the history of the 'stoical Australian', because stoical endurance here is not the war and death of the first advertisement, but lying beside a pool, waited on by a beautiful woman, and yet still fighting for Australia. 'It's a tough job but somebody has to do it'. The *symptomatic absence* in the Tourism advertisement is the place of migrants who *have* had to do in the Australian economy the tough things that others will not do, the issue which 'A Touch of Class' raises directly.

(c)   If we turn briefly to the third advertisement, for (Australian) Bundaberg Rum, we see the one eminent figure that the 'typical Australian' traditionally *doesn't* knock. Politicians are Hogan's target, but not sporting heroes (the sporting scenario in the Elnapress 'liberation' advertisement is no coincidence). In the Bundaberg advertisement we again begin with a woman diver (whose trajectory is taken up by the flow of rum into a glass). But this time she leads on to active, not passive males: the 'Mean Machine' Olympic swimming team, 'America's Cup' type yachtsmen, and phallically erect motor surfers. This is the Australian Spirit' pun: both youthful sporting spirit (this time untouched by war or unemployment) and Bundaberg Rum. The constituent parts of the 'Mutiny' advertisement have, in the two commercials which follow it, been re-worked with different major emphases: the laid-back image of Australian mutiny and endurance (Hogan); the active Australian spirit (Bundaberg) that volunteered 'men in greater numbers' than any other country for war.

These three commercials, then, ritually repeat and re-work in different combinations the same dominant cultural myth: of the active but stoically irreverent Australian. Together they present an unproblematic view of a white Australia, threatened and exploited once by a foreign war, but still a lucky country of sun-tanned, outdoors living—so different from the cluttered, exploited *indoors* of Mrs Belotti. Europe, where it exists at all in these advertisements, is an historically distant exploiter, and not the source of an exploited class that helped build Australian affluence.

Rowse and King, discussing Australian advertisements, argue that,

Hedonism is a problem ideology for Capitalism in so far as it works *for* consumption but *against* notions of duty and work. Television expresses this tension by constructing its audience in contrasting ways, favouring the hedonistic.[26]

The Hogan tourism advertisement works so well because it is hedonism which in the end *provides* work; it is *leisure* which is active. So the site of production (work) is displaced by the site of active consumption (tourism, sport), and questions of class, ethnic and gender exploitation are displaced by images of human and socio-natural reciprocity. Advertisements, Judith Williamson points out, 'obscure and avoid the real issues of society, those relating to work: to jobs and wages and who works for whom.'[27]

Yet television does, as Rowse and King say, construct its audience in contrasting ways, even if mainly favouring the hedonistic. *A Country Practice* is a top-rating prime-time drama, and in 'A Touch of Class' it does quite specifically deal with issues of class, and who works for whom. Further, it emphasises that leisure time is something that significant sections of the population *do not have*. It strips away cultural stereotypes to expose difference rather than multicultural uniformity (that 'new Australianicity'); and cultural difference is related structurally to social exploitation rather than to the plenitude and symbiosis of cultural or natural exotica.

Cultural difference, in other words, is seen less as a commodity to be exchanged, but as part of a global system of exploitation. Or at least, that is one potential voice for presenting counter-myths in a very popular television drama.

My argument for flow and contradiction in the construction of 'Australianness' in this sequence of 'A Touch of Class' and its advertisements is not intended to mark a clear distinction between a 'progressive' drama series (*A Country Practice*) and 'conservative' advertisements. In fact, in discussing 'A Touch of Class' I have, firstly, privileged a particularly 'radical' episode in a generally consensual series, and secondly, explicated certain dominant storylines in that episode at the expense of other much more conservative (even if more minor) ones. Moreover, it might well be possible to select a sequential relationship which works the other way: where the commercial is potentially more disturbing to hegemonic ideology than the drama. John Hartley, for instance, discussing a Del Monte Orange Juice commercial (where the power of a US 'gangster-style' corporation over Mexican orange growers is presented), argues that advertisements are sometimes 'outrageously honest about the relations of production' telling us 'the blatant truth about capitalism'.[28] What I have wanted to do is examine the 'structural marginality' of television in terms of its own institutional practices: in this case the sequential flow and contradiction in constructing 'Australianness' and 'multiculturalism' within the particular production practices of a specific series/serial[29] on a channel with an ambiguously focused notion of audience aggregation.

Notes

1   As I argue in *Television Drama* scheduling TV drama involves making
    choices according to both syntagmatic and paradigmatic relations: for
    further discussion of these 'scheduling spaces' see John Tulloch, *Television
    Drama: Agency, Audience and Myth* (London: Methuen, 1989), ch.1.
2   M. Budd, S. Craig and C. Steinman, 'Fantasy Island: Marketplace of
    Desire', in M. Gurevitch and M. Levy (eds), *Mass Communication Review
    Yearbook*, Vol.5 (Beverly Hills: Sage, 1985), p.297.
3   John Fiske, *Television Culture: Popular pleasures and politics* (London:
    Methuen, 1988), p.104.
4   John Hartley, 'Out of Bounds: the Myth of Marginality' in L. Masterman,
    Television Mythologies: Stars, Shows and Signs (London: Comedia, 1984),
    p.123.
5   Tania Modleski, *Loving with a Vengeance: Mass-Produced Fantasies for
    Women* (New York: Methuen, 1982), ch.4.
6   Ibid., p.101.
7   Sandy Flitterman, 'The Real Soap Operas: TV Commercials', in E. Ann
    Kaplan (ed.), *Regarding Television: Critical Approaches—An Anthology*
    (Los Angeles: American Film Institute, 1983), p.94.
8   Ibid., p.95.
9   Hartley, 'Out of Bounds', p.127.
10 John Tulloch, 'Approaching the Audience—the Elderly', in E. Seiter, H.
    Borchers, E.-M. Warth and G. Kreutzner, *Rethinking Television Audiences*
    (London: Routledge, 1989).
11 Robert C. Allen, *Speaking of Soap Operas* (Chapel Hill: University of
    North Carolina, 1985).
12 Ibid., pp.153 ff.
13 John Tulloch and Albert Moran, *A Country Practice*: *'Quality Soap'*
    (Sydney: Currency, 1986), p.200.
14 John Tulloch, 'Responsible Soap: Discourses of Australian TV Drama',
    East-West Film Journal, Vol.1, No.1 (December 1986). See also Tulloch
    and Moran, *A Country Practice*.
15 Tulloch *'Responsible Soap'*, p.39.
16 See Tulloch, *'Responsible Soap'*.
17 Allen, *Speaking of Soap Operas*, p.174.
18 Flitterman, *'The Real Soap Operas'*, p.94.
19 Tulloch and Moran, *A Country Practice*, p.181.
20 See Philip Drummond, 'Structural and Narrative Constraints in "The
    Sweeney" ', *Screen Education*, No.20 (Autumn 1976), p.26.
21 *The National Times*, 25–31 July 1986, pp.8,9.
22 cf. Tony Bennett and Janet Woollacott, *Bond and Beyond* (Basingstoke:
    Macmillan, 1987), p.247 (citing Michael Denning): 'Just as the narrative
    code of tourism represents peripheral societies as objects of spectacle,
    so the narrative code of pornography codes women as the object of a
    voyeuristic look...the "licence to look" becomes the key exemplar of a
    "licence to consume"...'
23 For discussion of the semiotic function of music in this advertisement I am
    indebted to Theo van Leeuwen.
24 Ibid.

25 Russel Ward, *The Australian Legend* (Melbourne: Oxford University Press, 1958), p.2.
26 Noel King and Tim Rowse, '"Typical Aussies": Television and Populism in Australia', *Framework* 22/23, p.42.
27 Judith Williamson, *Decoding Advertisements* (London: Boyars, 1978), p.47.
28 Hartley, 'Out of Bounds', p.123.
29 For a discussion of **A Country Practice** as series/serial see Tulloch and Moran, **A Country Practice**.

10

Continuous Pleasures in Marginal Places: TV, Continuity and the Construction of Communities

John Hartley

Tellyology

Some time ago, in wooden de-mountables on the wrong side of the campus, or on the other side of town across the binary divide of the tertiary sector, Television Studies was taking corporeal form. What a peculiar thing it was. Traditionally, people who take up textual studies of a given medium—literature and cinema for instance—are drawn to it because they think it's important or they *like it*. Television Studies, perversely, was peopled by those who thought television trivial and *despised* it: a ratbag collection of tired ex-professionals seeking serenity in early retirement and vanity publishing; psychologists relentlessly pursuing the victim in order to justify their own brutal methods and personal nightmares; Marxist sociologists schooled in false-consciousness berating the media in the afternoons and watching telly at night (and never noticing the connection); renegade literary critics desperately looking for a way to grab the attention of card-playing hulks who earned more than they did but who were forced to attend Liberal Studies before they qualified as mechanics and mining engineers.

People who actually did like TV and knew a bit about it were also despised. But then the general public never get much of a look-in when professional intellectuals gather in any number. Not that the general public was all that interested in despised academics from despised institutions looking at a despised medium, who couldn't even explain what they did for a living to the grocer or hairdresser.

Academic discourse, like knowledge of all kinds, grows out of institutional sites. But in the disciplined departments of the ivy league, television was not so much a branch as a *twiglet* of knowledge. Even now it isn't corporeal enough to have its own name—there are no Departments or professors of, nor degree programs in *Television*. So television studies appeared merely as marginal activities conducted by the undisciplined younger element within traditional departments, or, in downmarket institutions, as a block, unit, module or stream in Communication, Cultural, or Media Studies—anything but Television.

The first thing needful, in such unpromising circumstances, was *theory*. What better than to follow the fashions of respectable radicals, to borrow the cast-offs of cinema and literary theorists, especially as the labels were all in French, so who knows what part of the body they were actually designed for?

This was fun. After a while all the theorists were dressed up (they even went through a strutting-in-front-of-the-mirror phase), putting on *New* French *Accents* and asking 'Does it suture?'. 'I'm doing Lacan-can!', chortled one. 'Look at my Lyotard!' retorted another. 'Après moi, le Deleuze!' moaned a third. 'Rhizomes, simulacra, what's the différence?' agonised one more. 'Cherchez la femme!' warned the only woman present. Then everyone joined in the chorus: 'Hey-down, ho-down, derry-Derrida! Among the LeaviStrauss-O!'[1]

It was a foregone conclusion. Tellyology was born.

Rearviewmirrorism

When printing was first invented in the West, it was made to look as much as possible like the medium it was destined to supplant. The so-called *incunabula* didn't look like books at all, they looked like manuscript writing. Likewise, when concrete was first used to build a house (called Gregynog Hall, in Wales), it didn't look like concrete at all. It looked like Tudor half-timbering.

This phenomenon is called 'rearviewmirrorism', or so says Marshall McLuhan.[2] In the early days television's own mainstream genres were developed on the rearviewmirrorist principle:

This wonderful age
Goes to show that all the world's a stage.
First you heard,
Now you see,
And you wonder what the next thing on the list will be!

That song, called 'Here's looking at you,' was composed for the first-ever public television broadcast by the BBC at the Radio Olympia Exhibition in August 1936. Referring back to both theatre and radio, not to mention Shakespeare and technological progress, its incunabular rearviewmirrorism was confirmed in the items chosen for the show—current variety acts from the London stage and Pogo the pantomime horse.

Right from the start television displayed many of its later characteristics at the level of repertoire, scheduling, genre and style (not to mention the levels of corporate organisation and financing, regulation and control). But its diet was gathered almost indiscriminately from existing media—the legitimate and variety theatre, the press, cinema, radio, pantomime and popular music.

Broadcast television was officially launched by the BBC on 2 November 1936. After the opening speeches the continuity announcer, Leslie Mitchell, introduced an edition of British Movietone News (made for cinema), which was followed by the popular singer Adele Dixon. A magazine show called *Picture Page* hosted by Joan Miller had already been piloted and went on to become a twice-weekly regular. Drama was produced from the BBC's studio at the Alexandra Palace (the Ally Pally) from the outset, and within a year the BBC Television Service was doing outside broadcast specials of civic and sporting events like King George VI's coronation, the boat race and the Derby. Walt Disney soon rang up from Hollywood to offer the fledgling medium one of cinema's great successes, and indeed viewers were in the middle of watching a *Mickey Mouse* cartoon when the BBC unceremoniously pulled the plugs on television in September 1939 at the outset of the war.[3]

However, one ingredient was missing from this rearviewmirrorist recipe, perhaps the most important one—the audience. To begin with, television was transmitted for only two hours a day (3–4 pm and 9–10 pm), to a potential audience restricted to the reach of the single transmitter at the Ally Pally in north London, and restricted further by the prohibitive cost of a receiver. So careless of their audience were the radio-minded BBC management that they even failed to put out test transmissions during the hours when dealers could demonstrate TV sets to prospective customers. TV was a side-show foisted on them by government decision, and they saw no need for a campaign of audience building. The BBC's top brass didn't see television as a mass medium at all.

It was precisely at this point that rearviewmirrorism failed. It was a mark of television's coming of age as a medium when it broke free and developed beyond mere invention and form to become a cultural force in its own right. Despite the fact that the BBC was then and still is the biggest single broadcasting organisation in the western world, it played *no part* in the emancipation of television.

Appropriately this took place in the democratic vistas of America, after the launch of commercial TV in the mid-1940s. It was this that mobilised the beginnings of a mass audience, recruited to TV as part of the post-war wave of optimism and consumerism, a consumerism which included an unparalleled concentration on the home and domestic, private life. For the first time the home began to be defined as a space for leisure pursuits and life-style, as well as being seen as a secure refuge and an efficient machine for sustaining and motivating the workforce. New post-war priorities, after the demobilisation of women from active participation in the war effort, centred on the family, leisure, welfare, modernisation, hygiene and gadgetry. Television was a product and promoter of these forces.

Theorists of culture were uniform in their response. They were horrified.

The unselfconscious invention of television's own specific genres and forms went unnoticed, unaccounted for because the only respectable attitude towards television—for conservative and progressive radicals alike—was not even as forward-looking as rearviewmirrorism. Television's first critics simply turned their backs on it.

Since then, masked and gowned against contamination, one or two of them have turned round. But even now their purpose is often not so much to account for television as to demonstrate their own theoretical razor-sharpness. Eventually they think they've got it all stitched up, get bored and wander back to the leafier surroundings of high culture. But however deft they may be, surgical skills that have been honed for another purpose cannot anatomise television without making a bloody mess of it.[4]

What's TV all about? 'Suture self' they reply, munching a Twiglet.[5]

Left to its own devices at last, television theory can only take the advice of a departing well-wisher, whose words still echo down the corridor: 'Well, it's all over. We have to start again from the beginning, asking one another what's going on.'[6]

Marginal places

Some time earlier, in wooden de-mountables on the wrong side of the continent, or on the other side of the world, Western Australia was taking corporeal form. What a peculiar thing it was. King George III had entrusted Captain Arthur Phillip with a fair bit of land in 1787, but its western margin was defined as longitude 135 degrees East (not quite as far west as modern Alice Springs). The present State-line, 129 degrees East, shares with that original border the distinction of marking, from the top of the continent to the bottom, *nothing*. But in 1787 the nothingness extended westwards. There simply was no Western Australia. Nor did the New South Walians expand westwards, American-style.

The colony was implanted, directly from Britain, from the sea, twice (first at Albany, then at Fremantle–Perth) mainly to keep the French out. More than twice it failed, but teetered into the twentieth century on the back of convict transportation, Kalgoorlie and Aboriginal enslavement.[7] It was never confident of its corporeal integrity; there was once a plan to sub-divide it into northern and southern States, and its (white) citizens voted for secession from Australia before the Second World War. Even now it isn't unified into a community—its regions and its citizens still have less in common with each other than with their sources of immigration from over east or overseas.

Western Australia is an experiment, one of the last deliberately experimental societies on earth. Among the experiments is community building; done in a self-conscious *developmental* style reminiscent not of the old country but of, say, Singapore. Indeed, the creation of a public, of an image for the state and its capital city, an 'imagined community'[8] of Western Australians, is, as in Singapore, semi-official policy.

To newcomers from old-established countries, where communal selfhood is taken for granted, and where nationalist rhetoric combined with capitalist money and provincialist self-aggrandisement smacks of fascism, such policies are often dismissed as dangerous and naive, all the more so given that the main vehicle for the promulgation of positive, euphoric images of Western Australia is commercial television. Occasionally everyone does come to the party together (though not all to celebrate), most spectacularly during the 1986–87 America's Cup at Fremantle. On this occasion, however, the tides of people who flowed through Western Australia for the event ebbed away all too rapidly afterwards.[9]

Western Australia, like television itself, remains a marginal place, regarded by rearviewmirrorist observers as hardly worth bothering about.

But to dismiss self-conscious community building as quasi-fascism (*manqué*) would be a mistake. First, because it's often just a symptom of the effortless superiority of those who think they know where the centre of the world is. This usually turns out to be their home-capital for Europeans, a bad habit they've passed on not only to New Yorkers but even to the so-called *t'othersiders* of Australia for whom it's Sydney (or Melbourne). Secure in their own self-centred metropolitanism, such observers may not notice the lesson of the America's Cup episode for Western Australia. This effort, led by the media, failed to raise the temperature of a sufficiently critical mass of citizens to produce fusion into a self-renewing community. Everyone just went home. But that only demonstrates the need for investment in community building, not the failure of it.

Second, community building is a continuing struggle even in old countries, as anyone from *old* South Wales can testify. Wales, a neglected western margin, reduced to an economy of primary, extractive industries, with an indigenous population whose language, culture and land is under tremendous pressure from Angloid settlers, and where unity is impeded by the isolation of small communities connected not by roads but by sheep, is a *nearly*-nation having more in common with Western Australia than might appear from their relative physical sizes. Both have experienced a continuing struggle to define their small, internally divided communities as different from the much stronger states to the east, which control their economy and political structure, if not their culture and politics.

Where Wales differs markedly from Western Australia, however, is in the antagonistic rhetoric and action that defines it *in opposition* to England/Britain; an opposition led by professionals, intellectuals and the public sector. Western Australia, conversely, has tended to consign self-promotion to the private, commercial sector, where it more often takes the form of glossy publicity than that of adversarial politics. Wales might learn about euphoric self-constructing imagery from Western Australia ('Love You Cardiff' seems ludicrous, probably because no-one's tried it). And Western Australia might learn something from Wales, where a ten-year campaign co-ordinated by *Cymdeithas yr Iaith Gymraeg* (The Welsh Language Society) culminated in the only U-turn of the first Thatcher government with the establishment in 1982 of *Sianel Pedwar Cymru* (S4C), Channel Four Wales, dedicated to broadcasting Welsh-language programs at peak viewing hours, despite the fact that Welsh-speakers are a relatively small minority in their own land.

If we're to believe myths of typicality, prime-time TV coincides with those times when people cast off the cares of economic survival and indulge in a little self-building and family-bonding—creating micro-communities for which they can take personal responsibility. Television's intellectual and artistic achievement is to have found a way of contributing to this process. Although it turns millions of individuals into its audience, it's watched inside those micro-communities, each of which constitutes itself as audience in its own evolving way, and uses television for its own idiosyncratic purposes.

In modern societies there are a few communities which cut across demographic boundaries like class, nation, region, age-group, gender, race; prominent among them being intellectuals and artists. But by far the biggest such community is that of *popular culture*. Corporate television is impelled by its own institutional imperatives towards populism (or, if it's lucky, true popularity once in a while). It produces non-material commodities that no-one buys, bartering symbolic unity and diversity, novelty and familiarity, conflict and consensus, to a community it has itself produced, in exchange not for people's money but for their valuable time.

Among the products of that exchange are knowledge and art; not formal, professionalised intellection or 'fine' art to be sure, but popular knowledge and accessible art. In marginal places like Western Australia, the imagery that binds the micro-communities of dispersed families to their environment and to the wider community is supplied free, gratis and for nothing, by marginal television. Cute, euphoric and partial it may be (like so many *successful* pedagogic tactics), but it's just about all there is on permanent public display to differentiate *here* and *us* from all the other locations and characters in the global scenario.

Amnesia (Lest we forget)

Globally, television is one of the culture industries (like religion, pop music, tourism, education)—industries where the commanding heights of power and profit are not at the point of production at all, but at the point of distribution.[10]

In fact, TV never went through an individualist, entrepreneurial mode of production (as cinema did), and producers never had power over their products or over the industry. Now, traditional basic industries like food are in the same boat—owning the means of production is neither here nor there, as farmers from Illinois to Bangladesh can tell you. Even in food, it's trans-national *agribusiness*, controlling distribution, which has cornered not just the market but the whole vertically integrated industry from top to bottom.[11] But television started that way.

Just as Burbage's Theatre and Shakespeare's Globe were among the very first fully capitalist enterprises (joint-stock companies of capitalists, managers and actors selling popular drama on an entrepreneurial basis, outside the regulation of the City or the patronage of the Court, to the public for profit)[12], so television is the model for twentieth-century economies. Contrary to habitual thinking, which dismisses the cultural industries as mere Mickey Mice in comparison with the macho sectors of primary industry and manufacturing, culture is the cutting edge of advanced monopoly capitalism. There's more in common between the Swan of Avon and the Swan Brewery than you might think.[13]

The distinctive features of television are products not of any intrinsic or essential form but of an irresolvable contradiction right at its corporate heart. On the one hand, networks (controlling distribution) must maximise audiences in order to survive, and they must do it every day now that Mr Neilsen has instituted overnight ratings. On the other hand, people watch TV in the hope of seeing something new, or at least novel versions of the familiar. And this means that no-one can tell in advance what will prove popular. So the problem is to get viewers into the habit of re-consuming non-material commodities they've never seen before, a trick broadcasters must perform without having an accurate idea in advance of what sufficient numbers of the viewing public will find appealing.

Economic imperative coupled with institutional insecurity—this rather than aesthetics is the foundation of the *form* of television *as a creative medium*. It explains why TV offers a *repertoire* rather than one standardised product—hedging of bets raised to cultural policy. It explains *scheduling*, the art of capturing particular categories of bums on seats (or, since this is TV, potatoes on couches) at different times of day—mums, kids, families, dads, in that order. It explains why networks are more powerful than creatives, since no one producer can bear the costs of the number of failures it takes to sustain each success in the game of predicting the unpredictable. And it explains television's cultural forms—the *genres* most likely to offer novelty within a habit of reconsumption—drama serials and news, sport and mini-series, and not least the weather.

Fifty years after its first broadcast, few writers bother with television *as television*—neither journalistic nor academic writing has noticed the potential of the medium poking out between the programs, like concrete glimpsed through the illusion of Tudor timber. Indeed, like concrete glimpsed when you think you're looking at 400-year-old wood, television's own genres look tacky, duplicitous, kitsch and cheap compared with the supposed authenticity of former forms.

It's only when you start looking at them concretely, in their own terms, that their illusory veneer becomes interesting.

Anamnesia

Continuity is the television that isn't there. You cannot find reference to it in TV guides, and unlike news, drama, the weather and sport, it doesn't occupy an established place in peoples' conversation about television. No other medium has anything quite like it, not even radio, which has found other ways of being continuous. Interestingly the two media seem to be heading in opposite directions in this respect. Radio appears to be minimising the boundaries between programs and segments, and many shows have dispensed with their own theme music, so the listener is carried over the threshold in the least bumpy manner. TV continuity takes thresholds much more seriously, with full fanfare, confetti everywhere.

Continuity is the gap between programs, between whatever you're watching. You may not notice that you're watching it even while you are watching it. It's filled with familiar emblems, oft-repeated slogans, jingles, images and ideas. It's used to promote the channel that you're watching, the programs you might watch on that channel, and to promote the country in which all this is happening.

Its use value for the channel is strictly pedagogic: it teaches you what and when to watch; it teaches you how to watch, how to feel, what to look for, how to look. It's the yardstick against which all the other TV genres can be measured, because it assumes no prior commitment from you—not only does it have to work, or not, entirely on its own merits (no-one promos promos), but also it is vital to the interests of the broadcasters. They use continuity to keep you. It occupies the dangerous time when channel and viewer can go out of sync with each other; when repertoire, scheduling, capital investment and fat executive salaries can be countermanded by a squirt of infra-red from the disaffected Couch Potato: remote control democracy.

Its use value for viewers is more pragmatic: it lets you make a cup of tea. That is, it reinstates real time, and it restores to the viewer a sense of agency—a gesture of self-recollection. Viewers, multi-conscious,[14] can do more than one thing at once—as well as clearing your throat, your bowel, your mind, you can plan, desire, reject. You use continuity to position yourself in relation to television, to *sidle up* to it.

Continuity performs the rhetorical function of *anamnesia*—the opposite of forgetting—the function of *bringing to mind*.

Frottage

Nowadays, on commercial television, it could be argued that continuity is the norm, programs are the deviation. There are whole channels devoted to programming what is, formally, nothing but continuity—MTV and its clones, for instance, or the two cable weather channels in America.[15]

Even more remarkable is the propensity for continuity to distend; to become bloated, tumescent. This usually happens at times of self-induced national euphoria, brought on either by a sporting or a civic occasion—the America's Cup, the Bicentennial. On such occasions, there are shows lasting perhaps half a day, consisting entirely of continuity. They are the most costly, most complex, most technically sophisticated shows that TV can do, and only TV can do them.

Here postmodernist self-reflexivity is raised to the status of refe-rentiality—it's what such programs are about. *Australia Live* (1 January 1988): not 'Happy 200th Birthday Australia' but 'This is how many people at how many locations, using so many gew-gaws for such an amount, on so many channels in this many countries, that it will take, is taking, has taken to say "Happy 200th Birthday Australia"'. That's entertainment—literally the *big time*, in this case four straight hours simulcast on one commercial and two public channels.

Such shows, together with ordinary continuity and commercials, are the interface between television as an institution and its public. For the viewer, they are the moments when, in the privacy of the home, secure from public gaze behind decently draped suburban windows, we can take pleasure in *being* the public.

This pleasure is akin to *frottage*—traditionally defined as sexual excitement associated with rubbing up against another's clothed body in public. In the case of television continuity, the pleasure is not directly tactile but it is the pleasure of getting *in touch*, kind of furtive brushing, a glimpse, a frisson of excitement provoked by taking private pleasure from public contact.

Like frottage, this pleasure can lead to ennui if carried on for too long—a 60-second, unselfconscious stimulation can be surprisingly agreeable, but if the same type of stimulation is prolonged for hours, as in the *Australia Live* show, it can irritate more bodily organs than just the skin.

The private/public, clothed and furtive pleasure of frottage is ambiguous—if it is to be a pleasure at all, there must be some question about who is furtively brushing up against whom; a question not only of seduction but also of reciprocation. Does TV continuity caress us with its seductive surfaces, or do we perve on the symbolic contact it offers us with attractive others?

The contact of continuity, positioned at the interface of public and private, is the place of modern citizenship. Television, the modern forum,[16] is the place where we can jostle pleasurably, keeping in touch, to see, hear and participate in the otherwise imaginary community to which we belong—our nation. And it's the place where we can identify ourselves *as* the public, as citizens and as consumers, the source and destination of *publicity*.

Windscreenwiperism

Television's stratagem for differentiating sameness is a special part of continuity; the *trailer*. Trailers are the art form of time, locking the viewer's future into the here and now, erasing distinctions between fact and fiction, between the past and the news.

Trailers are quite unlike the genres that surround them; they're not the rearviewmirror but the windscreenwiper of television, the neglected but vital component for seeing into the future. Trailers are dialogic, participatory, explicit about who's talking to whom, ephemeral, conversational, focusing our attention on our personal future (will I, won't I?).

Trailers do much of their work using the very stuff of their opposite—observatory, third-person narration and drama. The trailer promotes time-based consumption while simultaneously subverting it—it can compress the longest mini-series or special to half a minute.

The sophisticated viewer takes as much pleasure or more from trailers as from the programs themselves, which often feel like coercive and tedious filler in comparison with trailers' fragmented, postmodern aesthetics of excess. From the viewer's point of view trailers are the *originals*, seen first and determining the *authenticity* (promise) of the narrative whose image they are.

And so the tail comes to wag the dog, or at least the trailer wags the drama. On US Network TV, one-off telemovies and documentary specials (the leading edge of mainstream experimentation) *are not commissioned* unless their genre, plot, characters, stars, action, mood and topic can be conveyed, euphorically, in a twenty-second grab repeated during the couple of days before TX—(transmission) time.[17]

i – Deas for i – Deal people

Time is relative on television. A TV-hour is 52 minutes, whereas a TV-minute is 62 seconds. The former leaves room for continuity and commercials, the latter leaves a margin to make sure continuity is *continuous*.

An ID (or ident) is anything from a 15-second logo to a 2-minute promo. A station or network uses its ID and logo, as well as graphics, movie openers, news openers, news bumpers, personality launch campaigns, nightly line-ups, seasonal promos and other presentation material, as the foundation of its public image. 'The "front man" for a TV station, the ident has to project that station's values and personality while appealing to a mass audience over a long period of time.'[18]

i–D is a magazine, the self-styled 'worldwide manual of style, the indispensable document of fashion, style and ideas', launched in London in 1980. Maria Del Sapio describes *i–D* thus:

> It announces a new art politics, an art of living, 'art as informational combat.' It is a politics that recognizes the role of the mass media in continually rewriting the past in the name of the present and turns this into a zone ripe for the individual art of adaptation and exploration: clogging the system, overloading the lines, scrambling the codes, generating new possible senses through the kindling of a plurality of meanings . . . It is an aesthetics that deals not only in the exhibition of the surface effect, but also in the exhibition of the process of creating, recalling, juxtaposing, manipulating, deforming, imagining, and thinking with signs . . . within a technological space where the intensified circulation of signs has problematized the primacy of the subject as the origin of meaning as well as such concepts as causality and linearity.[19]

If all this is so, and if *i–D* isn't just a magazine for bone-headed bimbos and postmodern hairdressers (or even if it is), then it's easy to see where it got its name from, not to mention its i–Deas.

IDs are stupendously costly, taking six to nine months to produce, using the very latest animatics, Quantel digital production, 3–D effects, computer software (and even, in a recent bold move by the ABC, live-action photography). According to insiders, Australian production companies are 'certainly world-class', and Australian

TV–IDs are 'most definitely the best produced in the world' (although many of them are produced in Los Angeles). Each channel's ID is broadcast many times a week, and each ID is designed for a long, evolving life-span—anything from a year (the Seven Network) to a decade (the ABC). Such repetition could easily become irritating and monotonous, making the audience see infra-red instead of the intended rosy glow, hardly a desirable outcome from the network's point of view—hence the investment.

Oddly enough, the insiders don't seem awfully sure if the investment pays off in terms of viewer response. One from the Seven Network, admitting that the different channels do compete for the best ident, said: 'I don't know how much the viewers care. It's just important to have a very classy image and a better profile than some of the country stations.'[20]

An ABC executive, commenting on the highly praised new logo for the national broadcaster, said:

> The contemporary feel can work as a tiny psychological trigger, reinforcing the identity the network wishes to project. We don't expect an immediate response to the colour-coding but over time it will become second nature to even occasional viewers and, as a bonus, it adds an interesting diversity to on-air presentation. The test will be how the idents look as they go to air in a package (there will ultimately be 15) and whether they have a different kind of effect in the lounge room. We believe they have a definite Australian feel without us having rammed it down the viewers' throats.

Network Ten is more self confident about the intention of their logo, but silent on its reception: 'The new logo was developed with specific goals in mind and in the briefing it was deemed desirable for us as a network to be perceived as exciting, dynamic, professional, energetic, entertaining and sophisticated.'

The Nine Network could only enthuse about the glass effect in their national 'travelling map' logo, in which each capital city can see itself reflected: 'The cities will each have their own look, which is very important to the local viewer.'[21]

Love you Perth

Conversely, of course, the local viewer is very important to the networks, for despite the global production and distribution of TV programming, the audience experience is always local. Australian TV stations, never more than so-so in their efforts to encourage local *production*, have got into the habit of flattering their audiences with local *images*. This can be seen for what it is—a commercial imperative to maximise ratings. Commercial imperative dictates that state– or city-based *program* production doesn't extend much further than the quotidian news and current affairs shows that inveigle their way into the local topography by means of giant advertising hoardings around town, sporting the visages of toothsome personalities whose job it is to introduce items generated *there* to people located *here*.

But to get a picture of *here* and of *us* you need also to look at the gaps between programs. In those margins which are nevertheless the *sine qua non* of commercial television, Western Australia itself and its citizens are constructed into legibility. TV continuity and advertisements exceed their commercial purposes even while fulfilling them, for to create viewers and consumers is also to create a community, to bring the global, national and local identities together into the home.

Until 1988 there were two commercial channels in Perth, Seven and Nine. They vied with each other to picture what it is that makes this part of the world loveable and shiny. Seven, with its 'Love you Perth' promo, concentrated on the city itself and some of its pretty, cute, friendly representatives, from policemen and nuns to the local band V Capri, who all signalled their community with each other by holding up seven fingers. Nine, made of sterner stuff, showed the country as well as the city, and work as well as leisure locations, with representatives of different ages and ethnic origins (though, like Seven, no Aborigines), in their 'Shine On Nine' series. Being Alan Bond's America's Cup station, Nine devoted much of 1986 to an evolving promo called 'Sailing Australia' (to the tune of **Waltzing Matilda**), which traced the history of the Cup back to the 1983 victory, and introduced us to the faces, syndicates and boats that were congregating off Fremantle. As the challengers and defenders were whittled down to the final contenders, so the promo was updated, until at last in early 1987 there was nothing left to euphoricise in that direction, and Nine's promos turned their attention away from local images to concentrate on images of television itself, in a series with the rather poignant title, under the circumstances, of 'Still the One'.

For their part, commercials interact with the local community in various ways. The most telegenic ones tend to be for (inter) national brands, which consumers will then see in the local supermarket or check the price of in the local papers. Among the best of the 1988 batch is an ad for Decoré Family Shampoo. This takes a classic rock and roll tune, puts Decoré lyrics to it, and sets it in the bathrooms of bright and shiny families. We see a pretty young woman singing in the shower while subjecting the shampoo bottle to the masturbatory gesture made familiar by raunchy rock singers. Other bathroom artistes join the fun, though not each other, until we end with a picture of a clean, healthy and thoroughly *sexualized* family. It seems to have gone down well in the suburbs, whose inhabitants are perhaps grateful to see themselves represented on the cusp between sex and driers and rock'n'roll, for a change:

> We would like to congratulate the makers of the Decoré advertisement. We think it's the best advertisement we've ever seen on TV. We love the music and can only wish all advertisements could be as good as this one. If they were, it would be a pleasure to watch them.
>
> Spitzer Family, Willetton.[22]

Here then is *frottage* incarnate, enacted, and located in the imagined community of ordinary family life. It's not an image of Western Australia, but of popular culture—which in Willetton at least means the same thing.

However, there are plenty of ads that do associate local products and places—stubbies and sunsets. But, this being Western Australia, 'local' doesn't always mean quite what you'd expect; for instance, viewers of the statewide country station, Golden West Network (GWN), might be treated to an ad for a local hardware store which is in fact a couple of day's drive away. Even so, you can sometimes get a glimpse of what does drive local preoccupations; another current GWN ad promotes silos for the farming community, showing semi-trailers trundling round a dirt track with the gleaming silver monsters strapped on their backs. As if this isn't curious enough for a TV commercial, a replica AC Cobra pops up at the end of the ad—a classic sports car of the 1960s frolicking in the wake of the semi-trailers. It turns out you can buy one of these from the same company. Sports cars, silos and semi-trailers—far flung, far fetched, far out.

In 1988 the third commercial channel (Ten) opened in Perth. Along with ownership changes and the move to national networking, this event has had its effect on both continuity and commercials. Increasingly, even these are produced in Sydney for national distribution. But there's still profit in appealing to the local viewer, it seems. Channel Seven has moved deftly into the new era by doing something I think no TV scholar has yet attempted—an *archaeology* of television promos, naturally its own. The 1988 promo shows a TV screen, on which we see—anamnesically—clips from Seven's promos going back to the days when it was Perth's first and only TV station (in 1959). This TV screen comes into bigger close-up as we come up to date, ending with the most recent and familiar images

and slogans: 'Love you Perth' and 'Say Hello'. Putting itself in
quotation marks, Seven proposes its relationship with the Perth
community as being *precisely* one of *continuity*.

It's the last word in rearviewmirrorist tellyology.

How to be an audience

I came to Western Australia in January 1985. I turned on the
television. It was an episode of Trevor Griffiths' first TV series,
Bill Brand, followed by an old *Sweeney*. I was reminded of something Trevor Griffiths had said years earlier about this particular
conjunction. This is what he said:

> I simply cannot understand socialist playwrights who do not
> devote most of their time to television... It's just thunderingly
> exciting to be able to talk to large numbers of people in the
> working class, and I just can't understand why everybody doesn't
> want to do it... If for every *Sweeney* that went out, a *Bill
> Brand* went out, there would be a real struggle for the popular
> imagination.[23]

Bill Brand is a drama serial about the career of a British left-Labour
MP, whose political and personal affairs provide a vehicle for topical
political and moral issues. *The Sweeney* also stars a couple of
working-class heroes. But between the unglamorous South London
locales and the protagonists' jokey relationship, class antagonism
somehow slides into defensive mateship. Political and moral issues
are there right enough (I once called *The Sweeney* the television of
recession[24]), but politics is rendered as the relationship between the
lads and their immediate environment, in which the vehicle for
moral issues is a Ford Granada.

I must say I was glad to watch these two worthy sparring partners
from long ago and far away struggling for the popular imagination in
the long, hot Perth summer. But what really caught my eye was
something I'd never seen before. It was Channel Nine's 'Launch 85'
promo, right after *Bill Brand*, and it spoke to me personally.
Actually it sang: 'There's never been a year like this before!' I
couldn't have agreed more, as this simple jingle prompted me,
windscreenwiperistically, to peer into my own imagined future in a
new country through what Channel Nine reckoned it had in store
for its thunderingly excited viewers.

On closer inspection, this pedagogic promo was a lesson in *reading
television*, if I can put it that way. The opening shots *performed* the
act of looking, and of preparing to look with a mood of excited
anticipation. It wasn't actors but dancers who played the role of the

audience, and I gazed on them, like some latter-day phrenologist, looking for the bumps that might tell me wherein lies Australianness.

In one television minute, I was guided in genre and scheduling, and shown how to be a young, attractive, heterosexual, energetic, euphoric, partying viewer with my smiling face lit up by the nearest source of visual pleasure. Meanwhile, more than a dozen personalities and as many shows were stitched recognisably together, embellished with Australian but not Aboriginal icons and presented through high-tech effects.

Now *that*, I thought, is struggling for the popular imagination in no uncertain terms: it's literally *enacting* the popular imagination, making it visible and hummable. It proposes the symbolic unity of viewer, nation and television, at one with Channel Nine; it's the viewers (live, jigging up and down) who take over from the stars, who end up literally as cardboard cutouts in their hands.

The odd thing was, no-one I spoke to about this promo seemed to have bothered much about it. It seems the popular imagination is *self-erasing*, although I did have the jingle rattling around in my head for weeks.[25] And, permanently marked for me by this augury incantation, 1985 did turn out to be quite a year. But that's another story.

Notes

1 Sorry about that. Perhaps a better way of putting it would be: Dana Polan, 'Film Theory-Re-assessed' in *Continuum: An Australian Journal of the Media*, 1988, 1(2), 15–30.
2 H. Marshall McLuhan, *Understanding Media* (London: Routledge & Kegan Paul, 1964).
3 The information on the first television shows is taken from a BBC radio program made to mark television's fiftieth anniversary: *TV Began Here*, broadcast on the BBC World Service, 27 October 1986.
4 An especially clear example of this would be John Ellis, *Visible Fictions* (London: Routledge & Kegan Paul, 1982).
5 I'm told these savoury snacks are unknown in Australia, which is fine for Australia, if not for my attempted calembour. Come to think of it, Twiglets are unknown to cultural theory too, so that's OK.
6 Umberto Eco, *Travels in hyperreality*, trans. William Weaver (London: Picador, 1987), p.150.
7 The term enslavement is Don McLeod's, who uses it explicitly to gloss the preferred colonial euphemism 'protection': Don McLeod (nd), *How the West was Lost* (Port Hedland: D.W. McLeod).
8 Benedict Anderson, *Imagined Communities* (London: Verso, 1983).
9 See John Hartley, 'A State of Excitement: Western Australia and the America's Cup', *Cultural Studies*, 1988, 2(1), 117–26.
10 Nicholas Garnham, 'Concepts of Culture: Public Policy and the Cultural

Industries', *Cultural Studies*, 1987, 1(1), 23–37.

11 This information, like so much really useful knowledge, comes from television—a British series called *The Politics of Food*, broadcast in Australia on SBS-TV in June 1988. The ABC science series **Quantum** has also investigated agribusiness along the same lines.

12 Christopher Hill, *Reformation to Industrial Revolution* (Harmondsworth: Penguin, 1969), p.89.

13 On the complexities and contradictions provoked by reading Shakespeare the popular dramatist as a capitalist landlord see Terence Hawkes' *tour de force* 'Playhouse–Workhouse', in Terence Hawkes, *That Shakespearian Rag* (London and New York: Methuen, 1986, pp.1–26.

14 This useful concept comes from S.L. Bethell, *Shakespeare and the Popular Dramatic Tradition* (St Albans, Herts.: Staples, 1944).

15 Jane Feuer, 'The Two Weather Channels', *Cultural Studies*, 1987, 1(3), 383–5.

16 Horace Newcomb and Paul M. Hirsch (1983), 'Television as a Cultural Forum', reprinted in Horace Newcomb (ed.), *Television: the Critical View*, [4th edition] (New York and Oxford: Oxford University Press, 1987), pp.455–70.

17 Todd Gitlin, *Inside Prime Time* (New York: Pantheon, 1983).

18 Camilla Mowbray, 'Bright New Identities', *Broadcast* (Australia), March 1988, 28–31.

19 Maria del Sapio, '"The Question Is Whether You Can Make Words Mean So Many Different Things": Notes on Art and Metropolitan Languages', *Cultural Studies*, 1988, 2(2), 196–216.

20 This and the ensuing comments on TV executives are all quoted in Mowbray, 'Bright New Identities'.

21 At the time of writing the fifth national network, SBS, had not released its new logo ID.

22 Perth *Sunday Times*, TV Extra Magazine, 24 July 1988, p.38.

23 J. Wolff, 'Bill Brand, Trevor Griffiths, and the Debate About Political Theatre', *Red Letters*, 1978, 8, 57.

24 John Fiske and John Hartley, *Reading Television* (London and New York: Methuen, 1978), pp.178–188.

25 And this is it:

> Eighty-five will come alive
> When Nine's stars step out strutting;
> When daytime turns to night-time,
> Hey! Here's the place to be.
> Downhill hitting top gear,
> Stealing hearts and falling clear,
> Sail into a brand new year with Nine.
> From today until next Sunday,
> And the Minutes in the middle,
> When will you see a team you trust like ours?
> When racquet, bat and boot hit ball,
> When Keke Rosberg hits the wall,
> Where Eagles dare we'll take you there;
> The super sports on Nine.

We're the people for the movies
When a movie's really moving,
When a special's super-special,
We're just the place to be.
We're flying high—The Aussie Flag!
We're climbing high—And we're proud!
We're still the one—To shout out loud!
There's never been a year like this before!

11

Children and Television

Bob Hodge

The topic of children and television stirs up more emotion with a weaker basis in research than any other in the field of media studies. In this chapter, I will try to explain why this is so, and what course can be safely traced through this minefield of controversy. Precisely because it is so fraught a topic, it exacerbates other important issues that impinge on it, issues such as censorship, sexism, racism and violence, and media ownership and control. With all these issues, people find themselves taking surprising and contradictory positions when children become a factor. In order to sort through this confusing picture we need first to be clear about the ideological forms that dominate the field, and then look carefully at what research has to say.

Children are the focus of contradictory viewpoints because of the strategic position they occupy in a number of systems of power operating at different levels in society. For any society, children are highly desirable objects of legitimate power, legitimating in turn other forces of benign control. Control over children in our society is exercised through the family, where parents claim their own power and autonomy over their children, and through the education systems, where teachers are the authorised agents. Children are also potential consumers, targets of advertising and the media, to be seduced rather than coerced. These different groupings within the community construct children in a similar way, yet within this consensus framework always aware of competing interests. Out of this similarity of ideological form and conflict of interests come the strange alliances that can spring up.

The dominant ideological construction of children itself has a double form, built on a contradiction that is not a temporary accident but is systemic and functional, and has a long history. On the one hand, children are seen as helpless, vulnerable and innocent, the passive victims of powerful and rapacious forces seeking to harm and exploit them. The function of this ideological message is clear. The more helpless the child, and the more evil the enemy, the more power its guardians can claim on its behalf. This part of the ideology legitimates the powers of a would-be guardian (parent, teacher, religious leader) against competition. But children are also seen as incessantly, wilfully seeking out pleasure, tending towards destructive and evil/anti-social behaviour. The function of this second ideological message is equally clear. It legitimates the would-be guardians' power over children themselves: their power to control what children should do and think and feel. Although as I've said, these messages are contradictory in some key respects, representing children as both good and evil, passive and active, they form a single functional whole, a single ideological complex.[1] These contradictions are necessary to serve the double interest of its ideologues: their claim to fight in the name of children and child-interests, while telling children what those interests are. This ideological complex has long roots—Christianity for instance has transmitted both halves of it for millenia. It has a strong appeal to many people, for many people have a vested interest in controlling children and exploiting their ideological potency.

The power and pervasiveness of this ideological complex, however, should not make us despair of arriving at an alternative position which is more genuinely grounded in children's needs and interests. This ideological complex has generated a large amount of relatively poor quality research. The position it describes is in fact anti-child, and cannot allow itself to recognise what children really are and want. There's a final irony about this ideological complex. There are many individuals—parents, teachers or citizens—who have a greater understanding of children and care more for their interests than the ideological complex allows. But such is the strength of the complex that these people often feel they are betraying children precisely on points where their responses are more genuinely in tune with children's real abilities and needs. Conversely, the fiercest lobbyists on behalf of children are trying to make sure that children get even less of what they want and value from television. With friends like those, who needs enemies?

The ideology of public regulation

Television is normally seen as part of the private sphere, but the ideological complex brings the issues into the public sphere. 'Children and Television' is a suitable topic to hold public inquiries on, and to justify lobby groups working to influence legislation and set up formal regulations and mechanisms of control. Children provide the most convenient pretext to get such legislation on the books as the thin end of a regulation wedge.

To illustrate the typical arguments and strategies I will look at the Australian experience, though this experience is by no means unique. Both Britain and USA have similar lobby groups arguing similar cases. Australia is somewhere between the two in terms of scale of regulation. British TV is more regulated by government agencies, and American TV by media corporations. As focus I will take the Australian Senate Inquiry into children and television of 1978.[2] This Inquiry by a joint committee of the Senate established a broad bipartisan framework which still exists as the basis for policy in this area. It is an important document for the study of ideological forces and government policy, an interesting parallel to the major American report on television violence by the Surgeon General's Committee of 1972.[3]

Both documents reveal the strength and effectiveness of public opinion as expressed through lobby groups. In the Australian report, a book of 179 pages, the contribution of published academic research is striking by its absence. Its footnotes refer to only 7 published books or articles, but 101 witnesses are listed and 251 written submissions, contained in over 4500 pages of evidence. Some of the witnesses had some academic expertise and other academic references are buried in the text, but even so there is no deference nor respect paid to this kind of evidence.

This initially seems in contrast to the American report, which lavishly funded some of its own research and provoked counter-research by oppositional groups. However, in both cases academic research played an equally peripheral role in forming views, judgments and policy recommendations, whether the cart went before the horse as in America or without need of a horse as in Australia. In both inquiries, the public body judged that the research community was not providing the clear basis for what it wanted to recommend.

The report states one of its key ideological premises in the first substantive chapter 'Television in Society'. It quoted from the Royal Commission into Television of 1953—the date of the source testifying to the unchanging authority of its premises: 'The objective of all television stations, from the outset, must be to provide programmes that will have the effect of raising standards of public taste'.[4]

This aim, we note, addresses all television (not at this point singling out commercial stations) and all audiences, not just children. 'Raising' then invokes the opposition between 'high' (as desirable) and 'low' (as undesirable), with 'standards' assuming that there is an objective measure of these things, even though what is at issue is 'taste', which is from the private sphere of pleasure and individual experience. The ideology behind this is familiar in cultural debates. It is an elitist view of culture in terms of which some people know and hold to high standards, and others (the public, the masses) do not even know what these standards are and need to be lifted up to glimpse them (or lick them). Behind this view are class assumptions emphasising the superiority of the culture of the ruling class.

This ideology has two targets. One is the ignorant masses. The other is 'the Industry', commercial television stations which, the committee declares, have 'failed...to live up to these ideals'.[5] But as it notes, the industry hasn't failed to live up to these ideals: it follows a different one, providing 'what the public wants'.[6] The Senate Inquiry regards this motive as inadequate and unworthy. But the logic of its position is interesting. The motives of the industry are seen as purely commercial (as it would agree) and therefore inherently dubious. But it is tacitly accepted that the industry is doing what it claims, giving the public what it wants. The assumption, then, is that the industry shares the elite's contempt for 'the public', but where the elite wishes to raise the masses, the industry simply wishes to exploit them for a profit. We thus see the presence, in a fused form, of the two halves of the ideological complex where there is an enemy (the industry) to save the helpless victims from, and there is an inherent tendency to what is low and debased in those victims, who need to be saved from themselves and given what others know they need, not what they think they want. At this point in the argument the 'victims' are not specifically children, but this is a report on children and television, and we can see already how beautifully apt children are for those arguing a case like this. If the masses are like children who need to be told what is good for them, so much greater will be the need to control the children of the masses.

The committee's next ideological move is to establish the vulnerability of the child viewers. The Senate Report announces this clearly:

> At the outset of this inquiry, our concern was felt for those
> children in the impressionable age categories or in their formative

years when they are most vulnerable to the various socializing influences that confront them in today's complex society.[7]

It also isolates three kinds of child viewer whom it sees as especially at risk: high-viewing children from low socio-economic backgrounds, children of low intelligence and/or with low levels of academic achievement, and children with 'low self-esteem', a category derived from one Australian researcher who made it into the magical circle of seven.[8] There is a fourth category implied: children who are not under the control of their parents. The committee quotes with alarm a study that showed children in control of what they watched for 41 per cent of their viewing time.[9] This seems a horrific figure to the committee, a parental betrayal of a whole generation; though children's right and ability to choose what they want to watch from another perspective could be seen as harmless, perhaps enjoyable, and maybe even a part of a desirable process of development. But this is connected by the report with high viewing and low socio-economic status as a sign of a crisis situation.

The report also isolates four issues of context, all of which are common objects of public concern and anxiety: violence, sex stereotyping, sex, and triviality. Violence is issue No. 1 and I will discuss it more fully below. The report shares the widespread concern that violent TV content will unleash violence in society. Sex it dismisses as a real issue, since self-censorship is already operating effectively within the Australian media. Sex stereotyping it sees as a problem, something that should be deplored, but its diagnosis and solution are, it could be said, a little naive. The chief culprits are identified as American sit-com programs. The cure is therefore easy, for patriotic Australians: 'greater emphasis on programmes that reflect the Australian life styles'.[10] Of course, this cure is only available in non-sexist societies like Australia. Less liberated societies presumably will have to buy Australian programs until they catch up.

I have discussed this report in some detail because it enshrines so comprehensively and authoritatively the set of attitudes that determine debate on children and television, not only in Australia but also in Britain and America. It shows the specific forms taken by the ideological complex. It allows us to see how implicated this complex is with the aspirations and anxieties of a particular class, in response to what it sees as a threat to its values and existence. The concern for children masks other middle-class fears: about violence erupting from below (the violence issue) and about the 'loss of standards' (their standards), in a public forum dominated by the mass media. But it is ultimately working-class children who are to be protected from being working class, and middle-class parents from being labelled irrelevant and out of touch.

Ideology and practice

A discussion of the ideological attitudes at play here would not be complete without looking at the recommendations of this report and what happened in practice. The striking thing to understand here is the gap between the range of concerns it expressed, and the effective recommendations it endorsed. This can be interpreted as yet another sad gap between ideals and reality, another example of politicians capitulating to the power of the media barons. Or it can be seen, as I will argue, as a systemic contradiction, growing out of the functional contradictions within the ideological complex itself: not an unintended accident but a typical instance of how children are used as counters in an ideological game which does not have their real interests as its major goal.

The gap can be seen especially clearly in the first of the seventeen recommendations, to do with TV violence. The recommendation is in three parts: first, guidelines must be drawn up, as a preliminary to see whether or what kind of problems exist. Second, programming should be monitored in relation to these guidelines. Finally (and here the teeth gleam ominously), this information should be 'made readily available to the public', and 'taken into account' in assessing TV stations' performance for licence renewal. This last sounds a real threat, but is only a token slap on the wrist, given the weakness of the Broadcasting Tribunal over licence renewals, and the vagueness over its powers which the report itself notes with disapproval. So TV violence is isolated as the major cause for concern, yet the report proposes no effective measures to deal with it. This double message of anxiety and ineffectiveness was similar to the situation in America, following the Surgeon General's Report of 1972, although media interests had to lobby hard there to neutralise the possibility of effective controls. In Britain, where the systems of control are more covert and responsive to middle-class pressure groups and less in need of legislative action, the campaigns of Mrs Whitehouse and her supporters were able to affect programming style with the BBC, with the 'violent content' of *Dr Who* a notable victim of this approach.[11]

There is one area in the report where this pattern of ineffectual protestations does not entirely prevail. The report gave a strong brief to the Children's Programme Committee of the Australian Broadcasting Tribunal to ensure regulation of TV programs for children during particular viewing periods. It also recommended that a children's production unit be established to produce 'good quality children's programmes'. Both these initiatives have been taken seriously. Commercial television stations have been required to screen a set number of programs classified as especially suitable for children during the period between 4.00 and 6.00 pm where children are generally the majority viewers. The Children's Television Foundation has been established and funded to foster the production of 'high quality' children's television.

The first development has had some problems, though to be fair to it, it is the most successful such intervention in the history of Australian television. That is because previous interventions have been total failures, as even former members of these committees proclaim. The consensus judgment on their lack of success is that their recommendations have been well-intentioned but powerless against the economic clout of the industry.[12] These earlier committees did indeed lack teeth. Their successor, the CPC, was given some dental implants, though it was still not exactly terrifying. It thus becomes interesting to see what they were or were not allowed to bite.

In effect, by requiring that the 'children's slot' (between 4.00 and 5.00 in the afternoon) should screen a specific proportion of programs classified as 'c' programs, and by controlling the issue of these 'c' certificates (as granted by the Australian Broadcasting Tribunal), the committee was able to police a time-slot, and give a higher economic value to the kind of television program it believed was beneficial to children. It has been able to establish a niche within normal programming where 'high standards' (or the middle-class elitist values of the children's lobbyists) can prevail. It is able to constrain commercial TV stations as public bodies, but it cannot, of course, constrain children to watch these programs, or have their taste raised by them. TV stations object that in spite of a number of exceptions, C-programs are not popular with children. The CPC concedes that many shows to which it has awarded certificates are not really as good as it would like, but compromises have to be made, and it can rightly claim that overall it has improved the 'quality' of programs in this slot, and that more children are now exposed to 'quality' television than before. Add to this the productions sponsored by the Children's Television Foundation and the verdict becomes clear. However circumscribed the scope of the improvement, however many compromises with political and economic realities they have had to make, the CPC and the CTF together have made a successful intervention, in their own terms, into the field of children and television. The Senate Inquiry and

Report, which mobilised and focused public opinion to support these initiatives, were successful in this respect in translating the ideological complex into practical effect.

In understanding the significance of this achievement we have to understand the political difficulties that would have been involved if the report had recommended decisive initiatives on all the issues it raised. Strategically it had to concentrate its recommendations along a narrow front so that it could achieve its small but real advances. Even so, we can step back and scrutinise the priorities expressed in the bastions it defended and those it left alone. Most of the problems it highlighted were not especially acute in the 4.00–6.00 slot. High-viewing, high-risk children were exposed to more danger (or so it was claimed) from watching well into adult viewing times, where they would be assaulted by violent content, insidious advertisements and American sexism. At best, the C-certificate strategy might implant 'high' standards in these viewers, though more realistically it would probably confirm their rejection of this kind of program, perhaps even driving them deeper into the unsavoury realms of evening viewing. *All* the main dangers affecting *all* the main viewers at risk, as identified by this report, are left unaffected by its proposals. It leads us to ask very intriguing questions. Were the anxieties expressed on behalf of children real—in which case the Senate Inquiry is guilty of betraying their interests—or were they only rhetorical? The first premise we looked at—the desire to 'raise standards of public taste'—turns out to have a higher priority than fears for the pernicious influence of TV.

Thus we come to the last contradiction associated with the ideo-logical complex—the gap between the ideological complex itself and the program of action it generates. This cannot be seen simply as the difference between high ideals and a recalcitrant reality, because the gap occurs too neatly along a line of cleavage within the ideological complex itself. Of two constructions of children, as innocent victims to be defended or as recalcitrant and wilful agents to be shaped and coerced, it is the second which is functionally primary, since this is how children must be constructed to legitimate them as objects over whom to exercise power. The notion of children as innocents justifies their defence against others (for whatever motive) but not any right to control children themselves.

This contradiction, I want to insist, is not unique to the Senate Committee. Nor do I see its members as a particularly devious and hypocritical group of people. The committee did not invent this set of contradictions. It simply took them from the community that it consciously tried to serve, and gave them an authoritative shape. In this role it was essential that it express grave concern about a whole range of issues but propose nothing effective about them, while achieving the limited set of reforms it addressed itself to. What is true on a large scale of the Senate Committee is true on a smaller scale (with much individual variation) of 'pro-child' lobbyists. Their central aim is more power over more children on behalf of their class, and their battle is waged against those (always including children) who resist that power or want to exercise their own. The pro-child lobby, then, is motivated by among other things a hostility to the actual wishes of actual children. That is not to say that the industry is virtuous or innocent. It too has a vested interest, its dominance of the market, and if it 'gives the public what it wants', that is only because what it wants is the public as its own commodity. We don't have a simple case of right versus wrong or might versus right. What we have is a struggle between competing interests, each of which constructs its own ideological complex to serve it in its struggle.

The 'facts' about children and TV

An emphasis on the category of ideology in a discussion of children and television is liable to give rise to two discouraging and mistaken impressions. One is that no-one who claims to be concerned for children could at all be sincere. The other is that 'facts' do not exist as a basis for deciding who or what is right or wrong. Certainly I would caution against naively accepting what people in dispute claim to be their motives, or what they claim to be 'facts'. This word has become somewhat tarnished by its misuse in such debates. Ironically, the TV industry group organising its case used the name Federation of Australian Commercial Television Stations, which comes out as the convenient but misleading acronym FACTS. But although people have complex motives, that does not mean that no motives that are expressed are genuine. And although ideological considerations are at work in every stage in the production of ideas and knowledge ('facts'), ideology does not work in an unfettered way. Research is constrained by two factors working in different proportions in different instances: constraints on the researcher (ideological and social) and constraints from the object of research itself.

I will illustrate this from the debate about the 'violent effects' of television on children, which is still the focus of greatest concern in this field. I was the member of a research team which investigated this issue in depth over a three-year period. The findings of that study have been published,[13] so that I am now identified with a particular position on this issue: essentially, that television violence does not have the general effect of producing a violent society. In terms of what I said above, the existence of this basis of research and publication doesn't simply give authority to what I have to say on the violence-effect ('it's been published, so it must be right'). On the contrary, in some ways it compromises it. My own text is ideologically constrained. But it's also constrained by the object itself. I couldn't, for instance, plausibly claim that there is no violence shown on television. The anti-violence lobby can't show pictures of brave researchers bitten by maddened children after watching **Tom and Jerry**. It is this refractory object, common to nearly all researchers, which I will try to describe, because it is this that the 'concerned' public wants to know and has a right to know, from academics who are funded by the community and ultimately responsible to it.

First, then, the matter of violent content. The Senate Inquiry quoted the following, which is a typical product of content analysis applied to Australian TV in 1977 (broadly similar results apply for Britain and America):

> In terms of the change from the bumper-crop violence-harvest of 1976 to the relative(ly) placid 1977, the declines in percentage of programmes containing violence fell from 90 per cent to 75.5 per cent; the rate of violent episodes per hour fell from 9.5 per cent to 6.7 per cent; and the rate of violence per programme fell from 6.2 to 5.0 episodes.[14]

With figures like this it is proper to question what counts as violence, and who is doing the counting under what conditions. Different criteria might produce very different figures. But an academic like Dr Murray can be trusted to try to count scrupulously by his criteria, and however the figures are adjusted, they are likely to show a substantial amount of violence depicted on television screens. We can add that cartoons typically come out near the top of any straight count. This aspect of the case, then, is not in dispute (nor could it easily be, since normal members of the public have access to the primary data). There is a lot of violence depicted on television. The big question, then, is: what (if anything) is/are the effect(s) of all this?

On this, the crucial question, I think that it's no bad thing to point first to the commonsense knowledge of the community, since on this matter they actually have some first-hand data, which they are normally encouraged to ignore. Middle-class adults (those most concerned about the violence issue) know that they themselves are not impelled to mindless havoc in the streets by five minutes of **Tom** *and Jerry*. All the children whom they see watching such shows are more likely to be calmed down by them than incited to violence. Yet still the myth persists that this danger lurks somewhere, for many children. What we have, in fact, is the very interesting phenomenon of large numbers of people claiming to believe something that at one level they know is untrue. This contradictory set of beliefs, I have suggested, is a product of the ideological complex. It is something shared by both the Senate Inquiry and by the community whose views that Inquiry represented. So that community wanted anxiety to be expressed but would not have been delighted and reassured if the government had taken on the industry and introduced stringent controls on 'violent' content.

It might still have been the case that television violence has powerful effects which are initially invisible to the ordinary eye, as is the case with bacteria or radio-activity or certain carcinogens. The possibility exists that 'commonsense' is not equipped to see the danger, and it is proper to turn to research to ask if its magnifying lenses have revealed surprising and unsuspected phenomena. My view is that so far this hasn't happened. And since different 'experts' seem to argue so strenuously on opposite sides, I will try to stay with a few 'commonsense' observations on the complex state-of-play: not because 'commonsense' is always a reliable guide, but because research findings remain inaccessible, incomprehensible and in-effective till they are translated into the current language and assumptions of 'commonsense'.

The first observation I will make is that there has been a huge expenditure on research effort trying to prove that television violence causes violence and aggression in viewers. Up till 1978, approximately 80 per cent of research on media effects was concerned with this issue, according to no less an authority than Professor George Comstock, former Chair of the Surgeon-General's Advisory Committee.[15] All this effort has produced very meagre results. That indeed is why there has been so much effort. There is an obvious commonsense response to this: if over 10 000 studies in more than a decade come up with such slim pickings, any 'effects' must be microscopic and negligible. If we compare this huge effort and its dubious results with research on smoking and cancer, or alcohol and a variety of medical conditions, there is a marked difference. The broad case has been proven with cigarettes and alcohol, whatever governments choose to do about it. The broad case isn't proven with TV violence.

If we tighten the microscope a little, we find further 'facts'. The studies which seem to show some effects of violence viewing tend to be short-term experiments under artificial conditions, not long-term studies under more everyday conditions. As a matter of commonsense, this is opposite to what we would expect, if TV has a cumulative effect. If small effects are revealed from individual programs, as detected in artificial conditions, we would expect large and visible effects from the massive exposure over many years that is commonplace for many members of the populace. This is what research has consistently failed to deliver. So it seems more likely that the 'effects' detected under artificial conditions are largely produced by those conditions. In any fair court of law, *Tom and Jerry* would have been cleared by law of the crimes for which they stand charged, for want of evidence by the prosecution.

Finally I want to deal very quickly with some other claims that have been made about the effects of TV on children. The lack of proof of the violence-effect will itself have an unfortunate effect if it persuades people that TV has no effects at all. 'Commonsense' is quite right to think that an experience that occupies more child-hours than school for many children must have effects. The Senate Inquiry was worried about sexist stereotyping, and also about what they perceived as trivialisation. There was also concern running through the Inquiry with children not doing, thinking and feeling what they ought to. I will label these three general areas of concern the ideological effect, the culture effect, and the resistance effect.

The ideological effect

Children's TV has been demonstrated to have massive biases in terms of gender and race (sexism and racism). It has equally massive biases in terms of class, which have been less extensively studied. Unlike the 'violence effect', these biases are generally reinforced by ideological structures in society at large, which complete this effect. Exactly what role is played by the ideological content of TV is not yet demonstrated, but on this matter researchers of all ideological persuasions agree that TV plays a crucial part.

The culture effect

TV has become an important component of contemporary culture. As such it functions as a marker of group membership, actively constructing communities of viewers, drawing up an alternative map of social relations that in some respects threatens the dominant map. In a class society like Britain or Australia, TV is stratified into 'National' (further subdivided, in Britain, into elite [BBC1] and super-elite [BBC2]) and commercial, reflecting basic class divisions in those societies. But in practice, children are exposed to the possibility of being declassed by their TV watching. The problem is in some ways more acute in America, where there is no clearly designated elite programming on the broadcast network. One significant further effect of the culture effect is the growth of lobby groups, whose basic aim is to reclaim space and currency for their own culture on the mass media, so that they will not lose their children to an opposing class.

The resistance effect

TV viewers, including children, are active not passive, and this activity can be expressed through a range of kinds of resistance. Critical or oppositional readings of TV are a paradoxical kind of effect, since they seem to go in the opposite direction to where TV seems to be pushing. They inevitably draw on knowledge, attitudes and skills from outside the immediate context of watching TV, so they are 'effects' of something other than TV. Yet they are still intrinsic parts of TV society, fundamentally determined by the nature and forms of the TV that they respond to. Incorporation of TV into education is one very important such effect. So are the efforts of lobby groups. So also are various age group, subcultural and familial practices. The resistance effect is both an important class of effects in itself, and also a randomising factor which obscures the clear operation of other effects.

I have argued against the ideological complex because it is so pervasive a force in shaping opinions and debate, making it difficult to think clearly about the issues of children and TV. But the complex is not simply a distraction from the 'real' truth about children's needs, interests and abilities as users of TV. The way children are constructed and appropriated for ideological purposes is itself a part of an important social phenomenon, even if it's a game that only adults are allowed to play. In this game children are expected to be seen but not heard. If anyone bothered to listen to what they see and say, it would quite spoil the game.

Notes

1 On this term, see R. Hodge and G. Kress, *Social Semiotics* (Oxford: Polity Press, 1987).
2 Australian Senate Inquiry, *Children and Television* (Canberra: Australian Government Publishing Service, 1978).
3 Surgeon General's Scientific Advisory Committee on Television and Social Behaviour, *Television and Growing Up: The Impact of Televised Violence* (Washington DC: US Government Printing Office, 1972).

4 Australian Senate Inquiry (1978), p.5.
5 Ibid., p.8.
6 Ibid., p.9.
7 Ibid., p.17.
8 P. Edgar, *Children and Screen Violence* (St Lucia: University of Queensland Press, 1977).
9 Australian Senate Inquiry (1978), p.24.
10 Ibid., p.42.
11 See J. Tulloch and M. Alvarado, *Dr Who: the Unfolding Text* (London: Macmillan, 1984).
12 See for example P. Edgar and U. Callus, *The Unknown Audience* (Melbourne: Channel 9 Publication, 1979).
13 R. Hodge and D. Tripp, *Children and Television* (Oxford: Polity Press, 1986).
14 Dr J.P. Murray, Macquarie University, quoted in Australian Senate Inquiry (1978), p.29.
15 G. Comstock, S. Chaffee, N. Vatzmann, M. McCombs, and D. Roberts, *Television and Human Behaviour* (St Lucia: New York: Columbia University Press, 1978).

12

Changed Times, Changed Tunes: Music and the Ideology of the News

Theo van Leeuwen

The Majestic Fanfare

Charles Williams' **Majestic Fanfare**, the short piece of music re-produced below (Example 1), is known to almost every Australian. For 32 years—from 1953 to 1985—it was played before every ABC news broadcast. We cannot hear it without thinking of the ABC and its news. It is without doubt Australia's best known 'news signature tune'.

What is the function of 'news signature tunes'? To call the list-ener to attention? To serve as a musical label, a kind of aural logo? No doubt news signature tunes do both these things, but they also do something else. They also tell us something *about* the news, and they do so in the language of music.

Why in the language of music? Because, although what these tunes tell us could also be conveyed with words or pictures, this would not have the same effect. Music is, in our society, primarily used as a means to address the emotions. We are not used to think-ing about music as having representational meaning; we more readily think of music as affecting us emotionally. Now music does, of course, affect us in this way. It is a language which speaks to our body, which 'moves' and 'stirs' us. But it also, and at the same

Example I: the 'Majestic Fanfare'

(harplike glissando's on
synthesizer)

time, can represent the world around us, give us, for example, a
musical picture of what ABC news is and does, and to this aspect
we tend to pay less attention. In other societies and other periods
than our own the meanings of scale choices, instrument choices
and so on, are often more explicitly known and discussed. We,
however, have to music the same romantic attitude that exists also
with regard to rhetoric in language, especially poetry: music must
be seen as directly coming from and directly appealing to individual
emotions. To intellectually recognise its conventions, and to see it
as a social product, enmeshed in the ideology of its social context,
somehow spoils the fun. This attitude, this denial of representational meaning in music, turns music into an especially effective
vehicle for the maintenance, indeed the celebration of social structures and their ideologies. Music can make people respond to meanings without them knowing what it is they respond to, make people
identify with messages without them knowing what it is they identify with. As an advertiser has said:

> Music is particularly good at changing attitudes because it
> somehow gets into the brain via the backdoor and it plants a
> thought in there. You can almost, if you like, have people
> humming your sales message before it's even really been
> expressed to them...[1]

We can, however, make ourselves conscious of the way music
represents the world around us. To do so we need to look at music
as a language, and at a given piece of music as an instance of it,
a combination of choices from the different musical systems that
constitute that language.[2] To use the term 'language of music' is
of course to speak metaphorically. Music does not work the same
way as language.[3] But language and music have this in common that
every utterance must be a combination of choices from different
systems and that the choice between different possible lexicogram-
matical or musical forms is always also the choice between different

possible meanings: the systems of a 'language' are its meaning potentials. Thus, to have a linguistic utterance, we must choose, for example, from the realm of possibilities offered by the system of mood (choose to make our utterance declarative, or interrogative, or imperative, etc., hence to make it a statement, or a question, or a command) and from the system of ergativity (choose whether to represent events as self-engendered or as caused by some agency, choose, e.g. between *he died* and *a fatal disease killed him*), and so on.[4] There are many such systems and choices must be made from all of them. Their combination in the utterance builds up the meaning of the whole. It is so also in music. The systems are different, but the principle is the same. It is in these terms that we will now look more closely at the **Majestic Fanfare**.

The system of tonality

The primary choice in the system of tonality in contemporary Western music is that between *major* and *minor*, and the **Majestic Fanfare** is written in a major key. There are other, more 'delicate' choices in the system, but these need not occupy us here.

What meanings are involved in this choice? A little historical background may help to make this clear. Major tonality came to the fore as the 'normal' and in a sense normative tonality in Western music in the late Middle Ages. The music which was ideologically dominant before that time, the music of the Church, shunned the Ionian mode (a scale corresponding to our present major) although that mode was widely used in secular music. The ascendance of major, then, was linked to the secularisation of society, to a gradual but irreversible shift in cultural hegemony from the Church to the rising merchant class, and major came to be associated with the positive values of that class: belief in progress through human achievement, science, industry, exploration, etc. Minor, by contrast, literally depresses the major scale, by lowering the third, the sixth and the seventh, and so presents the 'depressing', negative image of these values, and becomes associated with everything that stands in the way of progress and human self-fulfilment—for a long time pieces in a minor key had to have a 'happy ending' (the 'tierce de Picardie').

These meanings have remained remarkably stable. In this century Shostakovitch has been urged by the Soviet culture controllers to make greater use of the major triad, so as to 'give enduring expression to the heroism of people's lives in the period of the victory of socialism'.[5] After Independence, Indian sitar players began to add major thirds to the bass drone of *ragas*, which, until then, had always been a 'bare fifth'.[6] In the West we have, as said, increasingly repressed conscious knowledge of the relation between music and ideology, and thought of music as expressing 'private emotions' —hence we speak of major as 'happy' and minor as 'sad'. But music in fact creates a fusion between meanings and emotional states, linking pleasure to what is ideologically correct, and unpleasure to what is ideologically deviant.

The system of interaction within the musical group

The system of interaction within the musical group provides options for the ways in which the various parts in a piece of music can relate to each other. The primary choice is that between unison (monophony) and its absence. In monophonic music the parts are identical: all the players and/or singers play and/or sing the same notes.[7] The first two bars of the **Majestic Fanfare** are monophonic: the brass section of the orchestra plays in unison.

When unison is absent a further choice opens up, that between polyphony and homophony. In polyphony the parts of the players and/or singers are different but equal—equal in melodic and rhythmic value and complexity; equal also in that they would, by themselves, form musically complete and interesting pieces. Within polyphony many further choices are possible, based on the ways in which the parts can be different: they can, for example, form 'harmony lines', melodies of identical structure sung at certain intervals apart from each other; they can, as in counterpoint, be the inverse of one another, and so on. In homophony, on the other hand, one part becomes dominant, the others accompaniment, support. The parts of the subordinated voices are not equal in status to the part of the dominant voice, and when played by themselves do not form complete, musically interesting pieces: they are meaningful only in relation to the dominant voice and to each other; they have value only in terms of their function in the whole. This value in relation to the whole is harmonic value: the accompanying voices constitute the chordal pillars on which the melody of the dominant voice rests. But with harmony comes the possibility of disharmony—muffled tension, muffled dissonance/dissent behind the dominant voice. This dissonance the music must constantly resolve if it is to continue to progress forwards (note the metaphorical resonance of the technical terms 'resolution' and 'chord progression'). The second part of the **Majestic Fanfare** is homophonic in this way: the brass plays the melody, the other instruments, including strings, woodwind and a harp, play the accompaniment. Within this accompaniment the chord progressions are basic and simple. Dissonance is absent.

The choices that constitute the system of interaction within the musical group allow the expression of the relations between people and groups of people—relations of equality or inequality, of similarity and difference, of independence and conformity, etc. Lomax,[8] in his ethnological survey of song styles across the world, notes that monophony tends to dominate in societies in which decisions are made collectively and in which there is an emphasis on consensus and conformity. Polyphony is often used to symbolise gender roles and tends to occur in societies in which there is comparative equality and complementarity between the productive labour of men and women.[9] Homophony is a Western invention, intrinsically related to the development of capitalism: the way in which the subordinated parts in homophonic music relate to each other and to the whole, resembles the way in which the work of individual factory workers is meaningful only in relation to the whole, to a masterplan, and has no meaning in itself. It began in the work of the Italian opera composers, around 1600, and had become dominant, almost to the exclusion of everything else, by the time of the Industrial Revolution.

One other choice in the system needs to be mentioned here: the possibility of alternation rather than simultaneity of the parts of a 'leader' and the parts of the group 'led by the leader'. A 'call and response' structure in which the whole orchestra and/or choir 'responds' to a 'leader' who plays and/or sings solo, is common in many different kinds of music. It allows of further, more 'delicate' options: the parts of 'leader' and 'chorus' may overlap or be strictly separate; the group may repeat what the leader has sung or played, or respond in a more autonomous way, and so on. This subsystem, then, also models the relations possible between a leader and a group, but in a more dialogic fashion instead of directly subordinating the part of the group to that of the leader. The **Majestic Fanfare** in fact combines a 'call and response' structure and homophony: rather than independently responding to the part of the leader (which is represented here by a group of players rather than by an individual player) the group harmonically supports an 'answer' provided by the leader during the 'conclusion' of the melody.

The meanings made possible by this system are, in themselves, fairly vague and abstract. When we look at them in context, however, they acquire more precise and concrete definition, because it is the context which tells us, for example, *who* the 'leader' and the 'group' are. This makes it possible to see how music represents the relation between, for example, the priest and the congregation, the male rockstar and the female back up vocalists, the male and female characters singing a duet in an opera—or the 'voice of the news' and the listeners in a news signature tune. One could say that the music functions as a verb ('respond to', 'support', 'shore up', etc.) relating participants who are given in the context.[10]

The system of time

Time is a crucial element in social organisation, and the music of a society, or a group within a society, tends to express how that society or group conceives of and lives with time. In polyrhythmic music, for example, each voice or instrument has its own time, yet all fit together. Much Caribbean and South American music is polyrhythmic and, as Edward Hall[11] has pointed out, these are societies in which our punctuality, our timetabling, our ways of synchronising people to the mechanical time of the clock have not found anywhere near as strong a foothold as in the so-called developed countries, where everyone has become alienated from subjective, experiential time, and subjected to the clock, with its scientific division of time in hours, minutes and seconds, and where the regime of time is fundamental to most social institutions—the school, the factory, the hospital, the media, etc. The development towards this way of structuring time, which was very much in the interest of the newly dominant merchant class (if only because it allowed time to become the object of calculation) led to the disappearance of the unmeasured, 'eternal' time of plainchant, and to the introduction of the musical equivalent of the clock, the barline, and its concomitant subordination of all the voices and instruments playing a piece of music to the same metronomically regular beat.

More recently the influence of African music has, via jazz, challenged the classical Western order of time. In modern 'Afro-American' popular music the beat is often displaced, anticipated or delayed. The regular metronomic beat of Western music is subverted here, rebelled against, and this rebellion does not remain restricted to subcultures, but has become part of a large sector of the dominant entertainment music, which thus moves away somewhat from the discipline of the clock and the work ethic, in the direction of pleasure and leisure time self-gratification.

Given a choice for measured time and regular metre, another choice opens up: that between duple time (2/4; 4/4, etc) and triple time (3/4; 6/8, etc). These two have gradually become the dominant metres in the music of Europe, to the exclusion of more complex and less regular metres—which, however, continued to be used in folk music and would be rediscovered by the composers of the dominant music in the late nineteenth century. The significance of the choice between duple and triple time becomes more clear by looking at the kinds of dances with which these metres were associated—there often is a close connection between musical metre and dance, and, in turn, between dance and the main productive activities in a society.[12] Out of dances in which the dancers stood opposite each other in rows, or danced in a circle, there developed two new kinds of dance, the procession dance, associated with duple time, and eventually culminating in the *March*, and the closed couple dance, initially, as in the *Volte* and the *Minuet*, still involving gestures towards the group as a whole, later, in the *Waltz*, turning the couple into a world of its own, physically together with others in the ballroom, yet not communicating with these others, in the way that neighbours in a suburb may live close to each other, yet never communicate. So there is on the one hand the *public* time of the procession dance, symbolising, with its forwards movement, progress, exploration, expansion, and, on the other hand the *private* time of the closed couple dance, expressing the bourgeois ethos of privacy, the ethos of the self-contained 'nuclear' family which did engender so many new emotional ties and so much refinement of interpersonal sentiment.

The **Majestic Fanfare** is not only written and performed in measured, regular time, but also in 4/4, the time of 'public music', of marches and rousing anthems. But towards the end the tempo relaxes somewhat, and the marchlike beat of the 'leaders' becomes the broad forwards surging of the masses of listeners.

Systems of the melody

Three systems of the melody will be discussed here: directionality, latitude and durational patterning.

A primary choice in the system of directionality is that between melodies which are ascending, moving upwards in pitch, and melodies which are descending, moving downwards in pitch. According to Cooke[13] ascending melodies are more 'active', more 'outgoing', more 'dynamic' than descending melodies, and he links this to a physiological concomitant of singing: moving up in pitch requires increased vocal effort, while descending in pitch allows the singer to decrease expenditure of vocal energy. This motivates the meaning contrast involved: ascending music seeks to energise, to rally listeners together for the sake of some common activity or cause; descending music seeks to relax listeners, or to incite them to sharing their thoughts and their feelings. Hymns are a good example of the

Example 2: Australian Hymn Book No. 481

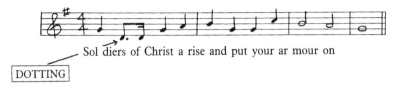

Sol diers of Christ a rise and put your ar mour on

DOTTING

Example 3: Australian Hymn Book No. 520

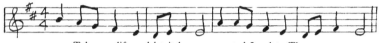

Take my life and let it be conse crated Lord to Thee

way in which this contrast becomes more concrete in specific social contexts. Example 2 shows a proselytising, missionary, 'public' modality of religion, Example 3 a more inward looking, resigning, 'pious' modality of religion. The former has a predominantly ascending melody, the latter a predominantly descending melody.

The system of latitude provides options for the size of the intervals between successive notes. The intricacies of this system cannot be discussed here, so we will restrict ourselves to an overall distinction: 'public' music tends towards large intervals between successive notes, large strides, energetic leaps; 'private' music tends towards smaller intervals—chromaticism, which uses the smallest intervals possible in Western tonality, is a standard device of 'sentimentality' in Western music. Examples 2 and 3 demonstrate this contrast.

The contrast between 'public' and 'private' is, in the Western tradition, also realised by the system of durational patterning of melodies. Public music frequently uses dotting, in which a note is repeated in such a way that the repeated note is long and the repeating one short (DAA–de–DAA–de–DAA). Anticipation, the use of an 'upbeat' note which precedes the first note of the first bar of the melody, has a similar effect. An example of dotting is shown in Example 2, an example of anticipation in Example 4.

'Private' music often uses suspension, the long drawing out of a note and concomitant delay and shortening of the next note. Imagine a rather slow and sentimental version of 'Yesterday', with the syllable 'far' drawn out extra much, and the next syllable shortened accordingly, to 'get back into step'.

The sonata form—the crucial form of the Western art music tradition—in fact posits and works through precisely this opposi-

Example 4: 'The Internationale'

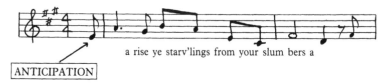

a rise ye starv'lings from your slum bers a

ANTICIPATION

Example 5: 'Yesterday'

SUSPENSION

Yes ter day all my troubles seemed so far a way

tion between the 'public' and the 'private'. A sonata has two themes, a first 'heroic' theme, and a second 'sentimental' theme, and, after stating the two themes, plays them out against each other in the 'development', so that the music becomes discursive, a kind of dialectic argument in which the opposing themes are eventually reconciled. In Example 6, the first few bars of Haydn's Piano Sonata 1, the first theme has large intervals and dotted rhythm, the second suspension and passing notes to diminish the size of the intervals, even to the point of chromaticism. Many musicologists refer to the two themes as the 'masculine' and the 'feminine' theme, which goes to show how many of the fundamental dichotomies of a society can be mapped onto gender.

The melody of the **Majestic Fanfare** displays many of the features of 'public' music just discussed. It has dotted rhythms, large intervals and a tendency towards ascending pitch. Towards the end, however, the opposition between the 'public' and the 'private' is somewhat diluted: though still ascending, the melody now uses smaller intervals, and the addition of other, more lyrical and 'sentimental' instruments, like the strings and the harp, further enhances this effect.

We can now summarise these observations and attempt to show how the combination of choices from the various systems, placed in the concrete context of ABC news broadcasts in a given historical period, constitutes a representation of the identity of the ABC news.

The **Majestic Fanfare**, then, is, first of all, 'public' music. Its musical language is the language of rousing hymns, uplifting anthems, marches—major key, 4/4 measured time, dotted rhythms,

Example 6: Joseph Haydn, Piano Sonata I, first 9 bars of 1st movement

(heroic theme)

(sentimental theme)

(return to heroic theme)

large intervals. Its structure is that of an instrumental (hence some-what abstract) 'call and response': the first motif, played by the brass in unison, is responded to by the full orchestra. But the response is not an independent response; there is no true 'dialogue'— the brass continues to lead, and the orchestra provides back-up by harmonically 'agreeing with' the melody, and this without any sense of dissonance. Thus the essence of the ABC news is represented somewhat as follows: the dominant, hegemonic voice, the voice of the Empire, a voice resonant with military and imperialist connotations, rallies behind it the whole nation, unified in harmony despite its diversity, and resolves in the process the opposition between the 'public' and the 'private' through its dilution of the former with smaller intervals, more 'sentimental' instruments, and the relaxing of the tempo. The theme then ends on a major third, which renders the piece unfinished, to be completed by the news itself, and so, together with the news, part of a larger text, and which also, because of its quintessential major-ness, lends extra prominence to the idea of 'progress', of the onwards 'march of time'. The theme represents the relation between the 'voice of the news' and the listeners as a relation between a dominant, extra-local, central power and those willingly falling in line with it. It overcomes the contradiction between the public and the private, always a potential conflict when public messages are sent into private homes. And it continues the old tradition of the herald, announcing important events.

Changed times, changed tunes

When *The National* was introduced, in March 1985, the **Majestic Fanfare** was at last replaced, be it again by a British theme.[14] The new theme was called **Best Endeavours**, and came from a record of 'contemporary orchestral brighteners', on the sleeve of which it was described as 'prestigeous' and 'industrial'. When *The National*, after a short and troubled existence, was withdrawn in December of that same year, Peter Wall, ABC radio manager and composer, was asked to write a new tune. It is reproduced in Example 7.

During the 1970s the ABC had led an increasingly troubled existence, and its news and current affairs programs had been centrally involved in this. Since Mike Willesee had defected to Channel 9, and, in 1972, achieved better ratings with his program *A Current Affair* than the ABC did with *This Day Tonight*, it had begun to lose its monopoly over information programs and started to worry about ratings. Gradually it introduced changes in types of programming and styles of presentation which moved it into the direction of commercial radio and television. For this it came under fire from two sides: it was criticised for being too highbrow, too elitist and too British, and it was also criticised for being too commercial and abandoning its standards. Within the ABC antagonism between the News Division, which guarded the traditional standards, and the Public Affairs Division, which was responsible for current affairs programs and more inclined to innovation, increased. Current affairs journalists were not only independent from their radio counterparts, this in contrast to news journalists, but also had more liberty in using interviews and film footage, and in turning journalists into glamorous 'personalities', and they saw it as their task not just to present the news, but also to interpret it. This, according to the News Division, made them into 'showbusiness

Example 7: ABC Television News Signature Tune by Peter Wall

boys' and 'editorializing journalists'.[15] The 'showbusiness boys' won. *The National* broke conventions by mixing news and current affairs and by using a glamorous presenter, Geraldine Doogue, and so managed to introduce an element of entertainment into the news. But *The National*, too, came under fire from two sides, and was criticised both for breaking with the traditional standards and for not doing this as well as the commercial stations. The program did not last out the year, and the separation between news and current affairs was reinstated, although some of the innovations would cling, e.g. the space age graphics.

The new style ABC television news, then, is characterised by contradictions—contradictions between the commercial emphasis on entertainment, 'drama', human interest, the foregrounding of the news team itself (the glamour of the presenter, the professional efficiency of its teamwork and technology), and the traditional ABC news values of impartially and more or less anonymously passing on 'intelligence' from the centre of power to the outposts of the Empire; contradictions also between an authority resting on the power of formalisation and abstraction and an authority resting on the 'credibility' of personalities.

These contradictions emerge also in Peter Wall's new news signature tune. At first hearing it has more in common with the **Majestic Fanfare** than with the theme of *The National*. In contrast to *Best Endeavours*, which was all-electronic, it combines synthesiser effects and traditional instruments, and, as in the **Majestic Fanfare**, the brass, with its 'public', military connotations, dominates. A call and response structure is used (though less prominently so) and the characteristic melodic features of 'public music' are in evidence. But there are also significant differences. To begin with, the piece is no longer in major, but in minor, as though something of the belief in the old-style values of the ABC and its news has gone, as though the notion of progress has become questionable.[16] Secondly, it opens with an amorphous synthesiser drone, and the connotation of this is anchored by the visual which shows the universe with a revolving satellite in the foreground: news no longer emanates from the central leadership of a human nation or Empire, but from space, in a dehumanised process, inevitable and inescapable because of its very technicality; the backcloth is no longer history, no longer the 'march of time', but the timelessness of space, an eternity bereft of meaning. Thirdly, syncopation makes its entry and shifts the music away somewhat from the classical Western discipline of time and from representing the news as an official, public message, moving it in the direction of leisure time entertainment. Finally, the boundary between the musical theme (ideological banner of the news) and the news itself (the 'facts') has become somewhat blurred: during part of the music a voice is heard, headlining the news. In this voice-over section the use of musical realism is extended: an ostinato pattern of repeated notes suggests messages coming in continuously on the teleprinter, and so signifies the *immediacy* of the news. This can be heard also in the news signature tunes of many commercial stations. Indeed, some use sound effects (e.g. typewriters) instead of a musical imitation thereof to achieve the same effect [this relative interchangeability of music and sound effects is an important aspect of realism in modern mass media music, and was in fact foreshadowed in musical experiments of the 1920s: Satie, in his ballet score *Parade* (1916), already added typewriters to the orchestra]. Overlaid on this ostinato pattern are short melodic fragments, alternatively played by the brass and the synthesiser, the former sounding harsh and abrasive, the latter, by comparison, more lyrical. In this way the music signifies the *variety* of the news, with its mixture of 'hard' and 'soft' news, of the public world of politics and international affairs and the 'sentimental', private world of 'human interest' and human 'drama'.

ABC news has changed and so has its tune. Echoes of the old identity can still be heard, but they are subdued, and they must do battle with the music of the satellite era. New, 'commercial' aspects intrude, 'advertising' the news as immediate, varied, entertaining, exciting. And so this tune speaks of a contradictory news, a news in transition. No doubt more chapters will soon need to be added to the history of ABC news signature tunes.

Notes

1 John Bevans, interviewed on ABC Radio, March 1980.
2 To avoid misunderstanding: by 'choice' I do not mean 'free, individual choice'. What may be 'chosen' is in fact restricted by conventions—not so much, however, by the conventions of the 'language' as by the conventions of the social context in which the utterance is embedded. This context may either be the actual context in which the music is performed, or a context represented by the music, e.g. in a drama accompanied by music, or both.
3 The French structuralist music semioticians of the 1960s and 1970s (e.g. N. Ruwet, *Langage, Musique, Poésie* (Paris: Seuil, 1972); J.-J. Nattiez, *Fondements d'une sémiologie de la musique* (Paris: UGE, 1976)) took this metaphor too literally and expected to find every aspect of linguistic structure reflected also in the structure of nonlinguistic, e.g. musical codes. In this they were, predictably, disappointed, and their work has not contributed much to the elucidation of musical semiosis. Modern systemic-

functional semiotics, however, is capable of overcoming the limitations of the structuralist approach.

4   The account of language on which I am relying is that of M.A.K. Halliday, *An Introduction to Functional Grammar* (London: Edward Arnold, 1985).

5   I.V. Nestyev, *Prokoviev* (Oxford University Press, 1961), p.458.

6   Cf. D. Cooke, *The Language of Music* (New York: Doubleday, 1959), p.55.

7   Western music has invented instruments (notably the keyboard instruments) which allow the musical group to become, as it were, internalised in one player. The role of that player thus becomes individualistic, complex and divided, rather than that it provides a unique identity. When I played piano in a salsa orchestra with South American musicians this way of playing was rejected: I was to play the same notes with both hands.

8   A. Lomax, *Folk Song Style and Culture* (New York: Transaction Press, 1968), p.15.

9   Ibid, p.165 ff.

10   It follows that (non-programmatic) instrumental concert hall music is a great deal more abstract than other forms of music: in terms of the foregoing discussion, it abstracts the representation of social relations from the concrete participants of these relations. Distancing and abstraction is, of course, one of the hallmarks of the bourgeois 'habitus' which fostered this kind of music (cf. P. Bourdieu, *Distinction* (London: Routledge and Kegan Paul, 1985)).

11   E. Hall, *The Silent Language* (London: Oxford University Press, 1959).

12   Cf. Lomax, *Folk Song Style and Culture*, p.224 ff.

13   Cooke, *The Language of Music*, p.102 ff.

14   The first ABC news signature tune had been a British military march, **The British Grenadiers**. When, during the Second World War, the Government decreed that radio programs should make 'subtle propaganda' for Australia First, it was replaced by **Advance Australia Fair**. But the British element was to return after the War. In 1949 'Advance Australia Fair' was cut in half, and in 1953 it was replaced by the **Majestic Fanfare**, played by the Queen's Hall Light Orchestra and conducted by the composer. In 1982, the year of the ABC's 50th anniversary, it was updated somewhat—given a faster tempo and some synthesiser effects.

15   K.S. Inglis, *This is the ABC* (Melbourne University Press, 1983), p.285.

16   When I interviewed Peter Wall he agreed with most of my interpretations: they reflected what he had intended when he wrote the piece. But when I asked him why the piece was written in a minor key he was taken aback, and, after thinking for a while, said: 'It must be because the news is more dramatic these days'.

13

Afterword: Approaching Audiences—A Note on Method

John Tulloch

Many of the chapters in this book mention audiences. None, however, takes current audience theory as a focus, and the various chapters conceptualise audiences in different ways. In his recent book on the English soap opera, *EastEnders*,[1] David Buckingham surveys its audiences in four different ways, usefully demarcating methods of approach. First, there are the producers' notions of audience in designing their product. Second, there is the audience inscribed in the text by narrative and other formal strategies. Third, there is the inter-textual operation of secondary texts (like newspapers and magazines) which work 'between text and audience' to establish 'reading' positions. Fourth, there are empirical studies of the *EastEnders* audiences—the people that actually watch the serial.

Looking back over the chapters of this book in the light of Buckingham's different audience approaches, it immediately becomes apparent where the gaps are. Buckingham's first notion of audience is the approach taken by Albert Moran and by Tom O'Regan in examining scheduling practices and viewing habits—part of television as an institution composed of 'elements in flux'. It is also the approach I take in examining the drama/advertisement sequencing of an episode of *A Country Practice*, in so far as the

187

chapter concerns itself with the ideological and commercial inten-
tionality of producers.

By far the most common approach to audiences in the book (as
it has been in screen and television theory until recently) is the
'audience-in-the-text'. The invitation within the text to some kind
of resistant audience reading is the feature of Graeme Turner's
notion of 'transgressive' TV operating ambiguously as both conventional and parodic form; and of Stuart Cunningham's analysis of the
invitation to the audience as 'knowledgeable citizen rather than
distracted consumer' of the 'multi-perspectival' and generically
'hybridised' mini-series. In some cases, even where the emphasis is
on audiences as socially and routinely subordinated groups, the
article still only analyses the 'audience-in-the-text'. Thus, although
John Fiske argues that the 'necessarily resistive' meanings of popular
culture 'exist in the moments of reading rather than in the structure
of the text' and that 'textual analysis can identify those spaces and
gaps where popular readings can be made, but . . . cannot, of itself,
describe such readings in any concrete form', he nevertheless does
not analyse empirically these concrete forms. So he says of **Perfect
Match** that the 'challenge to patriarchal power and social discipline
is explicit in the structure of the game and implicit in the title
sequence which establishes the discourse of the show and the
reading relations we are *invited* [*my italics*] to adopt towards it'.

Fiske's, Turner's, and Cunningham's emphasis on textual 'excess'
and ambiguity is in contrast, as Turner says, to the 'large body of
culturalist analysis that focusses on the way TV "smoothes over"
gaps in ideology, naturalising social conditions through the resolu-
tions of narrative closure'—as for example in Bell and Boehringer's
discussion of the 'passive spectator' of television scientism. Dugald
Williamson's 'rhetorical' approach to TV documentary is another
good example in the book of the analysis of the 'naturalising' effect
of audience positioning in the text. He argues that the very same
'semiotic excess' which Turner believes opens up a multiplicity of
audience meanings, in fact can generate a complex but mutually
supportive and unifying system of narration. This identifies cultural
history with individual biography, thus inviting the viewer to 'read'
a 'text as if its organisation of signs were a vehicle to express a
deeper meaning, usually guaranteed by authorial experience'. It is
the unifying experience of viewing (proposing 'the symbolic unity of
viewer, nation and television, at one with Channel Nine') which
John Hartley argues (in his chapter on promos and TV continuity)
gives audiences 'a lesson in *reading television*'. In Hartley's case, this
was a more inviting experience, speaking to him more personally

than the Trevor Griffiths text which immediately preceded the promo.

Curthoys and Docker's chapter on **Prisoner** draws on the notion of 'the audience-in-the-text' too (in its 'subversive' version, in so far as they discuss its 'carnivalesque' invitation to the spectator). But their article is also the main representative in this book of the third, 'between text and audience' approach, examining the role of high culture reviewers, critics and academics in establishing agendas for audience put-downs of soaps. Bob Hodge takes this approach further into the context of television policy, examining how such high culture views flow through into the ideology surrounding the public regulation of television.

Both Curthoys and Docker and Hodge refer to the 'resistance effect' of actual and active audiences, but (as with Fiske) neither chapter goes very far into Buckingham's fourth approach—ethnographic and empirical audience study. Curthoys and Docker refer to a piece of ethnographic research, but tend to rely otherwise on analysis of **Prisoner** itself as well as on impressions 'from personal observation, and from several interviews with children printed in the *SMH Guide*'. Given the currency of ethnographic audience analysis in television theory during the last few years,[2] this absence of a single empirical audience study seemed to us a major omission. Consequently, I want to conclude with a note on ethnographic audience analysis, and some of its problems of method. I will take as an example my own experience in attempting a small ethnographic study of the elderly British audience for Australian soap opera. As in John Hartley's case, this personal 'audience' experience was juxtaposed in interesting ways with a Trevor Griffiths text, as I will describe in what follows.

Researching the Elderly Audience

I will start with an apparent detour: a conversation about soap opera that I heard by chance on an Australian 'country to city' commuter train. Most of the discussants were young rather than elderly (this was the 7 a.m. 'workers' train); and I begin with this example to raise problems of method relevant to the kind of study that seems to me most useful in the current ethnographic thrust to 're-think the audience'. My question, put simply, is: why visit the homes of the elderly (with all the problems of interviewer 'interference' and 'artificiality' that this raises), rather than listen 'neutrally' to the ordinary conversations of the elderly? There are, after all, trains

later in the morning often packed with pensioners. Why approach
the audience at all? Why not catch their conversation randomly and
'objectively' in this way?

The conversation on the train was about *A Country Practice*; in
particular the episodes where Vicky gives birth to twins. Vicky,
typically, had been working professionally as a vet up to the last
minute, and so (in a show also noted for its comedy) went into
labour in a cowshed, helped by the teenage girl Jo, and the male
nurse, Brendan. The panicking husband, Simon, a doctor, arrived
in time to deliver the second baby.

The conversation I heard on the train began with Jennifer, a
16-year-old commuting to work, outlining what happened in this
episode to her companions, a woman and a man who hadn't watched
it. Next, she said about the twins: 'Charlotte and Tom—I can't
think of two worse names.'

There was some discussion of favourite names, and Jennifer
complained about her brother and his football-playing mates calling
her 'Jen', which she didn't like. Then she went on: 'It was such an
easy labour. My mother was in labour six to eight hours. For Vicky
it happened in two seconds flat.'

The others asked whether Vicky knew she was having twins, and
Jennifer described how she did, but Brendan didn't—and she
quoted his lines as he found out. Then she asked if they saw a movie
later in the same evening, and said she wanted to see it, but 'Dad
was out and Mum was too scared to mess up his video recorder'.
Jennifer then talked about work, and about 'being ripped off'
because her seventeenth birthday in October came a few days too
late for her to get a 17-year-old's wage next year. 'That's really
slack'; and the others agreed that she was being exploited at the
wage she was getting. Finally, an elderly woman got on the train,
who, to Jennifer's horror, had missed *A Country Practice*, but had
watched the film screened afterwards. She recounted the plot line of
the film for several minutes, before saying she missed the end
because she went to bed. At this Jennifer shrieked: 'Oh, we've
heard so much, we want to hear the rest of it. How dare you go to
bed!'

When I first discussed this conversation in a conference paper, I
analysed it in this way:

> The conversation reveals the way in which 'wanting to know what
> happened next' is interwoven with—often actually related to—
> personal experience (Jennifer's inability to use the video
> recorder); and how personal experience here represents areas of
> hardship in women's lives. Some of the hardships may appear
> minor ones: a sister's frustration at being unable to control her

own name in the company of a group of young men. Other hardships are spoken of by way of a commonsense discourse that naturalises them, such as women's supposedly 'inevitable' fear of controlling the video. Other areas of hardship, though—to do with difficult pregnancies, to do with exploitation at work— are recognised. So, if a first reason for viewers getting 'hooked' by soaps is cognitive (the pleasure of knowledge, the ability to discriminate between characters and events), a second is experiential, practical, and in some way political (the felt relationship of this 'shared' knowledge with the real world of hardship and oppression).[3]

My point here in describing both the conversation and my conference paper is to insist that no audience analysis even if 'natural' (in the sense of not being prompted by a conscious research design) can ever be 'neutral' or 'objective' (in the positivist sense).[4] Jennifer was, of course, making a new text out of *A Country Practice*, setting it in a new context, making it discursive; and similarly I, in my paper, was making a further text out of Jennifer's discourse, forcing it to circulate inter-textually, by way of the series of analytical texts (feminist work on soap opera by Dorothy Hobson, Charlotte Brunsdon and Terry Lovell;[5] work on gender relations in the home audience, particularly in relation to use of video recorders, by David Morley;[6] work on cultural competence and the cognitive skills in discrimination among soap opera viewers by Robert Allen[7]) that informed my paper. The 'to-air' *A Country Practice* text, once fragmented and reassembled by Jennifer, was now undergoing another stage of cultural 'bricolage', as I reassembled her text, making sense of it by way of a number of current theoretical discourses, making it 'mean'.

In this case Jennifer and her elderly discussant had no way of assessing my analysis; and I had no way of knowing whether what I said 'made sense' within their own systems of meaning. One way of getting around this problem is by ethnographic research; and in describing ethnography here in Caughey's sense of 'the importance of understanding any given group's lifeways by discovering the learned systems of meaning by which it is structured,[8] I would want to extend its application in television studies from its familiar use in audience research to include also production studies. The *A Country Practice* team, like any group of production workers engaged with a continuing genre, have a 'native point of view' about its necessary continuities, and discovering their learned systems of meaning is crucial to understanding textual systems and the way they are transformed.

The four distinctive features of qualitative research which Lindlof and Meyer have recently summarised in relation to ethnographic audience analysis[9]—reflexivity, contextuality, meaning system explication, and theory development—are all as significant to the relationship of researcher and production workers as for observer and audience. In other words:

1 the researcher is 'marginal' to both production and audience cultures, and must take account reflexively of the relationship between his/her 'second order' constructs and the constructs made by the actors in the social scene being researched;
2 the researcher needs to take account of the historical and situational contexts—production practices, audience routines—in which the subject of research interest is embedded;
3 the researcher needs to try to attain a sense of the intersubjective competence and 'mutual knowledge' which create the symbolic alignments of the group in question;
4 the researcher needs to be continuously concerned with the interleaving of concept formation, observation and 'data collection', in particular the relationship in his/her understanding between 'mutual knowledge' and 'critical distance'—the relationship Valerie Walkerdine has well described between the researcher as 'surveillant other' and the subject of research.[10]

So, with this in mind, let me return to my case study, and a particular incident in the processual relationship between media producer, observer and audience. I had gone to Bournemouth in England (a town famous for its elderly population—recall the headmistress in *Picnic at Hanging Rock*: 'My late husband and I always took our annual holidays in Bournemouth—delightful place. . .nothing changed ever, not for forty years. . .dependable, completely and utterly dependable'.) to look at old people's response to soap opera. In particular, I was interested in their viewing of the Australian soap operas *Sons and Daughters*, *A Country Practice*, *The Young Doctors*, and *The Sullivans*, which were showing regularly on daytime television. As it happened, I had also just spent some time with Trevor Griffiths and Ken Loach doing an 'ethnographic' study (in the sense of the four distinctive features summarised above) of their work as film makers. The incident I want to describe occurred at a point of intersection (temporally-speaking) *between* this study and that of the elderly Bournemouth audience.[11] And, as we will see, at certain key moments of my discussion of soap opera with the elderly audience, I—as interviewer—spoke from within the symbolic alignments of the Griffiths–Loach production.

In thinking about the audience study in advance, I had been concerned with two methodological 'limitations' (as Lindlof and

Meyer describe it) of ethnographic research: researcher obtrusiveness and status differences between researcher and subjects. 'Researcher obtrusiveness' is a concept related to the assumption of ethnographic research that the researcher needs to 'become just another member or an accepted part of the scenery';[12] and accounts for the further assumption that to get over initial 'intrusion' into the social situation to be observed (in the sense of violating ordinary routines) the ethnographic researcher needs to spend 'a large block of time with subjects to become accepted and, more importantly, to be trusted'.[13] This trust, as Lindlof and Meyer see it, can also mitigate the problem of status differences between researcher and subjects: otherwise the 'mere mention of the researcher as a "researcher" or "college professor" may be enough to make subjects in an ethnographic inquiry shudder, refuse to participate at all, try to act much differently than usual, or feel as if their every move is being scrutinised or analysed'.[14]

I chose Bournemouth not simply because it happened to be a location with a large selection of elderly TV watchers; but also because it was the place where my own elderly parents, uncle and aunt live, and where I had grown up and spent long periods of time since then. I chose the particular Shaftesbury Home for elderly people for my study because it is where my uncle and aunt now live, and where they could readily get me access to many other elderly people on a basis of trust (which I had singularly failed to do in Australia).[15] I was introduced to these elderly people first as 'Douglas' nephew' and only after that as 'a researcher from Australia who is interested in what television you watch' (though this 'researcher' tag still, of course, had a significant effect on interviews— as I've described elsewhere).[16]

Using my uncle as mediator would have, I believed, two advantages methodologically:

1 it would make it easier (as 'just Douglas' young nephew') to establish a status position whereby the subjects of research really believed they were valued as ' "experts" at doing what they do";[17]

2 since I had observed my uncle's, aunt's and parents' television habits as a family member in an ongoing way over many years, they were *already* "experts" at doing what they do', and comparisons between their television routines and the elderly cohort could be made on the basis of initial hypotheses, conceptualising in terms of class and gender differences, and so on.

I had, then, already spent 'a large block of time' with part of my audience group: I already had considerable 'data' and 'mutual knowledge' regarding their contextuality and symbolic alignments.

Nonetheless, while easing some problems, this approach did nothing to obviate the need for reflexivity about the researcher/subject relationship (the relationship between 'critical distance' and 'mutual knowledge').[18] Nor did it (if I was to avoid the positivist 'fly on the wall' ideal of much ethnographic research) do away with the need for theory development. So my second case study begins to explore these issues via an incident in the research relationship between myself (as researcher) and my uncle.

A particular feature of the elderly's negotiation with television is via a generational memory; and I have described elsewhere how the elderly construct their pleasures as a kind of 'guerilla activity' on TV genres, weaving together their pleasures as a *bricolage* of generic appropriations from different programs, different narratives.[19] My uncle was typical of my elderly cohort in consistently mobilising 'my generation' in his discussion of television programs that he liked or disliked. But here it was with a very clear class inflection. As well as discussing Australian soap opera, he explained his dislike of *Coronation Street*, in contrast to *Dallas:*

> MR T: Maybe it's snobbery, but I'm fed up with—I want to hear a series where people speak with a decent accent. . . I mean I wouldn't choose a pub like 'The Rovers Return' to go to, I couldn't bear it. . . In *Dallas* admittedly they're speaking American, but I would rather hear that than English badly spoken. I mean, they're not speaking English, they're speaking *American* English, aren't they? But these people in *Coronation Street*—I don't know, it's possibly my generation are getting old and crabby and thinking everything new is not as good as it was and that sort of thing, but a lot of the things I can't *help* feeling about. I don't think the stories are as good as they used to be. You don't find any stories like Edgar Wallace. . . The modern detective things don't appeal to me at all. *Starsky and Hutch* and that sort of thing doesn't interest me. . .

> INT.: With a show like *Dallas*, did you feel that was realistic?—you said you liked *Sons and Daughters* because you felt it was realistic.

> MR T: Well to me I can imagine oil magnates—although I don't think there would be anybody quite like JR, and I don't think Bobby as he was would ever have become president of a big oil concern—but the people that you saw, you could believe that they were there and that they did exist. But some of the people in *Coronation Street*, and in *Crossroads*, well I think they are very much a fiction of the author, and I don't think there are such people.

However, later he had changed his view about **Dallas**.

MR T: To me, **Dallas**—I get fed up with it because the girls, as far as I can see, all they can think about is parties and sex, and that's about all. JR, he meets a girl, he takes her out for a drink and the next thing you see them in bed. And of course it's the same with everything now practically... Not only television, it's life.

INT.: Do you think it's realistic in that sense then?

MR T: Oh it's probably realistic for this generation, but remember our world was a different world. We can't adjust ourselves, the other people can.

When I twice asked my uncle about 'realism', the question was partly, of course, informed by the discourse of screen and television theory. But it was primarily motivated by the fact that my uncle had himself initially chosen, without any prompting, the issue of 'realism' as the ground for debate and evaluation. Thus he began by saying that he liked **Sons and Daughters** because 'they seem to be real people in it. So many of these serials that one sees... most of them, the people aren't real'. It quickly became clear that 'the real' was not *necessarily* related directly to personal experience (or indeed to what other viewers might think plausible) since among the 'real' Australian stories he mentioned:

MR T: The one we enjoyed most was where the girl's caught by a crocodile... **Return to Eden**, where there's a tennis player who's a very unpleasant character and married this girl or was going to marry her and they pushed her out of this boat where there were crocodiles... But then she turned up—some sort of doctor somewhere who used to practice in the background.

Nor were series *simply* liked for reasons of memory and nostalgia, since:

MR T: I've looked at **The Sullivans**... but to me the war's forty years ago and you get a bit fed up with a series about it... It's out of date now somehow to me.

The conversation turned to English soaps, and my aunt mentioned enjoying **Coronation Street** and **Crossroads**. At this point my uncle intervened with: 'Again, some of the people in it don't seem real to me'. His discussion of the 'real' in relation to the 'proper' speaking of English followed, and became particularly clear when I raised the subject of **EastEnders**.

MR T: Again, you see, why can't they have something that is

middle-class, that is decent English? Why has it got to be all 'Chuck 'e aht' and all this business? I'm not *interested* in that class.

INT.: You don't think there's enough middle-class stuff on already?

MR T: I don't think there's *nearly* enough middle-class stuff—although, of course, now with modern education and everything, people are being educated up to a middle class, but the ones who were higher are coming down to middle class. The result is that there is no real difference between the yob and the duke's son, they all speak the same.

My uncle's family had been distinctly upper middle-class, with a family tree which he had researched over some years. He proudly revealed that this went back to the thirteenth century, including connections with Scottish royalty and French aristocracy. The family had been planters and 'pioneers' in India for over two centuries, during which time, he complained, it had been 'done out of its earldom'. Consequently, he felt a kind of cheated affinity with 'the duke's son'. As with many British Raj families, he and his brothers had been sent back to preparatory school in England at the age of seven, followed by boarding years at one of Britain's most exclusive Public Schools. Here his brothers (but not he) had shone at rugby, boxing and rowing.

Given this class background, it is perhaps not surprising that he spoke of his dislike of *Crossroads* in terms of 'that union person who started the strike there—he irritates me. I know he was only acting, but he took the part of a sort of person that I can't stand'; and then concluded our discussion with bitter anger over the recent British miners' strike and his opinion that Arthur Scargill should have been taken out by the troops and shot. When I raised the subject of socialist playwright, Trevor Griffiths' recent demystification of the 'Scott of the Antarctic' legend in the television series, *The Last Place On Earth*, he said he didn't like it:

> MR T: I enjoyed *Tenko* very much because they were real people again. I mean, they definitely have existed those people... *The Last Place On Earth* I watched—again it was a real story, though I think that the real Scott was a bit different from the one portrayed by the person who acted him there... The one here, I would never follow a man like that. Whereas the Scott that I imagine would be rather like your Uncle Cromarty, who one would follow—at least I would.

INT.: You don't think that the Scott that we were told about in history only partly existed? You see, one of the things that programme pointed out, quite truthfully, was that a lot of the diary of Scott was not published, the pages that exposed the mistakes he made and sheer mismanagement of the expedition. Whereas when we were kids we were brought up with Scott as a great heroic leader. That's what the dispute was about in the programme, wasn't it?

MR T: Well, I suppose like everything, there's always somebody ready to tear something down. Nobody ever wants to build it up, they always want to break it down. Now Churchill, to my generation, was a wonderful man. But there are already people who write about Churchill who weren't born when he was at his height, who belittle him.

Clearly, at this point of the interview, I had abandoned the ethnographer's 'mutual knowledge' position (in relation to the elderly audience) for a consciously more critical one, speaking here for the position of Trevor Griffiths, whom I had recently been working with. This quickly revealed that my uncle's own cultural competence extended well beyond Edgar Wallace. We engaged in the discussion of the writing and construction of history.

MR T: You're influenced if you read a book. Say I chose *Freedom* by Victor Krovchenko. You read that and think, 'Russia, my God, what a shocking place to live in, I couldn't bear it'; and then you read Sydney Webb's book on Russia, and everything's wonderful. Well now, what is the truth?

The truth, as my uncle went on to point out, was by no means relative, but was to do with the fact that 'the wrong people are writing history nowadays':

MR T: Take, for instance, Mountbatten; in his very young days he was a bit of a playboy, so one hears... But then in his later life he became a very great leader and he did a lot for the Indian independence going as smoothly as it did. Admittedly they had the troubles with Pakistan breaking away which Mountbatten didn't want, which nobody wanted. But you should forget about the times when he was a playboy and remember the times when he was doing his heroic bit. Why write about the other stuff as well?... As far as I can see nowadays one shouldn't have any pride in any of our past heroes. Nelson—yes he had his faults like everybody else, but he was a very great man. Why shouldn't he remain as a hero figure? Why have we got to bring the other stuff in to try and blemish that figure?... And remember, with Stalin, his main object was to build a country that was in a very poor state really into a great country. Which he *not*, and you cannot do that in a kindly way.

As an interviewer I had quickly been confronted with an apparent contradiction in this interview. On the one hand, my uncle disliked a unionist in **Crossroads** because 'unreal'; on the other hand, he clearly related him closely to real contemporary characters, active in the mining unions that 'I can't stand'. By adopting a more adversorial position as interviewer I was able to tease out his, in fact, quite coherent position.

This I would describe as grounded in a 'Boys' Own' reading formation (including, of course, Edgar Wallace), and in a 'history' of individual heroism on behalf of one's team and nation. This history had been activated (most closely and personally) by his own brothers, first at school and then as pioneers of Empire in India. His identification with the 'real' Scott, with 'leaders' like his older brother, was no coincidence. His brothers had distinguished war records against the Japanese in Burma; and, like Mountbatten, had stayed in India to oversee the transition (through 'the troubles') to independence. This was my uncle's 'real', now threatened and displaced by generational change: 'Our world was a different world. We can't adjust ourselves, the other people can.' My uncle was acutely conscious of a world where his own class was apparently downwardly mobile, unable to control even their own representations on the screen, while increasingly 'others' (the working class) could. It is important to understand his negotiation with television, his likes and dislikes (his early liking for instance of JR, but not of his 'much weaker' brother Bobby, who was therefore 'less real' as an oil tycoon), in terms of this residual memory and notion of reality.

Because I had, of course, known my uncle over many years I could 'check out' whether what he said to me in the interview situation matched what I had known of him (and my father) during that period of time. I could also (unlike my analysis of Jennifer's conversation earlier) share my interpretation of his response with him to 'help in assessing the validity of conclusions'.[20] I could also compare his generational memory of the 'real' with that of his close friend, the working-class Cockney Mr Gilroy, and elaborate further concepts and conclusions, so that (as I've described elsewhere):

'Realism' in television for both Mr Gilroy and Mr Tulloch was a matter of filtering this daily process through a generational memory, establishing connections (via their own experience) with TV characters (with JR as 'somebody doing something they're not supposed to, tricking one another out of money' in Mr Gilroy's case; as strong, if larger-than-life American hero for Mr Tulloch, until soured by JR's current-day permissiveness). Both, as elderly men born at the turn of the century, were conducting a guerilla activity with the present by way of their television pleasures and dislikes. Television was for them a site through which to understand and remember the world, a place where residual values could be made active, and new values resisted or switched off.[21]

I was, then, making my primary methods of choice those which, as Lindlof and Meyer say, 'are intended to apprehend the processual detail of social reality'[22]—a process of 'expansionist' explanation from the *situated* individual outward which is a hallmark of ethnographic work.[23] However, as Lindlof and Meyer also say, methods seeking the processual detail still 'should make explicit the roles of the researcher in interacting with social actors'.[24] It requires a reflexivity about the researcher's own act as *part* of that processual detail.

My uncle, it seems to me, was putting together a personal history out of a number of (public and private) discursive events. There was, first of all, Trevor Griffiths' own anti-empiricist discourse of history,[25] as contained within the 'to-air' *Last Place On Earth* (complicated by a range of processes of narrativisation and theatricalisation as this text was transformed from Scott's diaries to biography to screenplay to television series).[26] Secondly, there was *The Last Place On Earth* as *social event*—particularly the newspaper previews (which my uncle had read) which drew on the Scott family's rebuttal of the series because 'no-one would have followed a man like that to the Pole'.[27] Thirdly, there was my uncle's own history (which I had heard many times) as the youngest, least sporting, least 'macho' brother in a proud imperialist family, in which his brother Cromarty (who as bearer of that name, like me, carried the *sign* of that family history) was supreme emblem. Fourthly, there was the positioning and repositioning of my uncle (while at his exclusive English Public School) within the history of a 'Boys' Own' reading formation that did so much to generate, circulate and refurbish the Scott myth. Fifthly, there was my own position as interviewer, my own history as the first generation to 'fail' the family by going to a *state* secondary school, partially recuperated in my uncle's eyes through studying history at Cambridge, and later lost to him again through the experience of May 1968 and radical sociology. Sixthly, there was my particular discourse as interviewer, informed by my very recent history as academic, talking with Trevor Griffiths and watching him at work making a film with Ken Loach.

In my interviews with Griffiths a particular history (and mutuality) was mobilised;[28] in my interview with my uncle, quite another. Yet that engagement I had with Griffiths (via a post-1968 radical social theory) was one which, in a very different form, my uncle (as the 'soft', non-colonist 'intellectual' of the family) had had with Sydney and Beatrice Webb and with perceptions of 1930s Russia (Stalin was one of the 'heroes' that, together with Scott and Churchill, he didn't want 'knocked'). In my own case, too, going to university, 'staying with the schoolbooks' and so not being 'out in the real world' was regarded ambivalently within the family. So both he and I carried with us a set of desires (to understand *beyond* our family colonist order) and anxieties (as 'soft' near-outsiders to that order) which, as they intersected, became *discursive* around the discussion of Scott— a mutuality which was at the same time a profound opposition worked through different historical positions (the 1930s, the 1960s).

Which of these histories and discourses are 'trivial' and which 'important'? Clearly, all are significant. We must not, as Lindlof and Meyer insist, fall into the positivist 'parsimony' of seeking 'big causes' for 'big effects'—the search for 'causes and specified conditions' that 'will invariably produce a given effect which can be verified through nearly countless replication'.[29] The goal of ethnographic audience inquiry is 'thick' interpretation of cultures,[30] and of how social realities and constructions are themselves *interpreted* by their members. It is this agentive, reflexive relationship between researchers and researched, between 'critical distance' and 'mutual knowledge', that can never be attained by the 'fly on the wall' in commuter train or private household.

Notes

1 David Buckingham, *Public Streets: **EastEnders** and its Audience* (London: British Film Institute, 1987).

2 See for example papers from the 'New Tendencies in Television Research—Re-thinking the Audience' conference, University of Tübingen, Germany (February 1987), published in Ellen Seiter et al., *Rethinking Television Audiences* (London: Routledge, 1989).

3 Paper at 'Re-thinking the Audience' conference, Blaubeuren (University of Tübingen), February 1987.

4 I understand 'positivism' as defined by Terry Lovell in *Pictures of Reality* (London: BFI, 1980), p.10: 'Positivism consists basically in the belief that "positive knowledge" can only be obtained by the methods used by the natural sciences... It is also committed to an empiricist account of scientific method, the doctrine that the source and foundation of knowledge is in the experience of objects of the external world, through the senses.

5 Dorothy Hobson, *Crossroads: The Drama of a Soap Opera* (London: Methuen, 1982); Charlotte Brunsdon, 'Crossroads—Notes on Soap Opera', *Screen* Vol.22, No.4 (1981); Terry Lovell, 'Ideology and Coronation

Street', in R. Dyer et al. (eds), *Coronation Street* (London: BFI, 1981), pp.40–52.

6 David Morley, *Family Television: Cultural Power and Domestic Leisure* (London: Comedia, 1986).

7 Robert C. Allen, *Speaking of Soap Operas* (Chapel Hill: University of North Carolina, 1985), chs.4 and 6.

8 John L. Caughey, 'The Ethnography of Everyday Life: Theories and Methods for American Culture Studies', *American Quarterly* Vol.34, Part 3, 1982, pp.222–43.

9 Thomas R. Lindlof and Timothy P. Meyer, 'Mediated Communication as Ways of Seeing, Acting, and Constructing Culture: The Tools and Foundations of Qualitative Research', in Thomas R. Lindlof (ed.) *Natural Audiences: Qualitative Research of Media Uses and Effects* (Norwood: Ablex, 1987).

10 Ibid.

11 For an analysis of this Griffiths/Loach collaboration, see John Tulloch, *Television Drama: Agency, Audience and Myth* (London: Routledge, 1989), chs.3–6.

12 Lindlof and Meyer, 'Mediated Communication', p.14.

13 Ibid, p.16.

14 Ibid, p.15.

15 See John Tulloch and Albert Moran, *A Country Practice: 'Quality Soap'* (Sydney: Currency, 1986), p.10.

16 John Tulloch, 'Approaching the Elderly', in Seiter et al., *Rethinking Television Audiences*.

17 Lindlof and Meyer, 'Mediated Communication', p.16.

18 For a theorisation of these concepts, see Anthony Giddens, *The Constitution of Society* (Cambridge: Polity, 1984), pp.334 ff.

19 Tulloch, 'Approaching the Elderly'.

20 Lindlof and Meyer, 'Mediated Communication', p.8.

21 Tulloch, 'Approaching the Elderly'.

22 Lindlof and Meyer, 'Mediated Communication', p.6.

23 Ibid.

24 Ibid. .

25 See Tulloch, *Television Drama* (1989), ch.3.

26 Ibid, ch.5.

27 Ibid.

28 Ibid, Introduction.

29 Lindlof and Meyer, 'Mediated Communication', p.26.

30 Ibid.

Index

www.ingramcontent.com/pod-product-compliance
Ingram Content Group UK Ltd.
Pitfield, Milton Keynes, MK11 3LW, UK
UKHW020412010325
455677UK00029B/865